I'd Rather Be Wanted Than Had

I'd Rather

THE MEMOIRS OF AN

Be Wanted

UNREPENTANT BANK ROBBER

Than Had

Micky McArthur

Stoddart

First published in 1990 by
Stoddart Publishing Co. Limited
34 Lesmill Road
Toronto, Canada
M3B 2T6

―――――――――――――――――――――――――――――

CANADIAN CATALOGUING IN PUBLICATION DATA
McArthur, Micky
    I'd rather be wanted than had

ISBN 0-7737-2340-4

1. McArthur, Micky. 2. Brigands and robbers -
Ontario - Biography. 3. Prisoners - Ontario -
Biography. 4. Criminals - Ontario - Biography.
I. Title.

HV6653.M33A3 1990   364.1′552′0924   C89-090623-8

―――――――――――――――――――――――――――――

Printed in the United States of America

Contents

It matters not how strait the gate,
How charged with punishments the scroll,
I am the master of my fate:
I am the captain of my soul.
                    — William Ernest Henley

The characters, events and settings of this autobiography are real, but certain names and dates have been changed to protect the guilty.

Special thanks to my lawyer, David Smith, who dropped a pearl of wisdom in my ear; the police, whose inaccuracies, inflated by the media, resulted in over $1 million in free publicity; and the prison authorities, who taught me that to be creative one must suffer.

There is one person who has remained by my side throughout my entire criminal career regardless of my actions or whereabouts, never lecturing or scolding my choices, never subtly offering unsolicited advice as some friends are prone to do or, worse, becoming unconcerned, never deserting me regardless of my predicament, but offering support by just quietly being there.

This one's for you, Maw.

Preface

This book was not written by a con's con. It was written by a prisoner, a thief . . . and a human being. I make no apologies for the truth. For those who spend their lives living a lie, sometimes the truth is hard to accept.

I began working on this autobiography in 1986 after I was transferred from Edmonton Maximum Security Prison to Millhaven Maximum Security Prison. I was sentenced to fourteen years and four months for bank robberies and escapes, and locked up in solitary confinement because I was considered a security risk and dangerous. Between Edmonton Max and the Mill I spent fourteen months in the hole. To save my sanity I began writing. The guards wouldn't give me any paper because they hated me, but they had to issue complaint forms. I borrowed a stub of a pencil and began scribbling down the significant events of my life, ironically, on complaint forms. Eventually I transcribed the material into a more acceptable form!

For the past ten years my lawyers have urged me to write a book because of all the hell I've raised — and the tragedy and comedy of it all. For once I took someone else's advice.

I'm still in Millhaven, serving out my sentence, working on my Bachelor of Arts in Social Work and tutoring illiterate prisoners. I'm supposed to be the most watched man in the Mill, especially on foggy nights. In fact, the guards have a name for such nights, nights when the fog is so thick you can cut it with a knife and steal away — they call them "McArthur nights."

Micky McArthur

1

No Easy Way To Be Free

THE PRISON GUARD CAME BY FOR THE lockup, the crisp clack of his oxfords echoing off the concrete walls. He flicked on his night-light, bathing the interior of my cell in a bluish glow, and peered through the smudged cell-door window. Everything looked normal. I was sleeping as soundly and contentedly as a newborn babe. He didn't suspect a thing. Outside, the fog stole across the lifeless yard like a ghostly bride in a white silk wedding gown. The rush of air through the ventilation grille punctuated the evening stillness. Then, as always, the snap of a cast-iron key inserted in the punch clock shot up the long, dark corridor, and the solid barrier hummed electronically and clanged shut. Finally the guard's night-light blinked out, cloaking my cell in pitch-black, and the reverberations of his footsteps subsided until there was silence once more.

For the 364th evening in a row I contemplated the prison I was trapped in. Millhaven is a state-of-the-art maximum-security penitentiary surrounded by two fourteen-foot chain-link fences each topped by two feet of concertina wire and illuminated by a string of mercury-vapor fog lights. Both fences are protected by PIDS, a million-dollar Perimeter Intrusion Detection System. The first fence is equipped with a vibration alarm sensitive enough to be activated by a gust of wind. The eighteen-foot space between the fences is rigged with a pressure-sensitive alarm delicate enough to be triggered by a small animal. Tripping either alarm engages a series of remote-control cameras and alerts a prison guard monitoring video screens in a control room. Four thirty-foot concrete observation towers with spotlights are set equidistantly around the perimeter fence. They are complemented by four concrete outposts twenty feet high positioned between each tower. Each tower is manned by one guard equipped with a Colt AR-15 assault rifle and a Smith & Wesson .38-caliber revolver. The perimeter is patrolled by three roving trucks with spotlights. Each truck carries one guard equipped with a Browning twelve-gauge pump shotgun and a Smith & Wesson revolver. All towers, outposts and trucks communicate with one another and the control room with two-way radios. The guards are trained and instructed to shoot any prisoner attempting to escape, without regard for life. No one had beaten the fence in the Mill since 1975.

My thoughts slipped back to the last escape attempt seven years earlier. It was Thursday, October 27, 1977. The time was 8:30 p.m. The night was clammy but calm. Glenn Thomas Landers, thirty-one years old, born in Pembroke, Ontario, had been sentenced to eleven years for armed robbery. Glenn made a futile attempt at freedom and died between the fences. He was shot through the stomach by a 7.62 mm bullet blasted from a high-powered rifle as he scaled the second fence. The slug dum-dummed off the chain-link fence, tumbling and turning until it tore a gaping wound in his belly as it dragged his guts out through the exit hole. The bullet blew him right off the top of the fence, and he was dead before he hit the ground. He'd been so certain of his fate he'd written out a will predicting his death.

Silently I slid out of bed. I was fully dressed and had tucked in any clothing that might get caught on the razor-sharp concertina. Patiently I waited, watching for the guard outside on foot patrol. He was late. Time was precious and I had none to spare. My senses were heightened. I was keenly aware of any threatening sounds in the night. Carefully I took out the windowpanes, giving me access to the bars. They weren't ordinary bars. Tempered with titanium, they could reduce the best Swiss-made hacksaw blade to the usefulness of a butter knife in a matter of minutes. But everything has a weakness, even titanium.

Each bar was protected by a louvered window. I had taken one window apart daily for the past six days, breaking the frames into small pieces, wrapping them securely in newspaper and throwing them into the garbage, which I immediately took out of the area to avoid suspicion. The gray paint on the bars I'd coated with grime to give them a weathered look. Meticulously I'd gathered or constructed the necessary equipment for the escape: two twelve-foot pieces of nylon rope, four twenty-four-inch hardwood mop handles, four six-inch wooden blocks and a papier-mâché vest, with cuffs and shin pads.

In the cell to my left was the taciturn and aloof Marcel. He was a hit man from Montreal and had just been recaptured after a short-lived escape from the Hôtel Dieu Hospital in Kingston. I expected no problems from him. In the cell to my right was Patrick Harris, a prisoner I knew very little about. At least we were on friendly terms, which gave me some confidence in his silence. Directly opposite me was Steve Reid. A loner, he was also a bank robber. I had no doubts about his support. Still, aside from prison security, one of my biggest concerns was other convicts. Some would inform on another prisoner faster than a rat would abandon a sinking ship.

I took out the ropes I'd hidden in my drawer, wrapped the first one around the three upper horizontal bars five times, then secured it in a square knot. Next I did the same with the second rope and the three lower bars. After that I took one of the four mop handles and inserted it between the first and second upper bars. Tentatively I twisted the mop handle once, then twice, increasing the tension steadily. Then, placing a wooden block between the handle and the bars, I was amazed at the incredible amount of torque I was able to achieve. Previously I had snapped a steel cable trying to spread the bars. I now used the second and third upper and lower bars. The distance separating any two bars was exactly five inches, which wasn't wide enough to squeeze through. However, if past escape experience was any indication, all I needed was a half-foot gap. Using a six-inch ruler, I measured the space between the two bars. The ruler almost fell through; the opening was well over six inches!

Quickly I dressed in the vest and shields, which were made from twenty-ply newspapers glued together. They would protect me from the concertina. In earlier tests I'd found that the sharpest utility knife couldn't penetrate more than six-ply regardless of the force of the slash or thrust. The olive color of my pajamas blended with the light green grass in the yard.

Then something snapped. I hadn't heard the sound of the strands of rope separating in any of my earlier tests. Perhaps the rig wouldn't hold — a thought that gave me visions of my skull being crushed as I inserted my head through the bars. I had to hurry.

Poking my head through, I exhaled and forced my chest past. It was tight. Straining, writhing, struggling, I managed to get most of my body out. Suddenly my knee struck one of the pieces of wood, causing it to slip. If it gave completely, I'd be pinned halfway out, utterly helpless. Instantly I jackknifed, pulling my buttocks recklessly through just as the mop handle let go with a loud bang. It whipped around and caught me in the ribs with a dull thud. I felt a sharp pain and choked back a rising groan. Swinging easily, soundlessly, down from my second-story window to the ledge below, I caught sight of the glow from Donny Tyler's television set. He was still awake. I was positive he'd heard the noise, but I wasn't concerned. Donny and I had apprenticed in the barbershop together. He was only twenty-two, but he was rock-solid. He wouldn't blow the whistle on me.

I dropped noiselessly to the ground in the out-of-bounds area of the yard — the forbidden zone. Once in the yard I ducked behind the wheels of a transport trailer, which the administration used for storage. I scanned the prison perimeter for patrols, but they were nowhere in sight. If I was spotted by the trucks, I might get away with my life on this side of the fence, maybe, but I would have no chance whatsoever of escaping.

The mercury-vapor fog lights illuminated the neat, orderly coils of concertina, giving them the appearance of Christmas tree tinsel. I was completely exposed by the daylike lighting, but it was now or never. Jogging quietly toward the first alarmed fence, I kept the greatest amount of distance between me and the towers, which were 200 yards on either side of me. Just before reaching the fence, I veered sharply left, placing the impenetrable chain links between me and any bullets. Then, taking a deep breath, I raced for an unalarmed fence connected to the first alarmed fence. As I neared it, I glanced furtively over my shoulder, looking for the guard on foot patrol, accompanied by his attack-trained German shepherd. In that very instant I saw a large Doberman pinscher bearing down on me. In a panic I lunged frantically for the fence. He might get my legs, but he'd never pull me off the wire! I hit the chain links at full speed and scrambled for the top as if I were on fire. I didn't give a damn about the noise I was making. I fully expected to feel the gnashing teeth of the Doberman clamping down on my leg at any moment. Finally I reached the top, looked down expectantly and saw . . . nothing. No snarling, vicious, half-crazed Doberman pinscher, no guard shouting excitedly — nothing! It must have been my imagination.

Momentarily relieved, I inched precariously along the top of the unalarmed fence to the first perimeter fence. The fog was so thick I could just barely make out the dark shape of the nearest tower, and wondered if the guard could see me, too. Pausing to concentrate for a moment, I crouched and sprang, leaping cleanly over the two feet of concertina that crowned the first fence. I had bypassed the vibration alarm but had landed right between the two perimeter fences, which would trigger the pressure-sensitive alarm.

It would take seventeen seconds for the truck to reach this sector of the fence, but the tower guards would be alerted immediately. Their binoculars, if they were smart enough to use them, would eliminate thirty percent of the fog, which meant I had to hustle before the bullets started flying.

Counting on a little finesse and a lot of speed, I scaled the second fence for all I was worth. As I reached the top, my pants snagged on the wire. Desperately I struggled to free myself but couldn't twist loose. The more I twisted the more I became entangled. And time was running out.

The fence shook crazily as I wriggled to free myself. The bouncing rolls of wire screeched in the dense fog, acting as a point of reference for any rifle searching for a target. My flesh crawled. Any second now I expected to feel the impact of a tower guard's bullet.

It was do or die. I couldn't stay hung up on top of the fence any longer or I'd surely die. In a manic bid for freedom I threw myself headlong toward the ground, successfully wrenching my pants free. As I fell, I twisted my body sideways and grabbed the fence so that I landed on my feet.

Without a moment's thought I sprinted for the road. It was the last major barrier between me and safety. Still there were no bullets, no loud reports, no searchlights, no screeching tires and no wailing sirens. As if running an Olympic 100-meter dash, I crossed the road, knowing I had escaped again.

In the eerie silence I looked back in wonder at the orange glow of the fog lights. I removed the vest, noting that its outer layers were slashed, and stuffed it inside a nearby culvert. Then I jogged up the road toward freedom. It was 12:49 a.m., Saturday, October 13, 1984, exactly one year to the day of my arrest. I wondered how the cops would like that!

2

Stand Back, Stand Slack and Put the Money in the Sack

HOW HAD I REACHED THAT EXHILA-rating moment on the road to freedom? Before my rearrest and subsequent escape, I'd spent most of the seventies and the early eighties behind bars. Shortly after my parole in 1983, I was living peacefully with my lady in Ottawa's Hunt Club area. Life was progressing well for us. We had a modest but decent apartment and I was employed by a reputable printing firm. In short, I was living on easy street.

Jacquelyn was in her mid-thirties. I had met her while I was in Collins Bay Penitentiary. She was a volunteer worker for the John Howard Society, and I was chairman of the same organization when I was in Collins Bay. She knew everything about my past, but her upbringing had taught her not to discriminate. She treated everyone with consideration. An ex-model, ex-ballerina and the head teller of a bank, she was five feet two inches tall, weighed 105 pounds and had long blond hair. The first thing I'd noticed about her was her piercing blue eyes. She had a delicate nose, luscious lips and the softest skin I've ever touched. A good person with a caring heart who came from a decent Danish family, she was an excellent cook, a spotlessly clean housekeeper, a loving mother and an incredible lover.

After so many years of enforced abstinence, I had conceived a variety of very creative, if innocent, sexual fantasies, and Jacquelyn satisfied me completely. When a woman can make love to you and make you feel the full spectrum of emotions, you know she's a good lover. Each night I wanted a certain meal, dessert and her, in that order, and they were always there waiting for me whenever I came home late from work. When I was in her arms, I'd feel secure, and after a night of love, she'd give me a great big kiss and say thank-you.

The austere reality of prison had left me emotionally stunted and unprepared to cope with the jungle of daily life. The outside world was a scary place after the predictable routine of prison life. Even the most ordinary things disoriented me. Speeding cars looked like metallic monsters hell-bent on my destruction. Just crossing the street could be an ordeal. I was in a foreign land filled with strangers who seemed to look right through me and say, "He's an ex-convict who just got out of prison." I didn't know how to talk or act. My rough prison ways weren't appropriate for the real world. So I just withdrew into myself, saying as little as possible and staying as far away from everyone as I could.

Some people were prejudiced against me as an ex-convict; others were quite sympathetic. The majority, mercifully, just didn't care. The real problem I faced as an ex-con was the loss of my survival instincts, my ambition and my initiative. Prison had taken care of my basic needs for food, clothing and shelter for so long that I was left defenseless. While I was in prison the penal system as well as the National Parole Board had actively discouraged the social skills necessary to ensure my survival and success in society.

I hated prison with the quiet rage of a dormant volcano, and the mere thought of returning burned like molten lava in my soul. Even though I was free now, I was always haunted by my previous experiences. Jingling car keys on someone else's key ring became the keys of a guard, and dark ribbons of shadow on my bedroom wall created by the window frame assumed the shape of cell bars. My body might be free, but my mind was still shackled.

When I relived the more violent experiences in my dreams at

night, fighting unseen opponents in a life-and-death struggle, Jacquelyn would soothe me by stroking my brow and talking reassuringly to me. In her capable hands my invisible enemies vanished like morning mist at sunrise. She showed me through example that not everyone wanted to take advantage of me, that there were still a few hearts of gold in the ravaged Klondike of humanity. And she led me back into society the way a mother takes a reluctant little boy by the hand and leads him safely across a perilous street. Jacquelyn was as close to perfect as any one woman could come, and everyone loved her. All the neighborhood children used to come over to our place just so she could fuss over them, hugging, kissing and tickling the toddlers. I knew she was a jewel.

But there was one small problem. I was robbing banks like they were going out of style, while Jacquelyn held down a responsible position in a bank. Given Jacquelyn's sense of right and wrong, our occupations didn't exactly complement each other. Although I never told her I had become involved in crime again, she could feel that something threatened our relationship. There were too many peculiarities in our life together, like the missing footwear and clothing after my periodic absences. Those piercing blue eyes could see right through me. Before she even considered getting involved with me, I had had to promise her I would give up my criminal lifestyle. I regretted breaking my promise to her the most.

There were times, naturally, when it crossed my mind to ask her certain veiled questions to further my knowledge of the banking institution. But I had so much respect for her that I could never find the nerve even to broach the subject. Besides, she was too sharp for any such trickery.

Honesty formed the solid, unyielding foundation of her entire being. It was the basis of her entire philosophy. I came to realize that quite early, and quite bluntly, in our relationship. There was absolutely no larceny in her whatsoever. She never discussed her work at home. She refused to tell me the names of anyone who had ever harmed her. And she couldn't even say an unkind word about another person no matter how she felt. She treated me like a prince, unbidden. My life with her was peaceful and serene. She was my haven, my refuge, my shelter against the stormy waves and rocky shores of life.

But for all her decency and virtue she suffered tremendously. She had migraine headaches regularly, a minimum of one a week. The pain was terrible. She couldn't function at all. It just ground her to a halt. Sometimes they were so bad she would just cry and cry. And there was nothing she could do about them — painkillers were useless. To make matters worse, she had stomach pains periodically. She had three exploratory operations to determine why, but each time the doctors couldn't find anything wrong with her. Each successive operation just complicated her condition by causing lesions. Throughout all this, there was nothing I could do. I had the power and courage to rob a bank and hold fifty people at bay or shoot it out with the police, but I couldn't stop one little tear. Despite all she went through, though, she never complained. She was a saint in my eyes, and I think I loved her more than I realized. We led a very tranquil existence.

Until Steve Faust phoned, that is. Steve and I had met in 1967 when we were in reform school together. He had married my sister Janet. Now he was calling from Canmore, Alberta, to tell me Janet had fallen in love with another man, kicked him out and filed for divorce. He was heartbroken and had no money or place to stay.

My thoughts wandered back over the past. Steve and I had remained the best of friends, enduring more than fifteen years of freedom, prison, triumph and failure. Our friendship had parried the best and the worst that life could throw at us. It was a natural camaraderie. We were equally matched in prowess, had the same interests and thought the same thoughts frequently at the same time. We were like twin brothers even before he met and married my sister. As long as I had a home, he would have a home. And as long as I had money, he would never do without. I was certain he'd do the same for me.

I was financially secure. I collected $1,000 bills as a hobby from the proceeds of my bank robberies. Feeling sympathetic to Steve, I urged him to move to Ottawa and not to worry. He could find a job and live with Jacquelyn and me until he got back on his feet.

Once in Ottawa Steve never sought to secure employment. Nevertheless, we enjoyed his company, and when our birthdays rolled around together, Jacquelyn bought us gifts and we shared the occasion. On the weekends it was a regular occurrence for us to barbecue filet mignon on the front lawn. Only the best for Steve. And I always gave him $100 bills for pocket money when he ran out. However, Steve soon became restless and despondent, mulling over his marriage. He wanted to attempt a reconciliation. I flew him to Alberta and back twice — needlessly, as a reconciliation proved impossible. Janet had had enough of his immaturity. She was finished with him. Shortly afterward he left for Owen Sound, Ontario, to visit his family for a few weeks.

Then one quiet Friday evening I received another phone call from Steve. He was in Sauble Beach, Ontario, a mecca for tourists in the summer. He was bitter over his lack of employment and subsequent lack of funds. He intended to rob the Royal Bank in Hepworth, not far from the beach, in the morning. He had stolen a shotgun and knew where he could swipe a motorcycle. I advised him to reconsider his decision; after all, the banks were closed on Saturday. He insisted he would rob it on Monday morning, instead. I had little confidence in Steve's ability to rob a bank and get away with it. He didn't even know what day it was! I told him I didn't think it was a very good idea. But he was determined to rob it, anyway, and there was no discouraging him. In an attempt to avert a blatant mistake on his part, I promised to help him plan the robbery to ensure he wouldn't get caught, if he returned to Ottawa at once. He agreed, so I wired him the return fare.

When Steve arrived back in Ottawa, I attempted to reason with him, but it was useless. I was unable to dissuade him from robbing the bank. For some inexplicable reason I felt I was indirectly responsible for his predicament, since it was through me that he'd met and eventually married my sister. So, I reasoned, if I couldn't discourage him from robbing the bank, then I'd better help him. At least that way he wouldn't get caught and go to prison for ten years.

When I cabled the money to Steve through the Sauble Beach bank, there was a slight delay due to the transfer being routed through the Hepworth bank. Steve learned from speaking with a gentleman in a bar in Owen Sound that every Monday morning at approximately noon Brink's made a delivery at the Hepworth bank, which appeared to be the main branch of the two. Steve and I traveled to Hepworth to verify the occurrence as well as the time.

We were lounging beneath the shade of an old oak tree beside a church on a Tuesday morning. It was after the August civic holiday weekend, and we were waiting for the Brink's truck. With particular interest I noticed an Ontario Provincial Police officer in a Sauble Beach cruiser pick up the mail at the post office at 9:55 a.m. Then he drove back to Sauble Beach on Highway 8.

At exactly 10:45 a.m. the Brink's truck lumbered up to the front door of the Hepworth bank. I was curious to see the size of the delivery, so I walked up the street toward the armored truck. The guards climbed out of the vehicle, but to my surprise they entered the bank empty-handed. I followed them inside and engaged a teller in a minor transaction. Then I watched as one guard picked up two large white plastic-wrapped parcels and left. I exited the bank with a deep sense of disappointment, figuring we had just missed the cash from the last long weekend at Sauble Beach. Nevertheless, we could catch next weekend's receipts.

Since the bank vault remained open during business hours, the only additional piece of information we needed to know was who was entrusted with the combination to the vault treasury. I told Steve to go into the bank and purchase a number of money orders while I phoned and asked to speak to the head teller. She would be in charge of vault cash flow. When she came to the phone, I told her I was an American tourist who needed American funds now that my vacation was over. I said I would purchase them on a cash-for-cash basis and asked her if she had $2,000 U.S. on hand. She replied that she would check. After a short spell she returned to the phone and said no, but that the bank hadn't received all its shipments yet, though one was expected later on in the week. She said there could be American cash included and asked me to check back with her next Wednesday.

Then it dawned on me. It was only Tuesday morning. Not enough time had gone by in order to count the weekend receipts in Sauble Beach and transfer them to Hepworth in time for delivery. The money I'd seen had to be from the previous weekend. Elated, we calculated that with the Sauble Beach receipts, the payroll for the nearby Douglas Point nuclear power plant and the bank's reserves, we'd probably net $200,000. But we'd have to hurry.

We planned a basic escape route, but we needed a motorcycle and a car or truck. After searching the entire resort of Sauble Beach that evening, we finally located a 1981 Yamaha 250 cc dirt bike. It was parked on the front lawn of the owner's house with a For Sale sign attached.

The beach was dead at two o'clock in the morning. Most of the tourists had left town before sundown on Monday. The house was dark, its occupant no doubt sound asleep. Steve and I moved quietly across the lawn, the deep grass muffling our footsteps as we neared the motorcycle. I removed the For Sale sign and fastened it to a nearby tree. Then we cautiously pushed the bike across the lawn, through a ditch and up the road out of earshot. I picked the ignition and we roared away. Shortly afterward we found the perfect hiding place for the bike at an abandoned gravel pit protected by a rusty, padlocked gate. We lifted the gate off its steel hinges, cruised down a long road, cut across a field to a woodlot and wedged the bike beneath dense bushes.

Returning to Ottawa, we gathered our equipment: one twelve-gauge pump-action sawed-off shotgun, one 30-30 lever-action carbine, one portable crystalless Bearcat scanner, two motorcycle helmets, a change of clothing and disguises. Just to familiarize Steve with his 30-30, I took him out into the country to practice and gave him a crash course in bank robbery. I drilled him on every possible mishap and how to react responsibly to each. Being a bank robber didn't mean I was irresponsible, so I made Steve agree to two rules: first, no one was to get hurt regardless of the circumstances, and second, he had to follow my instructions without hesitation or question.

On the return trip to Sauble Beach, I stopped off in Toronto to purchase a book of matches from an Italian pizzeria, making sure I picked it up by the edges. Next, after scanning the Toronto telephone directory and selecting an Italian name and address near the pizzeria, I copied down the phone number on the inside of the matchbook cover. Left behind in the getaway car, the matchbook would serve as a "clue" to mislead the police.

After our arrival in Sauble Beach, we used the weekend to find a getaway vehicle. Late Sunday evening we still hadn't found anything suitable. Then we lucked upon a 1983 Datsun station wagon parked in a short dirt driveway twenty feet from the owner's house. In no time at all, Steve and I were on our way to the gravel pit in our new wheels. When we got to the pit, we recovered the motorcycle, loaded it up and drove to a stand of pine trees in a conservation area one mile from Hepworth next to the Whispering Pines Trailer Park. We carefully camouflaged the bike, helmets and clothing under pine boughs, then returned to the gravel pit to get some sleep.

Bright and early the next morning we loaded our weapons, checked the scanner and disguised our faces. I decided I would be a black and Steve a mutant. Using black theatrical hairspray and mascara, I altered the color of Steve's light brown hair, eyebrows, eyelashes and mustache. Cotton batting in his nostrils, a wart on one cheek, an ugly scar on the bridge of his nose, blackened teeth, disfigured ears and horn-rimmed glasses made him look pretty ridiculous. The only thing that would stop the bank tellers from rolling around on the floor with hysterical laughter would be the gun in his hand.

Any disguise I assumed myself had to be in sharp contrast to my normal appearance: a young Caucasian male with short black hair, light olive skin, average eyebrows, high cheekbones, an average nose, full lips, straight teeth and a round jaw. My disguise included an Afro wig and brown facial makeup. Nose inserts, a patchy beard, chocolate-brown contact lenses and brown makeup on my ears, neck and hands completed the masquerade. We knew we weren't fooling anyone. The best we hoped to get away with was two Italians disguised as a black and a weirdo.

I donned my gloves and carefully separated a few matches from the book I'd bought at the Toronto pizzeria. Quickly I lit and extinguished them, then deposited them in the ashtray. Next I wedged the matchbook between the driver's seat and the backrest. After reexamining our equipment, I checked my watch — it was time. We climbed into the station wagon, drove to Hepworth and parked in the bank's parking lot.

It was 10:15 a. m. on Monday, August 8, 1983. The town was quiet, the morning sunny and warm and the air still, causing me to wonder how many bank robbers had died with their blood splattered all over the street mixed with bits and pieces of bone, gristle, flesh, intestine and their last meals in a sleepy town on a nice day such as this one.

I entered the bank first, casually but purposefully. Steve was one step behind me. I checked the interior. Everything seemed normal. The employees were occupied and unconcerned. The customers were unaware. No one paid us the least bit of attention as we moved toward the center of the bank.

I walked past the service counter and through the employees' swinging gate. Then I executed an about-face, which placed me behind the counter and in perfect position to watch the desk employees as well as the tellers. Immediately I pulled the shotgun out of the large backpack I was toting. At the precise moment I was stepping through the swinging gate, Steve had put his large duffel bag on the floor. He withdrew the carbine, opened the manager's door and stepped into his office.

In a loud, firm voice I shouted, "This is a robbery. No one move!"

Everyone froze except an old man, who just turned around and began walking disinterestedly toward the door. It was as if he were saying, "Oh, hell, here we go again." I was surprised. Obviously he hadn't read his script. But I let him go, anyway. We weren't there to hurt anyone; all we wanted was the money.

By this time Steve had escorted the manager out of his office and ordered him to lie facedown on the floor. I asked Steve, "Where is she?"

He glanced around and replied, "She's not here."

The head teller, who had the combination to the vault treasury, wasn't there. Damn it! What the hell were we going to do now? I'd have to fake it.

"Okay, we're here for the Brink's pickup," I yelled. "Open the treasury. We're not leaving without the money. If the police come, we're taking hostages. We mean business — now move!"

It worked! One little lady began walking toward the vault. Once inside she spun a dial on the treasury box. After finishing, she came out and I met her at the vault door. Timidly she pointed her finger at another, slightly larger lady and said, "She has the other combination."

Up until that moment the second lady had been playing dumb. But now that her little secret was revealed she sighed and walked petulantly into the vault. She spun her dial and missed on purpose. "Darn," she said.

The woman was stalling for time, I thought. But I wasn't sure. She might just be scared.

"Don't be nervous," I told her. "No one's going to get hurt here."

She spun the dial a second time and opened the treasury safe, revealing bundles of Canadian currency. It was a pretty sight with all the colors of the rainbow. Money has a unique scent to it all its own, and the odor that issued from the interior of that safe invigorated me.

With the second woman's help I quickly shoved the money into my backpack.

"Let's go. We're running out of time!" Steve yelled.

I heard a transmission over my scanner. The Wiarton OPP dispatcher was notifying all cars of the robbery. A cruiser, approximately five miles away, was responding. Traveling at approximately ninety miles an hour, the police car would probably arrive in about three minutes.

I scooped the remaining bundles from the safe onto the floor and told the bank employees to help me fill the backpack, which turned out to be too small. To make some room, I threw out bundles of one- and two-dollar bills and replaced them with tens and twenties. Then, lifting the backpack, I found it much heavier than I'd expected, causing me to worry whether I'd be able to carry it with one arm and use the shotgun with the other if the need arose.

As we walked swiftly out of the bank, I bade the employees good-day, ever the gentleman. I was answered by dark scowls. It was a good thing I had a gun, or I would have been dodging purses and paperweights on my way to the door. Outside, as we ran around a corner toward the station wagon, we bumped into a young couple on their way to the bank.

"Excuse us," I said. "We just robbed the bank and we're in a bit of a hurry."

They were a little startled. Without further ado, we jumped into our "borrowed" car and sped off. The manager, crouching wild-eyed and wary behind a nearby car, madly scribbled down our license plate number.

I roared up the street and was suddenly surprised to see a late-model half-ton truck driving straight for us. It was on the wrong side of the road! I swerved up and over the curb, then down again, barely missing the truck. As we reached the intersection, I glanced in the rearview mirror. The half-ton had turned around and was now attempting to follow us. That was the last straw! I slammed on the brakes.

"You stalled the car!" Steve wailed in panic.

"Hit him," I said, meaning for Steve to step calmly out of the car, steady the rifle on the roof and shoot the front tire or engine block, halting the truck, exactly as we had planned in such a situation.

Just then there was a deafening boom. Steve had blown out the back window of our car, for Christ's sake! I started to curse and swear. "Of all the goddamn lamebrained stupid . . ." I stepped out of the car, leveled the shotgun at the truck's front end, pumped three shots into it, climbed back into the car and drove away, minus the truck.

Turning into the conservation area minutes later, I eased our car under the overhanging branches of the pines. As fast as possible we discarded our disguises, changed into Bermuda shorts and T-shirts and shoved the guns, money and accessories into the large duffel bag. We put on our helmets, climbed aboard the motorcycle and headed back to the highway, where we watched two OPP cruisers scream by.

"It's the cops!" Steve gasped, and dived off the back of the bike into the ditch with the duffel bag and the guns.

I couldn't believe it! What in hell was wrong with the guy? The police were looking for two weirdos in a Datsun station wagon, not two dudes in Bermuda shorts on a motorcycle. First he'd blown out the window; now he was flopping around in the ditch. I waited patiently for Steve to come to his senses. Eventually he climbed back onto the bike, mumbling sheepishly, and we sped right back into Hepworth.

I paused at the intersection one block from the bank. We could clearly see all the commotion. People milled about everywhere, jabbering excitedly. A black-and-white OPP car with its dome lights flashing was parked beside the half-ton, which was stalled in the middle of the street. An officer directed traffic as the driver of the truck wandered aimlessly around, looking at the damage. I drove out of town in the opposite direction of our getaway.

Approximately four miles later we turned off onto a trail and followed it deep into a heavily wooded forest. When we were far enough off the road, we stopped, spray-painted the bike green and hid it under tree branches, ferns and shrubs. Then we constructed two blinds on either side of the motorcycle and settled down to wait for nightfall.

On the scanner I could hear the police searching everywhere for two Italians. They even spotted four Italians in Sauble Beach and thought they might be the bank robbers. We counted the money . . . $79,000. We weren't disappointed. It might not be the $200,000 we'd expected, but after all, it was tax free.

At nightfall we rode the motorcycle up a railroad bed that detoured around Hepworth. The tracks and ties had long since been removed. Unfortunately we ran into an unexpected problem. A lone car was parked on the bed. We were half a mile from Hepworth on the only path that circumvented the village. Carefully we crept closer. Soft, muffled voices drifted out from the dark interior of the car. Two lovers were sharing a few moments of secluded intimacy.

Hell, I thought, even bank robbers should respect certain rites. Allowing them their privacy, we hid the motorcycle and gear and walked into town to purchase a few soft drinks.

The town showed no signs of the robbery or gunplay. It was tranquil and deserted. We had nearly $80,000, but we had to pool our silver reserves to buy the drinks. While Steve waited in the shadows I walked casually across the dimly lit streets, ready to bolt for darkness at a moment's notice if challenged. But the only bad thing that happened to me was the larceny of the pop machine.

Upon our return, much to our surprise, the lovers were gone, so we resumed our journey along the railroad bed and arrived shortly after in the small town of Allenford. Like Hepworth, this town was quiet and deserted, too. We raced through it quickly and continued on our way until we came to the end of the railroad bed. I'd figured we could take this route all the way to Guelph, but now we had to switch to back roads. At times, as we raced on into the night, we almost met with disaster, driving blind as we were. Finally, though, we emerged onto Highway 3, leading to Paisley, where I'd lived as a kid.

In Paisley we ran out of gas. After cutting a piece from someone's garden hose, we siphoned a tank of gas from a car and were on the road again. Shortly afterward we came to Tiverton, where we ditched the bike in the middle of a cornfield and bought two bus tickets to Toronto.

As we were waiting impatiently for the bus to arrive, an OPP car rolled up and parked on the far side of the street. We had unloaded the guns to avoid any ugly mishaps and stashed them securely inside the duffel bag with the money. If the officer approached I'd have no choice but to throw down on him with an empty gun. That would be a laugh. If he called my bluff, I'd probably die laughing, too. The cop climbed out of his cruiser, glanced once in our direction, no doubt noting we were strangers, then walked into his office.

I wondered what my best option was until I zeroed in on a girl sitting on the steps of a restaurant. She was probably waiting for the bus, too. It was love at first sight! I sat down beside her and began serenading her as if she were the town beauty, which she wasn't by a long shot.

By this time Steve had hightailed it around the corner out of sight. The cop just as quickly came back out of the office. As he neared his car, he glanced curiously in my direction again, paused for an endless moment, thought better of it, then stepped into his cruiser and sped away. We lost no time boarding the bus when it arrived.

After we got back to Ottawa, we buried the loot and weapons in a secluded woods behind my apartment building, leaving out $5,000 each to live on for the next six months. Anticipating the possibility of encountering police surveillance as a result of the robbery, I urged Steve to return promptly to Alberta and resume a normal lifestyle. The deal was that we wouldn't touch the rest of the money for at least six months to avoid police suspicion. Then we would open up two hairstyling salons out west and go legitimate.

By this time Jacquelyn was preparing to leave me. She'd decided she just wouldn't compromise her integrity, and she couldn't cope with my highly questionable behavior. In her own mind she knew I was committing crimes, even though she wasn't sure what they were. I thought she would accept the situation if I kept my business separate from our private life. I didn't want to lose her; I'd be a fool to and I told her so. But it was inevitable. She just couldn't handle the possibility of the police coming to our home to question me. She wouldn't tolerate that or the harm it might cause her eleven-year-old daughter.

I had promised her I'd never leave her, so I let her make the decision, which, after a great deal of soul-searching, she finally did. As soon as she was gone, I missed her terribly, and over the next month I phoned her repeatedly, trying to get her back. But it was no use, and I knew it.

Three weeks later I received a phone call from Canmore, Alberta. It was Steve. We had agreed earlier that we would use pay phones instead of our private lines for conversations in order to foil police taps. So I left my apartment, located a pay phone and got in touch with Steve again.

He'd spent his $5,000 on a fur coat for his wife and a minibike for his son. Now he wanted me to wire him an additional $9,000 to purchase a car for his wife. He was trying to buy her love, and it was for sale. I said no and told him he was probably under surveillance at that very moment. Any unusual expenditures or behavior would only serve to confirm police suspicions that we had robbed the Hepworth bank. He was jeopardizing our freedom. Again he begged me to send the money, telling me I could keep the rest if I did. I refused and urged him not to attract any more attention to himself. After an hour of trying to reason with him, I told him I'd come out to Alberta and break his goddamn legs if he didn't follow orders. He finally saw the light.

One week later I realized I was under surveillance. First my phone was tapped. Periodically it would ring, I'd answer it, hear a click and then a dial tone. Once the monitor, a young woman, even returned my hello before clicking off. Then I noticed a young, clean-cut gentleman picking up my garbage in a wheelbarrow, a very unusual practice indeed. Next I spotted a young woman on the third-floor balcony of a neighboring building with a camera and a telescopic lens.

Things were getting too hot in Ottawa. I decided to apply for parole transfer to my sister's home in Calgary. From there I intended to relocate to Vancouver six months later and open up the hairstyling salons. The Hepworth bank robbery had been a mistake. Up until then the police hadn't suspected me in any of the other bank robberies. They didn't even have a clue. Now it would be just a matter of time before something ugly happened. I resolved to push the robbery firmly into the past, where it belonged. I conducted a yearly profit-

and-loss estimate and concluded I had more than enough money saved to safely open two hairstyling salons. My sister Janet was a hairstylist. She'd taught me a few things about makeup application and disguises. She could help me get the salons off the ground. My criminal career was unofficially retired.

Four weeks later Steve arrived in Ottawa by car, accompanied by his now "devoted" wife. We had arranged that he would return to Calgary with the money from the Hepworth bank robbery, escorted by me on my motorcycle. We agreed to meet in Dorion, Ontario, Sunday evening. But my sister wanted to visit my mother in Kingston. She and Steve left for Kingston with the money and I headed out for Dorion Saturday morning. When I met my sister in Dorion Sunday night, she shed crocodile tears, and told me the sad tale. Following an argument, Steve had leaped from the car in the center of Toronto, having decided to take a train. My sister went back to Thunder Bay because of engine problems and I went on to Calgary alone. When I got to Calgary there was no one at my sister's apartment, so I phoned Steve's mother in Owen Sound to find out if he'd made it to Calgary all right. She told me Steve had been arrested in Toronto's Union train station five days earlier, drunk. The money from the Hepworth bank robbery had been recovered, and now the police were looking for me. Also, when I spoke to my sister, I discovered her apartment had been monitored by a police surveillance team in a dark blue van on the day of my expected arrival.

I wondered if Steve would betray my trust after all we had been through. Steve had married my sister and fathered a son. He was family. Hadn't I helped him when he was in need? Hadn't I treated him like a brother? I'd saved his life once and he'd saved mine. Didn't that create an unbreakable bond between us? No, Steve wouldn't betray me, because he knew I'd never betray him.

The police couldn't possibly convict me of the robbery. They had nothing. No positive witness identification, no fingerprints and no circumstantial evidence. I was free and clear. There was absolutely nothing that could connect me to the crime. I reported to my new parole officer, Dave Chapman, in Calgary. He took a long time to reach the office. I suspected the police had been called. I told Chapman I knew the police were interested in either questioning or arresting me, and I was there to meet either one. He admitted he'd phoned the police and that they would arrive soon. Shortly after, three plainclothes Royal Canadian Mounted Police officers entered the hallway and walked toward the office where I sat.

The parole officer came out and met them halfway. "He knows. He's waiting," he told the Mounties.

As they entered the room, the officer in charge said, "Mick, this has nothing to do with us. We're just here at the request of the Ontario Provincial Police to take you into custody."

I told him I understood. I was arrested, placed in the Calgary Remand Centre and four days later transferred directly to the Walkerton, Ontario, jail.

With a big grin plastered across his face, John Armstrong, the investigating officer, quipped, "Well, Mick, you're done like a dinner now."

I was placed in solitary confinement to soften me up, sort of like basting, I guess. They strip-searched me daily and I never once saw the exercise yard. I was supposed to receive an hour of exercise per day. They didn't follow their laws any more than I did. For security reasons they transferred me directly to Millhaven forthwith. A few weeks later Steve was released on bail, a bad sign for sure.

In the Mill I wrote a letter to Steve, which was smuggled out through a visitor and mailed near Oshawa. I needed it postmarked from near or in Toronto, the loan shark capital of Canada. The letter simulated a threat from a loan shark involving the exact amount of money Steve had been arrested with from the Hepworth bank robbery. I hoped he would read between the lines, realize it was from me and bring it to the attention of his lawyer. The lawyer could then present it to the court on Steve's behalf. I purposely misspelled certain key English words similar in composition to Italian words and commonly misspelled by second-generation Italians. It wouldn't take an Eddie Greenspan to link the letter to the matchbook the police had no doubt recovered from the getaway vehicle, thereby creating a reasonable doubt in any juror's mind. As it stood right then, Steve had absolutely no alibi whatsoever to explain where the money had come from.

Two months later Steve pleaded guilty to the Hepworth bank

robbery and was sentenced to six years. But in the interim he'd signed a statement implicating me in the robbery and had led the police to every piece of circumstantial evidence they needed to convict me, including the weapons cache. When he was arrested, the police had to slap him twice: once to get him talking and once to shut him up!

It all made sense now. Steve had been a Judas all along. He'd promised to break me out of the Walkerton Jail in April 1973 while he was out on bail. But he hadn't. And the rope that had slipped out of his hand when I finally did escape? He was trying to sabotage me. He'd surrendered too easily when we were surrounded by the police in his cousin's apartment in Kitchener. He hadn't even attempted to conceal himself. There had been a rumor that he'd been a rat at Collins Bay when his friend Jimmy Binko had taken a knife in the chest meant for Steve. Steve had been transferred to Warkworth Medium Security Institution while everyone else involved in the incident had been shunted to the Mill. The evening before Steve's arrest in Toronto the police had visited a sister of mine in Kingston. She had relayed to me the message intended for Steve: "Tell Steve we'll make a deal. Mick's the one we want. He's the dangerous one."

Six months later Steve testified as a Crown witness against me at my preliminary hearing. He'd struck a deal and sold me out along with his own soul. I thought the only witnesses against me would be the bank employees and the driver of the half-ton, who'd tried to run us off the road. So I appeared in court thirty pounds lighter, wearing my classic Fu Manchu disguise.

I shaved my entire head, plucked my eyebrows to make them slant and let my mustache and beard grow out, cutting them Fu Manchu style. Then I bleached my beard and mustache yellowish-white. Finally I used a mixture of yellow and light brown leather dye diluted with water to give my scalp, face, neck and hands a weathered appearance.

I was ready. I had pulled every trick in the book. I was so confident of my disguise that I knew even my own mother wouldn't have recognized me at first glance. Then my lawyer told me the Crown attorney's only witness would be Steve. I couldn't believe it.

Steve scurried up onto the witness stand, pointed his furry little paw right at me and squeaked, "That's Micky McArthur. He's ten pounds lighter, his head's shaved and he has a beard and mustache, but that's him. He robbed the Hepworth bank."

Then he went on to tell how he'd blown out the rear window of our getaway car and how he'd been arrested in Toronto in the train station with all the money. He'd been so drunk the previous two days that he couldn't remember half of what had happened. It was so damn funny I had to look out of the courtroom window to keep from laughing.

My lawyer, David Smith, said, "Jesus, Mick, this guy's incredible. You ask him one question and he answers three."

It was perfect. Steve couldn't have set me up any better had he planned it from the very beginning. He was the lock on their chain of circumstantial evidence. And when he left that witness stand, I could hear the prison cell door clang shut on me.

Following the preliminary hearing, the judge asked to meet with the Crown and my lawyer in his chambers. With Steve's testimony I had no chance whatsoever of an acquittal. The judge knew it, and he credited me with enough intelligence to know it, too. He was prepared to address sentencing on a plea-bargain basis. The judge offered a four-year consecutive sentence. My lawyer relayed the tentative offer to me and I accepted without hesitation. The Crown, after consulting with Inspector MacGregor, who was in charge of the case, insisted on a fifteen-year consecutive sentence. David Smith overheard Inspector MacGregor vehemently asserting that I'd shot a police officer in 1977. Once you shoot a police officer they never forget you, and they never let you forget, either. The plea-bargain negotiations collapsed.

I was transferred back and forth from the Mill a half-dozen times via Toronto, London and Walkerton on a number of court appearances for nearly a year. On every occasion I was escorted in a belly belt, handcuffed and shackled by two OPP officers armed with side arms and a Ruger Mini 14 submachine gun, plus a karate instructor. And in every jail I was locked up in solitary confinement as an escape risk. And every time the only way I could obtain any information concerning a transfer was to act totally irrational.

I tried speaking intelligently and acting reasonably, but the administration always dismissed my requests. They scrutinized me suspiciously out of the corners of their eyes, as if my inquiries were prompted by some devious and equally insane ulterior motive. Hell, all I wanted was to get out of the hole. Only after I raised hell by continually banging on the cell door all day long did they respond with any sense of responsibility. My behavior was demeaning, but ironically enough, in every case, it was the only way I could compel them to act sensibly.

Life in Toronto's East Detention Centre was hilarious after one of my typical conniption fits. Two guards checked the solitary confinement cell through the tiny observation window and couldn't see me on the bed. The first guard tapped repeatedly on the door. I didn't respond. Of course I was awake, but I was in an irritable mood because of the shabby way I was being treated.

"Is he there?" the second guard asked.

"I think so," the first guard replied. "I think he's under the blanket."

"Is he moving?" the second guard asked.

"No," the first guard answered.

"Well," the second guard said, "I guess you'll just have to go in there and check."

"I'm not going in there!" the first guard cried. "You go in there!"

"I'm not going in there!" the second guard replied quickly. And then they both walked away, bickering over whose responsibility it was to go in, thus ending their security checks.

The next morning the assistant superintendent personally escorted me to the waiting police cruiser with no less than eight guards. They were all nervously lined up in the corridor as though I were about to come whirling out of the cell like a Tasmanian devil, snarling, attacking and frothing at the mouth. What angered me the most was that their criminological education and training were so limited that I had to act like an animal in order to be treated like a human being.

The attorney general's office changed Steve Faust's name to Steve Foster and transferred him to Bowden Medium Security Institution in Alberta. Just to throw a little wrench of my own into the works, I wrote a letter to Revenue Canada, informing them of a bribe of $20,000 missing from the original $79,000 taken in the Hepworth bank robbery. Steve and I had spent $10,000, burned $6,000 in consecutively numbered "bait" bills, and Steve had given $4,000 to Janet in Toronto. In the letter I said I'd paid the $20,000 to Inspector MacGregor as a bribe, and he'd subsequently failed to meet his obligations. I said the money was probably hidden in a safe deposit box or secret account. I was notifying them to make sure that he declared it on his income tax. Then I signed the letter Steve Faust.

It wasn't that I was blind to Steve's faults. I rationalized them because I loved him like a brother. He betrayed me against all logic, against all common sense, and even against his own self-interest. Had he pleaded not guilty they couldn't have convicted him. He wouldn't have labeled himself as a rat. And they would have had to give all the money back! That was what really pissed me off.

Steve's testimony against me really hurt. I would have consented to his turning Crown witness if he'd asked me, if it had been the only way to save him. I would have accepted my fate. Our friendship was more important. But not betrayal. He could even have sucked the police in right up until the preliminary hearing, securing a minor sentence for himself first, then recanting his statements implicating me in the robbery. But like a drowning man, he panicked. The more he opened his mouth to gasp for air, the more water he swallowed. He didn't care whose shoulders he had to climb on, who he had to sacrifice to save himself. And I knew his testimony during the preliminary examination was just a drop of water in an ocean compared to how desperate he really would become.

Steve was the biggest mistake I ever made. I lost Jacquelyn, my apartment, my motorcycle, my money, my parole and my freedom, and all because I didn't want to see him go to prison for ten years. I'd taken him into my business and he'd stabbed me in the back with my own knife. He'd informed on his own partner — his own brother-in-law. What kind of person would do that? What kind of morals would that person have to have? If you betray society, at least have enough moral fortitude not to betray your confederate. But he didn't have even that.

When I got to Millhaven, I engaged in a few preliminary examinations of my own. I had no intention of accepting the fifteen-year sentence Inspector MacGregor was so adamantly attempting to foist upon me. When I combined the fifteen years with the seven years I was serving on parole, and still had to serve, it would give me a twenty-two-year sentence. To hell with that!

I had a strategy that would pay off, provided it was carried out by the right person with appropriate equipment, the proper technique and under the correct set of circumstances. I began to train myself accordingly, gathered the appropriate equipment, tested the proper technique and studied the correct set of circumstances. I developed my endurance so that I could run a twenty-six-mile marathon with ease, and perfected my speed with sprints. To complete my training I lifted weights and worked out on various gym machines. I acquired a pair of soccer shoes with cleats and collected the necessary escape tools. In the library I studied weather patterns, talked to a few older cons who had been in the Mill for years and listened to radio and television reports.

With a stopwatch, and by throwing rocks to trigger alarms, I checked the response times of guard trucks from various locations to each sector of the fence. Then I located all the surveillance cameras and calculated the lens angles and distance clarities. I gauged the distance to the first fence, and beyond the fences to the safety of the trees bordering the penitentiary, and the time it would take to run each distance. I found out which guard supervisors were scheduled for each eight-hour shift, and their individual attitudes concerning strict or lax supervision of their crews.

I determined the schedules and routes of cell block patrols, exterior foot patrols and trucks. I climbed to the top of the fence near the gym and tested the sharpness and tension of the concertina coils. I conducted a test climb over the tennis court fence, which was a duplicate of the perimeter fences, and completed it in six seconds flat. In the evenings the truck patrols waited until the last half hour of their shifts to fulfill their mileage requirements. Then they raced around the perimeter of the penitentiary as fast as they could possibly go. I thought that was just wonderful, because every night I would be there with my stopwatch, clocking their rounds. Afterward I stayed awake all night long to determine the period of least activity of the patrols and tower guards with their searchlights. And during the day I conducted tests on the bars of my cell.

The prison authorities, as well as John Armstrong, knew I was preparing to make a move, but they didn't know how and they thought the Mill was escape-proof. The visiting room was wired for sound. They overheard me tell my mother that after I escaped I wouldn't be able to visit her because of police surveillance. And they also heard her reply, "I'd rather see you free than in prison." That was my maw, as solid as the Rock of Gibraltar.

Still, for all their intelligence it didn't do them one bit of good, because where there's a will there's a way, and I'd rather be wanted than had. A year after my transfer to the Mill, I broke out. I ran eleven miles to Highway 401 with a broken rib and a sprained ankle, and stowed away on a truck parked momentarily at the side of the road — the driver was asleep. He awoke, and six hours later I found myself in rural Quebec. I caught a ride to Montreal with a French Canadian who later tried to get me to go to bed with his sumo wrestler wife, but I managed to escape her, also.

Little did I know how frantically the police were beating the bushes around Millhaven for me, and would be for the next two weeks, investing $1 million dollars in trying to hunt me down. My escape had caused a mad panic in the region. Whole families moved out of their homes to stay with relatives. One hundred Ontario Provincial Police Special Weapons and Prison Tactics team members scoured the Kingston area with machine guns and sniper rifles. The army was put on red alert.

It's a good thing I didn't know all this at the time, because after I escaped the Frenchman and his wife, I was off on a less perilous adventure — to rob a bank.

3

A Time of Innocence

I STILL VIVIDLY RECALL THE VERY FIRST thing I ever stole — a tiny golden baby chick. I was fascinated by it, so I brought it home. I was five years old. I remember walking along the dirt driveway to my house, with the chick cupped carefully in my hands. After a hasty parental tribunal was held and I had pleaded that my motivation had been purely humanitarian — after all, I'd rescued the lost chick from God knows what monsters lurking in the woods — I was allowed to keep it. I don't exactly recall what happened to that chick, though I do know it grew up to become a rooster and then disappeared. I suspect we had it for supper one night.

I spent the first few years of my life living with my aunt in Galt, Ontario. My father deserted the family prior to my birth on June 16, 1952, and my mother moved us into my aunt's. It was an enchanting place: scents, aromas and sounds in a flurry of dogs, cats, birds, running feet and reaching hands. I remember a soft white shag carpet, the deep brown baseboards and the first eighteen inches of the light green walls. Then my mother met a handsome young man named Harry McArthur, and when I was three, we all moved to Orrs Lake, Ontario.

This period of my childhood was pleasant and fairly stable. I spent a great deal of time fishing, exploring and collecting turtles, snakes and frogs, like any kid. The shores of the lake and the surrounding woods were like an untamed wilderness to me, full of mystery, danger and magic. My stepfather would take me on hunting trips for small game and we'd set snares for rabbits on Crystal Mountain, a fairy-tale place. During the summer holidays, I would climb with great difficulty to the top of the mountain, where I could see across the smooth, untroubled lake waters to the distant shore. One day I was wading in the lake with my older sister, when I slipped off a narrow reef and slid underwater. I couldn't swim, and if my sister hadn't dived in and pushed me back onto the reef, I would have drowned. At the time, though, it didn't occur to me that I was in any real danger. Those days were a time of innocence and trust.

There was one person from the village who had gotten into trouble with the law. He tried to break into a factory and then struggled with the watchman when he was caught. He was only an eighteen-year-old kid named Tommy, but all of us kids thought he was a real criminal. His crime seemed so terrible. I never thought that one day I would be a bank robber and children would look at me that way.

I had two aspirations back then. The first was to become a Mountie. This idea disappeared along with my Mountie hat, which was stolen by another kid. He was the kind of mean kid who would sneak over and kick holes in our snow fort walls after we all went home at night. We used to play war games and throw snowballs at one another. That was acceptable. Sabotage was quite another matter — akin to spying. So one day I just walked over and totally destroyed his whole goddamn fort.

My second ambition was to become a doctor. I got that idea from watching television. But I quickly abandoned it when I learned that doctors were subject to being kidnapped by gangsters and forced to provide medical attention for wounded hoodlums.

When I was seven we moved again, this time to Paisley, the hometown of my stepfather and the whole McArthur clan. Allowing my stepfather to move back to Paisley, where he would be influenced by his manic family, was the biggest mistake my mother ever made. When I think of Paisley, three things come to mind instantaneously: rednecks, drinkers and fighters. At one time, in ages past, there were no less than seven hotels for a population of approximately 700 persons, a historical fact everyone seemed quite proud of. It was a dirty little town — not the streets, just the people.

The years between seven and ten were a very chaotic stage in my life. I had frequent minor brushes with the law and major familial conflicts, since my stepfather was a sadistic drunk. When he was sober, he could be a nice guy, reasonable, sensible and fair. But as soon as he started drinking, he turned mean, twisted and violent. He tortured my mother and whipped us kids with the cords from electric irons for the slightest of reasons, if any at all. He wasn't a stupid man, just crazy.

One time he accused us of stealing some fruit from a grocery store. Hell, I didn't know anything about any goddamn fruit. But the three of us were herded naked into a corner as if we were cattle and whipped with a rubber ironing cord. We all ended up with big red welts all over our bodies. Afterward we huddled together and, in the spirit of gallows humor, compared welts to see who had been fortunate enough to get off the easiest.

The last thing our stepfather would say before whipping us was "This is going to hurt me more than it's going to hurt you. You'll thank me for it one day." We became very close as a family then, my sisters, my mother and I. It was us against him. It was always us against him. The bastard.

I could deal with the physical pain. I just mentally curled up in a fetal position and healed myself. But the constant threats of murder and beatings were sheer terror, something I couldn't escape from. I realized then that something was definitely wrong with a society that allowed this kind of thing to happen.

I never accepted Harry as a father, but the police seemed to tolerate our domestic situation. They'd make an appearance at the house whenever the neighbors complained about our screams, give my stepfather a mild rebuke, then leave. No one in Paisley ever stepped in to stop him from hurting us. No one ever said a word. Many years later, after my mother left Harry, he actually murdered his own father in our house.

I learned from an early age to be fast on my feet. I outran my stepfather many times when he tried to beat me. But the best solution of all was to stay away from the house altogether, down in Lovers' Lane, a rough-hewn dirt road that passed by our house and traversed a small patch of woods. It was then that I came to a very logical, if erroneous, conclusion, which was to serve as a basis in my reasoning for a long time to come, namely, whatever I did was right. Fuck everyone else. I would take care of myself. The rule I learned was this: do it, but don't get caught.

I couldn't look up to any of the real men in my life, so I looked for alternative mentors. The heroes of *Mission Impossible* and *The Fugitive* completely captured my imagination. On *Mission Impossible* the IMF team always managed to prevail against all odds, and the Fugitive was always, at the very last moment, able to escape his unjust captors and win his freedom.

One time when I was in the fifth grade my teacher, Mrs. Wilson, had two other boys and me run around at night with flashlights like the Hardy boys. She wanted us to recapture her pheasant, which had flown the coop and taken refuge in a strip of conifers bordering the Saugeen River. Mrs. Wilson was afraid that if she didn't catch the bird before winter set in, it would either freeze to death or starve. I did what I thought was the next best thing — I shot it.

On Christmas Day of that year my mother had given me a pellet gun, which I carried around hidden in my pant leg. I didn't know if it was legal to carry a gun through the streets of town or not, plus I didn't want anyone to suspect what I was up to, either. I walked the five blocks across town to the Saugeen River as if I had a wooden leg.

I found the pheasant all right. It was perched in a juniper tree, looking quite satisfied with itself. While I broke open my rifle, put a pellet in and clicked the gun shut, the bird just sat there. As I raised the weapon and aimed at the pheasant's chest, it just sat there. And even after I fired, it just sat there. I thought I'd missed, so I reloaded and fired again. Then the bird flew away. I searched everywhere for an hour but couldn't find it. Finally I located it lying on the ground going through its last death throes. Its mouth opened and closed, as it gasped for air. The forest seemed very still then, very quiet. At that moment I knew I should never have shot the bird in the first place. I wanted to help the pheasant, but it was too late. Instead, I loaded another pellet into the gun to shoot it in the head and put it out of its misery. Just then it died.

Not long afterward I was scouting the hills for hostiles up on my stepgrandfather's hobby farm. The land was mostly knolls and hollows and not much good for anything other than poor grazing pasture. But to me it was the breeding ground of lone rabid wolves and concealed renegade Indians. I scampered from hillock to hillock, crawled up the rises and slithered down the gullies just like Davy Crockett. Suddenly I spotted a hostile — the front kitchen window of my stepgrandfather's house! I hadn't forgotten the spanking he'd given me once, so I raised the pellet gun, aimed and put one right through the center of the window — bull's-eye!

All of a sudden there was one hell of a commotion from the house. Unknown to me, my stepgrandfather, his common-law wife and my stepfather had been watching me from the kitchen window. They thought my antics were quite amusing. The pellet passed through the windowpane and narrowly missed my stepgrandfather's wife's head.

I dived for cover. Then I heard my stepfather calling me in the distance. Wise in the lore of the forests, animals, birds and wind, I was well concealed. I knew he'd never find me. I could stay there all day and he'd never find me. I could stay there —

"Give me that gun, you little son of a bitch!" a voice roared at me.

Before I could do anything, though, my stepfather grabbed the pellet gun and smashed it, ending my hunting days for a time.

I was pretty much a loner. No one in Paisley had much sympathy for us, my stepfather being a drunk and all. Parents told their children not to play with me. I was nothing but trouble. One day while I was down at the public swimming hole at the fairgrounds I almost drowned. Everyone just stood there, chatting and watching. I wondered what kind of people could just stand there and watch another person drown. But that was Paisley for you — steeped in loving kindness.

I had more fights than I could shake a stick at. It was always open season on a McArthur. If I wasn't engaged in fistfights, I was wrestling in the dirt or throwing rocks. No matter what the odds, I always fought back. I never ever let anyone kick me around. Besides, fighting with kids was child's play compared to what I had to put up with from my stepfather.

One summer, on my way home from school, a local seventh-grade bully named Wayne began to pick on a little third-grader walking just ahead of me. I asked him why he didn't pick on someone his own size.

"Like who, you?" he replied.

"Yes," I said, knowing that if he called my bluff I'd be in big trouble.

Well, he did and I was. He backed me into a corner, and the only way I could keep him away from me was to put my fist in his face every time he came too near. After he tried to close in on me five or six times, his nose started to bleed and he quit, much to my relief. But his nose wouldn't stop bleeding, even after he went home, so I received a hearty rebuke for that one. In the process, however, I earned the reputation, quite undeservedly, of being a pretty good fighter. You see, when I fought, I fought out of pure fear. I fought for my life. My stepfather taught me that. But after I acquired the reputation, I fought my little heart out trying to live up to it.

Once my cousin was grabbed by four older teenagers. He was always being picked on. It wasn't that he ever did anything to antagonize anyone; he was just easily intimidated. The older teenagers forced him to go to their clubhouse. I gathered up a half-dozen good-sized rocks and began to bounce them off their heads, yelling for my cousin to make a run for it. They let out a couple of yelps and ran for their clubhouse. Incredibly my cousin ran with them.

Now it was a hostage drama. But I didn't have anything to negotiate with, except for rocks, which I more than liberally proffered. The bullies tried to make a break for it twice, but they never got farther than a few steps before I dinged one of them, and back they'd scamper. Still, they wouldn't release their captive, so I brought out the big guns. After a few brick-sized rocks threatened to cave in the walls of their clubhouse, they surrendered.

Even though I was only eleven years old, I was the unofficial but undisputed rock-throwing champion of Paisley. I could throw a rock farther and more accurately than anyone else in town. After my cousin rejoined me that day, I chucked a few more rocks at the bullies' clubhouse for good measure, and off we went. That night I dislocated the jaw of another neighborhood bully after he picked a fight with me, an act that put me in hot water yet again. Such incidents and my problems with my stepfather landed me in numerous foster homes, my first taste of jail. In 1964, reunited with my "family" again, we moved to Walkerton, just eighteen miles away.

My very first day in school in Walkerton I had a fight and wound up in the principal's office. After numerous fights and an equal amount of strappings, I threw a brick right through the living-room picture window of the principal's home. I got away with it, though, at least as far as the law was concerned. But after that I was blamed for anything and everything that happened whether I did it or not, though usually I did. Still, there was nothing like a false accusation to make me scream "Foul!"

Both my parents were employed in the Canada Packers poultry processing plant. I remember watching sympathetically as they slaved their guts out six days a week. My mother literally worked her hands raw. And at the end of five years all they had to show for it was nothing. What the government didn't take the landlord did. From that time onward I was convinced work was for fools.

I kept raising hell, and the Children's Aid kept kicking up a fuss about it. So at the age of thirteen I found myself on a dairy farm. I hated it. The smell was repulsive. After six months I was allowed to return home again. Then one day, right out of the blue, my stepfather punched me in the face and broke my nose for the first time. He didn't have any particular reason. Long ago I had learned not to question his motives. The man was just sick, and I accepted his abuse as a natural debt you had to pay when you were locked into a dependent relationship, the way my mother was. She needed him as a periodic financial supporter of the family, so that gave him the right to hurt us whenever he wanted to — no questions asked. We were forever urging her to leave him, but in those days it just wasn't done, not with seven kids.

Back home on Halloween night with a group of pranksters, I threw a tomato at a neighbor's screen door window, breaking the glass. That got me sent to a foster farm again, but this time it didn't seem so terrible. They were a regular family with one teenage son as well as four variously aged daughters and three budding teenage foster girls. I took a new, particular interest in the female members of the family.

The head of the household, Vern McFadden, asked me if I liked horses. When I said I did, he told me they had a couple I could ride. As well as riding the horses, I also rode the cattle, much to Vern's consternation. I even made the German shepherd pull a small sleigh. But I never rode the bull. He looked a little mean, and I didn't think he'd be too thrilled about my ride-'em-cowboy routine. When I wasn't chasing the girls, I was chasing the cows or the dog with the farm truck, or someone was chasing me. I smashed one tractor into the other and almost burnt the barn down. I admit I wasn't a paragon of responsibility.

My first love was Vern's twelve-year-old daughter. I was fourteen. She was well developed way beyond her years, much more so than me, and I went through the act rather unwillingly at first. Afterward I couldn't get rid of her. She kept following me around, and all she ever wanted to talk about was what we'd done up in the hayloft. Then her mother caught wind of us and started to chase me around the house with a broom. I had to jump right through a screen door window to get the hell away from her.

The farmhouse was situated at a crossroads, and one early summer evening everyone heard a tremendous crash. I was standing on the side lawn with an unobscured view of the intersection 100 yards away. As soon as I heard the noise, I looked over just in time to see two cars separating after having collided. I ran over to the accident. Apparently four intoxicated native gentlemen between twenty and thirty years old had barreled right through the stop sign and smacked into a passing vehicle at sixty miles an hour. The natives' car had bounced off the other vehicle, plowed through the ditch and smashed into a tree. The front end was badly crumpled. The second car was still on the highway, bent into the shape of a horseshoe.

The natives were stumbling around in a daze, but there was a young woman lying on her back on the asphalt. She was conscious, but she couldn't move. A young man knelt beside her, drenched in his own blood, holding her hand gently and crying, "Please don't die. Please don't die" over and over again.

The woman appeared to be seriously hurt, and whenever anyone came too close to her, she pleaded, "Don't touch me. Please don't touch me."

The ambulance had already been called as soon as we'd heard the crash, so we brought a blanket over for the woman. After a short while the ambulance arrived, and the woman was taken away. Later, we found out that she survived, despite a broken back and massive internal injuries. I'll never forget that young man weeping and begging her not to die. It really confused me. It was the first time I'd ever seen a grown man cry. Where I came from men didn't cry. They fought and hurt people, but they didn't cry.

Eighteen months later my sister phoned, but I wasn't allowed to see her. So I forged a ten-dollar check in Vern's name at the country store across the road. Then I called a taxi and traveled the thirty miles to Walkerton to see my sister. It was my first real crime, and I felt absolutely justified in committing it. I'd been taken away from my family. I'd been made to suffer for a situation I was not responsible for. I hadn't created the mess I was trapped in, so why the hell should I have to pay the price for it? Perhaps the foster home was for my own protection, but that wasn't the way I saw it. I was paying the price for someone else's mistake, and that concept was the basis for all my future criminality.

Anyway, the police met the taxi on the outskirts of Walkerton and I was hauled off to the local jail. Vern McFadden's wife had seen the taxi heading south to Walkerton instead of north to Southampton and had phoned the Walkerton police. Still, I adamantly refused to go back to the foster home until I saw my sister. But the McFaddens were called to take me back, nevertheless.

Going back didn't bother me. I figured I'd sit in the back of the car and kiss the girls on the way. And when I got back I intended to leave again, anyway. However, when Vern arrived to pick me up, his wife looked all set to tackle me, as if I were about to go on the lam at any moment. That was it. I lit out for higher ground. They captured me a week later by tricking me into going to the Children's Aid building for an interview with a social worker. They said they were going to let me go back to my real home, but they lied.

The McFaddens didn't treat me meanly, except for a couple of times. Once Vern tried to strangle me. His wife was a big fat surly thing, five feet four inches tall and 230 pounds. She used to bully everyone just by her sheer weight and size.

One day she rushed at me, and I instinctively put my hands out to hold her off. Well, my hands just happened to land on her big flabby breasts, so she told her husband that I'd punched her in the tits. Before I had a chance to explain what had happened or skedaddle, he grabbed me by the throat, picked me up and shook me like a rag doll.

I always felt there was a bit of sexual jealousy in the whole matter. Vern's wife was definitely envious of the other girls I paid attention to. I hated her and I wasn't shy about letting her know it. Hell, if I'd wanted to touch a pair of breasts, it sure wouldn't have been hers. After all, I had her daughter.

On another occasion Vern pushed my face into some cow manure. That time it was pretty much my fault because I'd become indignant over his telling me what to do. Who the hell was he to tell me what to do, anyway? He was just a goddamn shit farmer. Anyway, I told him to go fuck himself. That must have really hit home, because with a wife like his he was probably forced to play with himself the majority of the time, anyway. I didn't realize just how close to the truth my insult might have come.

Except for those two incidents I actually liked the man. He treated me fairly, he was easygoing and he was reasonably stable. He used to tell me the corniest jokes, but in his own way he was pretty smart. I had a respect for him that remains to this day, may he rest in peace. Anyway, I was taken to juvenile court for forging the check and sent to Bowmanville Training School, thirty miles outside of Oshawa. That was where I met Steve Faust.

At Bowmanville I learned that some men, due to spending so much time in prison, become institutionalized, dependent upon the system for their welfare. I was horrified and swore to myself I'd never let that happen to me. I'd always want to be free and I'd never accept prison. Never. Not as long as I had a breath of life in me. After six months I was released from Bowmanville. But the die had been cast.

4

What Was Mine Was Mine, and What Was Yours Was Mine

BACK IN WALKERTON, ALONG WITH two other boys, I stole four cars and traveled to Toronto and back. Between car thefts we hitchhiked and broke into two country schoolhouses, which we smashed all to hell. We smashed absolutely everything: the windows, the doors, the teacher's desk, the picture of the Queen, everything. We didn't do it to be vindictive or out of anger. We did it just for the sheer hell of it, and we had a riot doing it, too. We smashed the hell out of the stolen cars, as well. A few months later I was sent to Guelph Reformatory for a period of twenty-one months definite and twelve months indefinite, convicted of three break-and-enters. At Guelph I renewed my friendship with Steve.

Reformatory reforms a person all right — for the worse. It turns a mean little training school kid into an insensitive, totally amoral and vicious young punk. My first day there I was set upon by two other boys, but managed to fend them off. Not because I possessed superb fighting skills, but because they had none whatsoever. It was a common occurrence to see someone with all his front teeth knocked out. And more than once I witnessed group assaults and saw the results weeks later with the person's jaw wired back together.

While working on cell-cleaning detail one day a black thirty-year-old homosexual named Hazel came into the cell behind me. He tried to grab me by the family jewels but wasn't quick enough. We danced around a little. He was determined to have his way with me. I couldn't dissuade him, so I punched him.

"What, you think gays can't fight?" he snarled. "The only thing I like better than making love is fighting."

It turned out he was an ex-boxer. He hit me so many times I thought I was fighting four men. The only way I could get out of that cell was to knee him in the groin. So I emerged with my privates intact. That lesson was a tough one, and a little too close for comfort. Not long afterward I began training as an amateur boxer myself and found out I possessed natural speed. I could hit a man before he could blink.

At Guelph I was bounced from one job to another until I finally wound up on the "special" gang, busting rocks with a twelve-pound sledgehammer in a quarry under the tough but wise rule of Corporal Knapp.

He was a stately middle-aged gentleman who displayed the bearing of a naval officer more than that of a guard. Knapp tolerated no nonsense, but he was also keenly aware of the practical limitations of his authority. Fights were frequent, tolerated, but controlled. The special gang was reserved for individuals with aspirations.

One morning in the smoke shack I had an altercation with another older prisoner. He was built like an ape — squat, with muscular shoulders and long arms — and had a reputation as a good scrapper. He threatened to bean me with a log when I wasn't looking. I thought he just might do it. He certainly looked mean enough to. So, rather than have him lurking behind my back forever, I brought him right out in the open with a good crack. I gave him my best right cross to the chin, hoping to take him out quickly and avoid an ugly scene, particularly one I'd have to wake up to and look at in the mirror the next morning.

My punch knocked him back a pace or two, more out of surprise than the shock of the blow, and I followed up with a combination. He lashed out blindly with a right haymaker and caught me in the temple, and down I went. I hit the ground facefirst, but before he could put the boots to me, I popped back up again and the battle raged anew.

I must have hit him a good half-dozen cracks, but he just kept right on coming. After he gave me a solid boot to the breadbasket, the other prisoners jumped in and broke it up. And I don't mind admitting I didn't object too strenuously, because I figured he'd have beaten my brains to a pulp eventually.

Still, I'd given him a fat lip and two black eyes while remaining unscathed myself. I was the hero of the day. But I was just happy to be alive.

In Guelph I was instructed by Tony, a young Toronto car thief, in the art of hot-wiring cars. The technique is easy. First the ignition wires are pulled down from under the dashboard and cut. Then the rubber is removed with a wire stripper. After that the wires are twisted together, except for the black one. When you touch the black wire to the rest of the wires, you get ignition. The only minor setback to this technique is that the electrical options don't work, such as the radio and windshield wipers. But the headlights still work, so you're in business.

Eighteen months later I was released from Guelph. Not long afterward I phoned Steve and asked him what he was up to. The usual, was his reply, so we decided to travel to Galt and appraise an old Studebaker my uncle had for sale. As it turned out, the car didn't even have an engine, and we'd frittered away the money for our return trip, so we figured we'd hitchhike back to Owen Sound. But it was a chilly fall evening, so we decided to "borrow" a car instead.

After we arrived in the Sound, we parked in an alley behind a row of stores, planning to break into one of them. A police officer on foot patrol came by and noticed our empty car with its engine running. Meanwhile, Steve and I were using the bank of a nearby canal as a hideaway. The cop saw us and ordered us to get up, which we did. As soon as Steve reached the top of the bank, he ran like hell. The officer blew his whistle so loud that it scared the living daylights out of me. Then he pulled his gun out and aimed at Steve. As I stood there watching, I was positive the cop was going to shoot, but at the last moment he hesitated. Then he turned and pointed his gun at my stomach and ordered me to "assume the position." I was more than happy to do so and obediently placed my hands on the hood of the stolen car. Just as he was about to clasp the cuffs onto my wrists, I whirled around and ran up the street after Steve. As I said, I was fast on my feet, and I managed to get away.

Nevertheless, we were both caught by early morning. Steve was arrested at his mother's house, while I was nabbed in the front seat of a taxi. I was planning to use the cab to get back to Walkerton, but a bunch of cabbies jumped me and held me until the police came.

Steve and I were both charged with car theft, and two months later we were sentenced to fourteen months. So, for the next nine months, with five months off for good behavior, I took up residence at Burwash Reformatory, while Steve went to Millbrook Reformatory. The one thing I learned from my experience in Owen Sound was never to stop when the police drew their guns or threatened to shoot. It was a good bet that they wouldn't really fire.

In the Wash I was initially employed on the dairy farm. Three events stood out in my new home. One was sad, one was typical and one was more comical than anything else.

The first happened one cold winter day when a large, fully grown Holstein milk cow had given birth to a calf. Through some quirk of fate the calf came out backward and became lodged in the mother's birth canal. The calf was left to hang there halfway in and halfway out for the longest time. Then the assistant farm manager pushed it back inside to turn it around. In doing so, he suffocated the calf and injured its mother internally, paralyzing her legs.

I fed and watered the Holstein religiously, but her legs remained useless. She seemed to accept her doom, or perhaps she just didn't have the strength to try anymore. The assistant manager never even bothered to phone a veterinarian. Then one day the farm manager arrived with a .38-caliber revolver. He shot the cow behind the left ear, and she died.

I never saw so much incompetence in one place in my entire life. Of all the cows that had given birth in the two-year period I spent on Vern McFadden's farm, we never lost one. And not a single calf died, no matter how complicated the birth was. We had them coming out frontward, backward, sideways and not at all. And sometimes we had two men straining on a rope tied around the calf's ankle just to help the mother in her labor.

Anyway, the reformatory farm managers slapped a rope around the dead Holstein's leg, towed her out behind the barn with a tractor and left her there for the bears. I kept going back again and again to look at the tiny hole in the back of the dead cow's skull. It was so difficult to believe that such a small object could lay such a large, powerful animal so low.

I never had much respect for the assistant manager after that, not as a farmer or as a person. It was little wonder he was employed by the government rather than working his own farm. I never considered myself to be a bleeding heart, but in my books, anyone who let an animal suffer unnecessarily was not only cruel, he was also stupid.

The second incident occurred when another convict punched me in the mouth for the usual reformatory reason, which was no reason at all. He was just a nasty character. Well, I considered the matter and decided I'd have to do something about it. If I let it go, pretty soon everyone would be wanting to take a poke at me. And then of course there was the matter of my injured pride. So, after work, I invited the hood into the barn to "talk" about the incident.

We went into the feed room and took off our jackets in preparation to do battle. My adversary was five feet eight inches tall and built like a tree trunk, with a thick neck and sloping shoulders. As he confidently and purposefully rolled up his sleeves, revealing muscular forearms, he said, "When you wind up in the hospital, don't say I didn't warn you."

Oh, my God, I thought, what have I gotten myself into? He was talking about the hospital! All I wanted was a little scrap. If there had been a way out, I probably would have bolted for it then and there. But he was standing between me and the only door, so I gave him two crisp jabs to the chin and drove a hard uppercut into his solar plexus. But he just smiled the kind of twisted smile that says, "I'm not smiling because I'm happy. I'm smiling because I'm going to thoroughly enjoy beating your goddamn brains in."

I tried everything. I wrestled him. I booted him. I elbowed him. I head-butted him. I kneed him. I gouged him. I even fought dirty and bit him. But nothing had any effect. All I did was make him madder.

Finally, when he had me bent over backward on top of the feed mill and was about to deliver the coup de grace, I found his weak spot — the base of his skull. I hammered a half-dozen right-handed punches at his head until he grabbed my arm. But it takes two hands to hold one arm, so I went to work on him with my left. Then I heard a groan and I knew he was mine. A few more blows told the tale and he quit, but not without a warning: "This isn't over yet. I'll stab you with a pitchfork." Just then the guard came along, so we agreed to go to it the next day, same place, same time.

The next day I walked over to the barn where he was pitching manure with a five-pronged pitchfork. I was a little worried, I can tell you. To reassure myself, I took a firm grip on the sheet metal plate I'd secreted in my hip pocket. I was ready to draw and throw if he rushed me with the pitchfork. But to my surprise he didn't want to have another tussle. It was a good thing, too, because if I'd missed with the plate, I'd have looked pretty silly hightailing it out of the barn with him just one step behind me, trying to jab me in the ass with a manure fork.

The third occurrence took place following my transfer to nearby Camp Bison. It involved my education in the fine and delicate art of locksmithing, which included a course on designing and manufacturing picklocks given by my mentor, a smooth old burglar named Jerry Hines. Midway through the term Jerry decided a proper test would only be valid if conducted under normal circumstances. Therefore, he decided we would surreptitiously enter the canteen, relieve it of a small, unnoticeable quantity of items and relock the door upon our departure.

The day of the midterm exam Jerry successfully picked the exterior door lock, gaining access to the interior canteen door. My job was to pick the interior door lock, which I proceeded to do, while Jerry remained outside to keep an eye out for guards. I began finessing the second lock and was making fine progress, too, when I heard a muffled voice behind me demand, "What are you doing there?"

I glanced over my shoulder and met the black scowl of a correctional officer. He opened the door and planted himself directly in the doorway, repeating his question. I walked toward him, mumbling some jabberwocky about being employed in the canteen and the lock being jammed. He knew it was utter rot but still tried to make sense of it, anyway. Naturally he stepped aside.

The locksmith's pick and tension bar were evidence enough for me to be arrested, convicted and sentenced for possession of burglary tools, which carried a maximum five-year prison term. As soon as the guard moved aside, I bolted, and the chase was on. In stocking feet I slid down the waxed concrete corridor, with the guard in hot pursuit.

By the time we reached the end of the corridor we were going full tilt. The guard was a mere ten feet behind me. I spun around the corner, trying to slam the barred door shut behind me, but I wasn't fast enough. The guard ran right into the frame with his forehead and almost knocked himself out. I didn't know whether to laugh or run. I took off running again, leaving him wobbling around as if he couldn't find the ground with his feet. After negotiating another corner, I found Jerry strolling nonchalantly down the hallway as if he didn't have a care in the world. I handed him the tools relay style and he jackrabbited down the hallway as fast as he could. The guard came tottering along a few minutes later, rubbing his head, more hurt than angry now. He found me waiting for him in my cell. I just couldn't help myself; I had to laugh. He looked so ridiculous.

I received ten days on bread and water in solitary confinement for that one. And then it was back to classes as usual. Having a propensity for perfection, method and meticulousness, eventually I excelled in locksmithing. I came to understand and appreciate the individual characteristics and idiosyncracies of every type of lock, at any age and under any condition. After graduating with this latest degree, my talents for getting into excrement really began to bloom.

Following my release from the Wash, I lived in Toronto. Whatever had a lock was subject to my dexterity. I didn't work. I stole instead. I was always driving a hot car or bike around. Whenever I needed money, I just broke into some place.

The police were hot on my trail in Toronto, so I moved to the suburbs of Galt a short while later. Every Saturday at 9:00 p.m., like clockwork, I strolled up Saint Mary's Road on my way to the conservation park garage to select the vehicle I wanted to drive to Toronto for the evening. Usually I chose the dark green 1969 Buick Le Sabre. I knocked loudly on the front door just to be absolutely certain no one was working late. Then I walked around and picked the back door spring lock. First I checked for the keys, which were usually in the ignition or on the keyboard. Then I opened the back door and drove the car around to the front gasoline pumps to fill up. The laneway had a huge padlocked chain stretching across, so I simply drove down into the ditch with enough speed to shoot up over the other side. I was always careful to return the car before dawn, and I readjusted the front seat, inside and outside mirrors and the radio station before I left. Not the slightest hitch was ever encountered in borrowing or returning any of the conservation park vehicles. I synchronized my movements with those of the private security agency's patrol car. And never once was I stopped by the police en route to or from Toronto. I think I probably stole that same car two dozen times.

Once, in the wee hours of the morning, I borrowed the conservation van, loaded up two motorcycles, a 1969 Triumph 650 cc and a 1970 BSA 650 cc, and took them both to Toronto. Instead of equipping the bikes with another set of license plates, I reversed them, matching the plate colors, blue on white, and altering the numbers and letters to match the license plates of legitimate motorcycles. My artistry was almost perfect. Even I couldn't detect a flaw, other than the slight elevation of the original numbers or letters.

One afternoon, riding the Triumph, I took the exit to Toronto's main airport. I passed an unmarked police car parked on the opposite side of the road. The detective was detaining a motorist. The instant the cop and I locked glances, I knew I was in trouble. In a matter of seconds he disposed of the matter with the motorist, made a 180-degree turn and started tailing me. I exited into a service station in an attempt to discourage him, but it didn't help. He continued to follow me steadfastly as I reentered the flow of traffic. Soon he passed and signaled for me to pull over, which I did, after a fashion. I pulled right over four lanes of traffic to the far side of the road, then rode down through the ditch and across a field, leaving him sitting there on the side of the road all by his lonesome.

One evening I was double-parked, discussing directions with my sister in her Mustang, when a Toronto police cruiser pulled up behind us. I sped away on my Triumph and my sister followed suit in her car. But it was me the officer zeroed in on. I exited stage right into a dead-end alley and the cop followed. I wasn't in any position to change course or decelerate and still make good my getaway, so I jumped off the bike, which kept going until it crashed into a brick wall and exploded into flames. I jogged around the corner and intercepted my sister, and we left the area in a hurry.

The second motorcycle, the BSA, simply died on me one day on the 401 entering Toronto. I removed the license plate and entrusted it to a nearby ditch, then hitchhiked the remainder of the way into the city. On the way, someone took a shot at me from a passing car. I was standing under an overpass, and the bullet ricocheted off a concrete pillar ten feet away. If the shot hadn't hit the pillar, I would have mistaken it for a backfire. I was a little suspicious of any passing cars after that, ready to dive for cover at the sound of the first bang.

On a farm near Woodstock one night, a few hours after dusk, I quietly attempted to relieve George Bedard of his dark green 1969 Chrysler 300, which was parked in the backyard. The dog put up an awful fuss. The first time Mr. Bedard curiously opened his second-story farmhouse window and yelled, "What are you barking at, boy?" The second time he just looked out. The third time he told the dog to shut up. And the fourth time I stole his car.

If I wasn't stealing someone's car, I was stealing someone else's motorcycle. So many cars and bikes disappeared from Galt the cops thought a theft ring was operating. Eventually they realized it was all the handiwork of just one culprit — me. But they couldn't catch me in the act, so eventually I became involved in a highly entertaining game of fox and hounds as I was chased all over the countryside by the Galt police.

It all began one fine morning when I took possession of a new 1972 Mercury Cougar XR7. It was a gold two-tone job with a cream leather interior, basically a working man's sports car, but I grew fond of it.

For two months I drove the Cougar around as if I owned it. But this exceedingly hot day in July I decided to take everyone to the conservation park lake for a refreshing dip. As usual, I didn't bother to stop at the toll booth to exchange pleasantries; I merely drove around the back. A highly ambitious park employee observed this peculiarity and gave chase in pursuit of his four-dollar entry fee. I told him that I'd paid it earlier on in the day, but he didn't believe me, so we went back to verify it with the female cashier, which she did with a mischievous smile.

I proceeded to the lake and my sister challenged me to a swimming contest. We began to swim to the far shore past the buoy markers, but were intercepted by the same park employee, this time in a canoe. Following an exchange of views, the Lone Ranger left and I returned to shore for the sole purpose of giving him a good shellacking. We had both agreed to settle our little dispute with our fists.

Upon my arrival, however, I spotted the police taking an unusual interest in my car. My sister spoke to the gentlemen and relayed to me their innocent concern. They merely wished to clear up the minor difference of opinion between me and the Lone Ranger. I might have been slow but I wasn't retarded. I had absolutely no intention whatsoever of going anywhere near that car. Aside from the fact that it was hot, it contained three rifles in the trunk, which were hot, also. No doubt the police had radioed in the license plate number and had discovered it, too, was hot.

I headed for home, barefoot, bathing-suited and none too happy with the situation. I followed a secluded creek leading right by my apartment, then stopped and sent a neighborhood youngster over to my sister to find out if the police were in the area. My sister ran straight to me. With a desperate sense of urgency and bated breath, she gasped, "Run! The police are here!" Just as she gave me this warning, an officer walked around the corner, spotted me and blocked my escape. I was positioned between two vehicles parked snugly against a wall. At the last moment I swerved and vaulted over the hood of a car.

The cop was quite chubby and realized I would soon outdistance him in a footrace, so he drew his gun. I thought he just might be frustrated enough to shoot me in the back, so I ran right through a group of youngsters playing London Bridge Is Falling Down. They were all quite unaware that there was a maniac behind me waving a gun around that he didn't quite know what to do with. Then I ran smack dab into another officer in a squad car. It was touch and go there for a few seconds. I wasn't sure who would reach the end of the dead-end street first, him or me. But he wasn't quick enough, so I beat him to it. I hurdled a guardrail and disappeared through a series of backyards, eventually concealing myself beneath a canvas tarp in a neighbor's backyard for the remainder of the day.

That evening I returned to my apartment and learned that the police had impounded the Cougar and taken it to their yard less than a block from the apartment. They must have been slightly less than amused when they learned that that was where I'd stolen the license plates for the Cougar. They left a large German shepherd on guard, an animal that supposedly had a reputation for viciousness.

I had a spare set of car keys, so with a gallon of gas I decided to repossess my wheels. The Cougar was there all right, and so was the German shepherd. The mad dog was sitting in the front seat of a dilapidated wreck. I sneaked up on it, and when it saw me, it took off out of there as if it had seen a ghost. First it tried to climb the fence, then it bolted across the yard, tripping over everything in sight. I couldn't help laughing, and without further ado I took my car and left for Toronto.

A few weeks later, on a Saturday night, I returned to Galt and parked the Cougar behind an auto body shop. The next morning I went to pick it up. I found the car easily enough. It was sitting right out in the middle of the lot with the hood, doors and trunk wide open. The police were there somewhere, but I wasn't sure just where. A few auto body repairmen were sitting around eating lunch. I walked smartly over to the car, closed the hood, trunk and doors and drove away. They all sat there looking befuddled, trying to put it all together. I stole that same car three times, once from the owner and twice from the Galt police.

One night I drove up a side street to my sister's place and saw a police car in front of her apartment building. She was speaking with the officer. As I approached, he glanced once in my direction, then dashed to his cruiser and started to chase me as if I owed him money. I didn't bother to stop and chat. Instead, I quickly negotiated the nearest corner, ducked into a conveniently hedged driveway and turned off my headlights.

A short while later I returned to my sister's and found out what the officer had said. The police were becoming quite upset with me and intended to shoot me the first chance they got. Well, I thought, if they wanted the car that badly, they could have it. Some people just had no sense of humor.

I was back in Galt again in possession of another stolen car one evening, intent upon leaving the city, when an officer in a cruiser attempted to intercept me. I made a run for it — right into a tree. Abandoning the vehicle, I exited stage left with the officer in hot pursuit. In hopes of discouraging him, I scaled an exceedingly high fence and vaulted over the top. But the cop surprised me by simply running around the fence. I headed for a patch of woods and managed to lose him, but when I hopped over a stream, I ran right into another uniform carrying a flashlight.

I was up to my ass in police! They were everywhere! This one growled at me, so I retraced my triathlon route. I splashed back across the stream and dived into the woods. Realizing by now that the police had been lying in wait for me, I tried to tiptoe quietly through the trees and come out the other end. However, every which way I crept I inadvertently stepped on a twig or broke a branch. Each snap was followed by the corresponding hue and cry, "He's over here!"

I didn't want to present my pursuers with an opportunity to cordon off the area, so I charged out of the woods. Only one officer in the race was in contention now. I ran for a nearby house and circled it once. The second time around I ducked out, leaving the cop running around the house by himself. But then I ran right into a cruiser, which gave chase, too.

I couldn't keep up this ironman nonsense much longer without becoming exhausted, so I headed for high ground. The police, no doubt, were just as tired as I was. I made one last, all-out effort to climb a huge hill. Finally I staggered to the top and collapsed against a tree. Then I heard someone shout from below, "McArthur, you son of a bitch!" followed by a loud boom. They were shooting at me! I decided I wasn't as tired as I'd originally thought, so I got the hell out of there as fast as my legs could carry me.

On one of my trips to Galt I became trapped in my mother's apartment, specifically the washroom. There were two police officers right outside the door, and they wanted in. Although I tried my best to disguise my voice as a girl's, they didn't buy my ruse. Eventually they forced their way in. I, in turn, attempted to force my way out. What ensued was a comedy worthy of the Three Stooges.

One officer was quite strong, while the other was quite pudgy. I battled it out with the first one while the second one kept getting in the way. Twice he was knocked into the bathtub, which was full of hot water. Each time he let out a squeal. The tussle went on for the longest time, and eventually we were all quite exhausted and just going through the motions of fighting. It all ended when the first officer bit my finger to the bone. I tried to stick my hand in his mouth to pinch a nerve, but he wouldn't let go until the handcuffs were on.

And so, in such a manner, I was arrested. A day later I was escorted by two OPP officers to the Walkerton County Jail. I was to stand trial for a robbery I'd committed in Burgoyne, Ontario, in 1971. I had just walked into the convenience store, opened the till, scooped out the money and walked out again. I didn't think I'd get much time for it. Nevertheless, I decided that at the first opportunity I was going to make a run for it. That would in all probability be as soon as the cruiser door opened when we arrived in Walkerton at 10:00 a.m. I had no reason or desire to remain in jail and considered any man who did to have something wrong with his head.

In preparation for my escape I told the officers that my shoes were uncomfortable and that I wanted to take them off. The actual reason was that they had two-inch heels. Sprinting with them on would be extremely difficult. The cops didn't think I was going to try to escape. Instead, they thought I might try to bean them with my shoes. They didn't object to me taking my shoes off, but insisted I put them on the front seat. I agreed and chatted with them occasionally to allay any suspicions.

Lady Luck smiled upon me as we were passing through Harriston. The two officers just happened to spot the town's chief of police out for a spin in his cruiser. They parked, climbed out and began shooting the breeze with him, leaving me all by my lonesome in the back seat of their cruiser. My handcuffs weren't tight enough, and it took approximately two seconds for me to squeeze my hands out of them and hop out the front door. They couldn't believe it! All I saw were three pairs of big white eyes staring at me in astonishment. I did my best 100-yard dash diagonally across the road and almost into an oncoming car. It screeched to a halt, but I didn't. As I headed for the badlands with the police stampeding behind me, I still recall the mournful cry of one officer, "Micky, come back!"

Bruce County isn't internationally renowned for its dense rain forests. Consequently I had to put considerable distance between me and my cuffless captors. I ran cross-country well into the afternoon. As I tore through a cornfield, I tripped on a rock and ripped a good half-dollar-sized piece of skin off the ball of my foot. The pain was terrible, and I couldn't walk on that part of my foot at all.

I paused to rest around 4:00 p.m. and hid in a farmer's barn. After constructing a small shelter from bales of hay, I lay down to rest for a short spell before resuming my trek. Just as I was about to drift off, I heard whining and digging sounds coming from outside my shelter. I took a peek and spied a lone police dog trying to arrest me. Eventually I managed to discourage the dog and it left.

I had exhausted the long paw of the law. However, not to tempt fate twice, I soon left the barn to put a few more miles between me and that baleful bloodhound. And, as insurance, I used all the evasive maneuvers for disguising one's scent, the kind of tricks that are supposed to work in the movies but never do. I thought they might work in real life, but they weren't too successful there, either. I climbed trees and leaped from treetop to treetop. I walked along the top of wire fences and doubled back on my tracks. I jumped off bridges and ran through creeks. But the only way I lost the ten-man OPP canine tracking team following me was when I ran up the middle of the highway.

Later on that evening I borrowed a car from a farmer, after filling it up with gas, of course. The owner just stood there in the window watching me drive away. Naturally I waved. Country folk have always had a tendency to leave their keys in the ignition. I could always count on a car being available in a pinch. At the first city I bought a ticket and boarded a train to the west coast. I was freedom bound.

5

Fine Young Reprobates

I TRAVELED EXTENSIVELY THROUGHOUT western Canada by train, bus and thumb. But after two months I was back in Ontario. I figured the heat had died down by then and that it was safe to return. In the summer of 1972 Steve Faust was released from Millbrook Reformatory, where he had been doing time for our last car theft. He came to see me. We had nothing to do, so in an adventurous mood we decided to go west to seek fame and fortune.

Setting off from Toronto, we arrived in Kenora, thanks to a succession of rides. The town bordered an Indian reservation, and we were quite amazed at what we encountered. The streets were littered with drunks who staggered around all over the place, giving the town a strange, carnivallike atmosphere.

The first night we were there Steve was approached by an intoxicated woman who offered herself to him for a few paltry dollars. The police just cruised by the whole charade. After numerous inquiries, it became apparent that this was the established, if not accepted, way of life. The drunks cashed their welfare checks at the liquor store every month and barely survived between each drug-induced stupor.

But the most heartrending aspect of the entire setup was the police brutality. It was rumored to be so blatant and commonplace that it far exceeded, per capita, that of any other town or city in Ontario.

I'm sure smashing someone in the face really helped a person understand his alcoholism. We moved on with great haste.

One evening we received a ride from a native. A big native, and he was drunk. He slammed on the brakes, the tires screeched, and the car slid 100 feet. It performed a ninety-degree turn, almost flipped over sideways and finally came to rest halfway out of a ditch. "Climb in boys," he said. We had just completed a seventeen-mile hike, and if we hadn't been so desperate for a ride, we wouldn't have gotten in. But we were, so we did.

Our driver flattened the gas pedal. The tires spun, kicking up dirt, then caught the pavement. The car lurched forward, sideways and then straightened out. The first thing he said was "I'm Cree, full-blooded, and I don't like white men. I killed one once. He was messing around with my wife. I beat him to death. Got two years in the pen for it. Manslaughter. I didn't like white men even before that, never have, and I'll never like them as long as I live." Then he squinted suspiciously at us in the darkness and asked, "You boys ain't moonyasses, are you?"

Now, I was proud to be white. I respected my heritage. I wasn't responsible for taking the land away from the Indians and putting them on reservations. I respected my people. I wasn't ashamed of my race. I said, "We're Ojibwa. We're from the Southampton Reserve. This here's Steven Yellowbird and I'm Michael Blackhawk. We're on our way to visit my great-grandfather. He's chief of all the Ojibwa tribe."

The Cree wasn't such a bad driver, actually. Once he got the car in motion, he managed to keep it out of both ditches, which I thought was surprising. There was one thing I did find quite disturbing, though. He zigzagged down the road, playing accidental chicken with oncoming traffic. I was pretty sure he was going to kill us. I could almost hear my own requiem playing.

I glanced over at Steve, and he gave me one of his "It's been good to know you" looks. But the Cree's driving had a vaguely discernible pattern to it. Somehow we always managed to miss an oncoming car. Although I must admit I remained poised to lend assistance in the form of yanking the steering wheel if required.

After the longest ten miles I had ever ridden, he finally reached his exit and we were released. We tumbled over each other trying to get out the door. As he roared away around the corner, he drove part of the way through the ditch in order to compensate for the sharp turn. That ride was the most harrowing experience of my life up to that moment.

Two days later we received a ride from a respectable-looking elderly gentleman driving a well-maintained, late-model car. Now most senior citizens are usually sensible individuals. They realize they don't have an awful lot of time left and they want to preserve and enjoy what little time remains. When it comes to hitchhiking, they are the most reliable bet. Not so with this one. He wasn't your run-of-the-mill grandfather.

We were winding our way through the rock cuts of northern Ontario and it was raining hard. But that didn't prevent our driver from speeding and passing every vehicle in sight, regardless of the obstacle. Still, there was a method to his madness. He would gain on the vehicle from behind, hesitate for a brief second, unable to discern any immediate approaching vehicle, then hit the gas and go for it. But the most unsettling thing of all was that after each successful bid he'd cackle insanely.

God knows I don't mind a little excitement to spice up my life now and again. And at times I've even been known to extend the limit, bordering on danger. But this old geezer had a reservation at the Celestial Hotel, and he was banging the service bell at the front desk for attention. Worse, he wanted us to be his guests!

I suppose all the fun he was having gave him an appetite, because he pulled into a roadside café for lunch. To ensure our continued company, he tried to bribe us with a snack. But although we were a might hungry ourselves, we respectfully declined the offer and went on our way with a sudden change in plans and direction.

Eventually we reached Winnipeg, Manitoba, with decisive proof of how unreliable hitchhiking was. We decided to change our mode of transportation and hopped several freight trains traveling west. I was climbing from car to car one day, easing my way around a transport truck trailer unit on a flatbed, when I saw the train approaching a narrow, rock-walled underpass. Steve quickly grabbed my leg and pulled me in just in time. The authorities would still be scraping me off the rock today if he hadn't acted so quickly.

One night the train was rolling down the tracks at about fifty-five miles an hour. The air was warm and I was filled with exuberance. I stood straight up on the roof of the boxcar with the wind in my hair and lashing away at my clothes, the car rocking from side to side. The next day I did a little sunbathing on top of the car. I was mesmerized by the clear blue sky, so close I could almost reach up and grab it. Then there was a flick. Then another flick. Curiously I looked back along the tracks and saw telephone wires running right across the tracks, not more than three feet from the top of the train!

Not long after we were unexpectedly arrested coming into Moose Jaw, Saskatchewan. Apparently some motorist had seen us on top of the train and notified the RCMP. We were charged with the theft of train fare from the Canadian National Railway, brought to court, found guilty and sentenced to six days in jail all in the same afternoon. We used aliases and our fingerprints weren't taken. Nevertheless, despite our insignificant sentence, we were flown forty-five miles to the Regina Correctional Centre. After serving five days, we were flown back to Moose Jaw. That evening we hopped right back on board the first train heading north to Saskatoon.

Once in Saskatoon we fell back on our thumbs again. On a Sunday morning, as we were hitchhiking, it began to pour. We ran for the nearest shelter, a tractor dealership's storage garage. Out of mild curiosity, born of boredom, I tried to pick the lock on the rear door of the dealership with my comb, and succeeded. Once out of the bone-chilling drizzle, we thought we might as well stay awhile and warm ourselves up a little. While Steve prepared himself a coffee, I wandered around and found a large double-door safe.

There is an eccentricity prevalent among safe owners that was related to me once by an old safecracker. According to him, they left their safes on single-digit or day-lock overnight. Most regular safes have a three-digit combination — right, left and right respectively. All anyone knowing these two facts has to do is maintain downward pressure on the handle and carefully turn the dial to the right, number by number, until the third digit is reached, at which point the handle will fall and the safe will open.

More out of inquisitiveness than actual expectation, I tried this technique on the garage safe, and it worked! The heavy door swung open, and I could see why, too. There was another steel door requiring a large key. I tested the handle and discovered the door wasn't locked. Then I let out a whoop for Steve. He hustled into the office thinking the police had arrived. When he saw the open safe, though, he nearly did cartwheels. Our take from the safe netted us well over $1,000 dollars. We were rich now, since twenty minutes earlier we'd hardly had a dollar between us. Leaving the dealership with some haste, we headed for the nearest town and purchased two bus tickets to Hay River in the Northwest Territories.

Hay River is the twin sister of Kenora, except for the police brutality. Here everyone is drunk or wants to be, red and white alike. The pattern of lifestyle is: work the whole week, get off early on Friday, stay drunk the entire weekend until Monday morning, then drag yourself in late for work. Almost everyone we met wanted to leave the frozen, godforsaken place. But the living expenses kept skyrocketing, so that by the time a person settled his bills and sobered up come Monday morning, he never had enough cash left to buy a ticket out. It was like a merry-go-round. Actually, I wondered if anyone really wanted to leave. Perhaps it was the only place they could wallow in the kind of haphazard lifestyle they actually wanted while having a good reason to do so.

One night we went to a lounge, where we met two girls. Even though I don't drink, I sampled one or two rum and Cokes just to be sociable. After leaving the establishment, accompanied by the girls, we stood out on the street and waited for our taxi to arrive. Just then two sailors walked by, laughing. One was telling a joke to the other, which I overheard and found amusing, causing me to laugh, too. Then, quite unexpectedly, the sailor turned mean and asked me what I was laughing at.

I was feeling pretty relaxed and wasn't in the mood for a scrap, ladies being present and all, so I tried to be a little more polite than I would usually have been. Whether he was jealous because we had two women and all he had was his fat friend, I don't know, but he wasn't content to let things be. No, he had to give me a little lecture. Just as he was beginning to expound upon his second point, I interjected with a theory of my own, a right cross to the lips.

Well, he got quite excited about that and we started to go to it like a couple of fighting cocks. I was pretty fancy on my feet and equally so with my hands, and even though the sailor was tough, he was slow. All of a sudden, though, the drinks I'd had hit me and my legs turned to rubber and my arms to lead. Needless to say, he made short work of me, practically punting my face for a few hundred yards. And be damned if I didn't want to have another go at him as soon as I staggered to my feet again. But Steve, the taxi driver and both girls piled on top of me and that was that.

Our next major stop after Hay River was Edmonton, Alberta, to the south. We did a relatively small amount of pilfering on the way. One night we slipped noiselessly into a funeral home through an unlocked window. It was dark and so quiet that you could hear yourself breathe, or someone else! The air, heavy like a shroud, stank of the sickly sweet scent of flowers. I walked on my toes the entire time we were there.

Steve went off somewhere to check something while I searched the contents of a safe, finding only a number of the deceaseds' personal possessions, which I quickly replaced. At that point I realized that Steve hadn't returned yet, so I went looking for him, tiptoeing through the rooms and whispering, "Steve, Steve." But I couldn't find him anywhere. Something was wrong! I had visions of a seven-foot-tall undertaker, dressed in black, walking behind him with his hand on Steve's shoulder, taking him to God knows where! I was going to get the hell out in a hurry. In the semidarkness I dashed for the window, around a corner and ran right into Steve, scaring the hell out of both of us. "Where the hell were you?" I snapped, angered now by my fright.

"In the car," he replied, a little embarrassed.

We had a choice of two cars at the funeral home — a hearse and a Cadillac. We picked the Caddy. It was an outstanding luxury car with power everything. After a few hours on the highway, though, I grew tired of all the gadgets and climbed into the back seat to sleep as Steve drove. A little later the car's jostling woke me up and I found Steve laughing. He had fallen asleep at the wheel, waking up just in time to see the Caddy heading straight for the dividing guardrail. Yanking wildly on the steering wheel, he made the car swerve dangerously, then head directly for the opposite ditch and an unsuspecting hitch-hiker with his thumb out. The hitchhiker took one look at the Cadillac roaring toward him, threw his backpack into the air and dived headfirst into a ditch. We laughed like hell over that one.

By this time we had pointed our Caddy east, heading back to

Ontario on secondary roads in southern Saskatchewan. Steve was driving when we passed a small, squat building all lit up in the middle of the road. What a strange place to put a building, I thought. Nevertheless, we continued on into a little town, parked the car in a hotel lot and climbed out to see where we were, just as a police officer in a cruiser pulled up and began to look around. I stopped a gent leaving the hotel and asked him for directions to Winnipeg. "First you go back into Canada and — " he replied. That strange little building parked in the middle of the road had been the customs booth. We were in the U.S.! Driving back the same way was out of the question, so we waited for the border patrol cruiser to leave, then drove through someone's backyard, down through a ditch, across the border and back onto the highway again.

We drove all night and reached the outskirts of Winnipeg by dawn. As we were entering the city, a police cruiser started tailing us. We turned a corner immediately, and he followed suit. So we reversed the car and hightailed it out of the city until we found a secluded place to shelter the vehicle. We discovered such a place off a dirt road in a stand of poplars next to a river. The day was exceptionally warm, and we spent the remaining hours of daylight relaxing on the sandy shore in quiet reverie.

Due to our close brush with the law, we thought it prudent to change license plates. Leaving the car hidden near the river, we went in search of likely prospects. After a few miles, we turned into a long, paved driveway and spotted a car. As we approached, Steve cautioned, "There's a German shepherd on the porch."

"Don't worry about the dog," I growled. "I'll wrap this tire iron around his head if he messes with us."

"He's big," Steve commented.

"I don't care," I replied gruffly.

I wasn't afraid of the dog. I'd grown up with dogs. All you had to do was show them who was the boss.

Steve picked up a good fist-sized rock along the way. The dog was lying on the porch like a marble statue, its body tense. I knew it could sense I meant business. I was bad. I was mean. I could almost smell its fear. But when we got halfway down the driveway, it bounded off the porch like a bullet, no bark, no growl, just one smooth motion.

Steve and I performed a synchronized about-face in about one-hundredth of a second and ran for our lives! Yeah, we were mean, real mean, as we stampeded in terror down that driveway, the dog close on our heels. Ironically the only thing that saved us was the owner's voice calling his canine monster back.

After that brush with death, we lifted a pair of plates from a less dangerous target. Soon we were back on the road, driving all night until we were in northern Ontario. In a small town at a stoplight, we had the misfortune of seeing a police cruiser drive up beside us and signal us to pull over. Steve, who was driving, just kept smiling at the officer until we were able to reach the edge of town, then he hit the gas. By the time we reached 120 miles an hour on a downhill, we knew we were losing our pursuer, so we started whooping and hollering . . . until we saw the roadblock!

Two cruisers were positioned crosswise, obstructing the highway. Steve drove straight for them, reducing speed to sixty miles an hour at the last second. Without warning he swerved sharply left to squeeze by on the shoulder of the road between the cruiser and the ditch. Almost in unison, the left-hand cruiser reversed into our path and we neatly crunched off three feet of his rear end, sending him spinning like a bottle top as the second officer, who was standing behind his cruiser, dashed for the far side of the road to get out of the way. The front end on the passenger side of our car was completely smashed, but the Cadillac persisted in its state of uniform motion well past the roadblock, eventually grinding to an abrupt halt.

Steve sprang quickly from the vehicle and ran down into the roadside ditch as I jerked frantically on the inoperative passenger door handle. Sliding with maximum haste over the seat to the driver's door, I sped after him, disappearing into the bush while one cop yelled, "Come out or we'll shoot!"

In the pitch-black he'd probably shoot his partner in the butt, I thought to myself. Still, I appreciated his sense of humor and reciprocated by yelling, "Don't shoot! We're coming out!" as we continued blindly battling our way deeper into the trees.

After an exhausting run, we finally reached a rail line. Walking up the tracks and crossing a bridge partway, we saw a flashlight beam bobbing in the distance. It had to be the police! We retreated in a hurry, cautiously stepping onto each railroad tie, trying to prevent a spill and possible sprained ankle. Meanwhile, the flashlight beam got closer and larger until it was almost upon us. A train!

We threw caution to the wind and bolted. The headlight illuminated everything in its path, including us as we dashed for safety. My hair stood on end at the nearness of the train whistle as it shrieked at us. We weren't going to make it. "Jump!" I yelled. As we leaped off the bridge, the express train roared by. We tumbled down the embankment and came to rest near the bottom. Clawing our way back up the bank, we made sure there were no more bobbing flashlights in sight, then crossed the bridge and continued on our way up the tracks.

Without our Caddy, we decided to try our luck on the rails again. One cold night as we were passing through hilly countryside the train stopped briefly, yielding the right of way to an oncoming passenger train. We jumped off and ran stiffly up to the engine, where it would be warmer. At that moment the train began to chug away, leaving us standing there out of breath in the middle of bear country. We'd seen a few rooftops just a few miles before the stop, so we set off, feeling like a couple of midnight snacks walking down the railroad tracks. A while later we found a dilapidated old shack and spent the remainder of the night there.

In the morning we spotted a well-used railroad worker's boxcar parked on a side track. Finding no one at home, we settled in. Scrounging around for food, I found some homemade ragout in the refrigerator. I sampled it and it tasted pretty good, so I heated it up and ladled out a couple of generous servings for us. Just like home!

The boxcar was placed in an ideal setting on a lush hillside with a huge sapphire-blue lake below. But after two days we decided to resume our journey. Attempting a shortcut through the trees, we came across a canal leading to the lake. Although it was cold, we decided to swim across. I dived in first, clothes and all, and after a prolonged flurry of strokes, reached the distant shore. Steve was next. I watched with mild curiosity as his feet and arms sliced the water like knives. He didn't seem to be having an easy time of it, but I thought he'd make it. About three-quarters of the way across, though, he started gasping for help. Having nearly drowned a number of times myself, I knew that when you think you're out of strength, you can still swim a quarter of the distance you've already come. But Steve didn't know this, and by the time he was about twenty feet from the shore, he started to go under. So I thought I'd better go in and pull him out, or I'd never hear the end of it.

He wasn't so much waterlogged as freezing to death. We returned to the boxcar — this time by a bridge down the canal a piece — and I lit the stove and piled blankets on top of him until he stopped shivering. The following day we again headed out, this time taking the bridge. We walked five miles to the nearest highway and started hitchhiking once again.

Our first ride let us off in a typical northern Ontario town. We visited the local car dealership and helped ourselves to a new, no-frills car, planning to use it for the big stretch back to Toronto. Pausing at a motorcycle shop to check out the latest models, we also thought we might take advantage of the nearby gas station. Just as we finished our business, an inopportune police cruiser flashed by, catching our act. But he didn't catch us! We leaped into our new car and roared straight for him. As the cop tried to get out of the way, we slowed, hopped out and let the car roll down the road by itself — empty. In the bush lining the highway we ran in the opposite direction, took a secondary highway and stole another car.

By the time we got back to Toronto, after stealing everything we could lay our grubby little hands on out west, we figured we could do just about anything we wanted. The way I figured it, the world was just one great big shopping mall, and everything in it was free.

6

Doing Ninety in a Thirty

BACK IN TORONTO I BEGAN TO WORK as a hairstylist under an assumed name at the House of Lords on Yonge Street. That was during the day. At night Steve and I continued our criminal activities, a double shift that was really beginning to wear me out. Discussing the matter with Steve, we decided to find him a hairstyling job, also, and put an end to our larcenous lifestyles. We figured it was just a matter of time before we both wound up in jail, so we'd give hairstyling another shot. We liked the atmosphere and the women. There were always plenty of women wanting to look beautiful. We figured it was only right to sacrifice our criminal careers for this cause. Then one day a customer walked into the shop and sat down. As I was washing his hair, he said, "Hi, Mick." Although I didn't recognize him, he remembered me from our school days in Walkerton and knew all about my "legal" problems. That was the end of my short but sweet hairstyling career.

Now Steve and I set about crime in earnest. Leaving Toronto every night, we'd select a highway and break into every business along a ten-mile stretch or until it became light out — ten miles or ten hours guaranteed. One night we stopped in Stayner. We'd taken a bus this time, leaving the 1970 Chevy Nova SS we'd swiped in Galt at home. So our first order of business in Stayner was to break into a garage and secure a new set of wheels. After parking our new chariot in an alleyway, we broke into a men's wear store. Selecting only the items we liked in the correct sizes, we filled a number of heavy-duty plastic garbage bags and hid them outside while we broke into a combination hardware and jewelry store down the street.

After we collected the diamond rings and expensive watches, I went over to the hardware department and picked out a high-quality shotgun. We were in no rush. No alarms had sounded and we were alone in the store. There seemed no need to be careful. Then Steve noticed a stairway leading up to the second floor, no doubt the store owner's apartment. We hurried to the back door and slipped out just in time to see the flashing lights of an arriving police car. I ducked behind a nearby camping trailer, but Steve, incredibly, continued to walk swiftly down the sidewalk. As I eased myself along the far side of the trailer and peeked around the corner, I was startled to see Steve sprint past with the cop in red-hot pursuit. Not knowing if the constable had a partner lurking about, I pushed the shotgun under the trailer, having no desire to give the police an excuse to shoot me on sight. Then I made a break for it, expecting to hear a warning shot or at least the thud of pursuing feet, neither of which happened.

Where Steve had fled I had no way of knowing. I wasn't all that concerned about him, though; no one had ever caught Steve in a footrace, let alone a police officer with ten-pound boots. So I cautiously trotted through the back streets of town to the outskirts and into the countryside. As I jogged from farm to farm, checking for car keys and being dissuaded once or twice by a watchful yard dog, I eventually came across a 1965 Ford Mustang. Shifting the car into neutral and releasing the emergency brake, I steered it quietly down the long gravel driveway, climbed inside, started the engine and drove straight back into town.

By this time a few hours had passed since the break-ins. So, on the off chance the police hadn't discovered the clothing store break-in or recovered the clothing, I drove past the alleyway leading to the rear of the store. It was deserted, but our original car was gone, of course. Parking the Mustang, I retrieved the clothing and loaded it into the back seat. However, in order to return to Toronto, I first had to bypass the OPP station on the edge of town. Regardless of which route I chose, every back street always merged with the main street, which passed right in front of the station. Since it would soon be morning, I decided to run the gauntlet.

Driving toward the station, I spied a cruiser parked out in front. Two officers were sitting in it, talking. Too late to reverse direction or duck down a side street, I cruised by, keeping an eye on the rearview mirror. Two winks of the police car headlights told me I was in trouble, so I hit the gas, and the Mustang came alive with a roar. I brought the speedometer up to 130 miles an hour three separate times, each time easily outdistancing the pursuing cruiser. But I almost shot off the highway into the trees while negotiating the bends, since the steering capabilities didn't match the horsepower. Fearing an accident at the rate I was going, I abandoned the vehicle, clothes and all, and jogged through the fields. I slept the remainder of the night as well as the following day in the hayloft of a farmer's barn. The next day I swiped his car and made my way back to Toronto. Steve, of course, eluded capture, and found his way back to Toronto a few days later, too.

Not long after the Stayner adventure, the police began to get wise to us. They had put numerous break-and-enters together with car thefts and come up with none other than Steve and yours truly. They even visited all our relatives, making futile inquiries about our whereabouts. Slipping into Owen Sound one night to visit Steve's family, we found his mother out but stayed anyway to talk with his sister. We told her all about the wild times we'd been having, laughing and joking for hours. Steve considered staying the night, but I had an uneasy feeling about even being there, so we all went out into the backyard to sit around the picnic table.

Soon it was time to go. We bade Steve's sister goodbye and began walking up the street, when a carload of gentlemen in a dark, nondescript vehicle approached. We returned their gazes innocently enough and they shot up the street. Then we realized we'd just eyeballed a carload of detectives. Needless to say, we left town in a hurry.

Later, we found out the police had been tipped off by an ever-vigilant neighbor across the street. The cops had come crashing through the door of Steve's family's house, missing us by only a few minutes. Logic would have dictated that we leave Ontario or shift our crime spree into low gear, but neither of these options occurred to us. We knew the police could definitely prove certain crimes because we hadn't always been careful about not leaving our fingerprints behind. Still, like the reckless types we were, we shifted our operations into high gear.

Barely within the city limits of Galt one evening we found ourselves scrutinized by a police officer passing in the opposite direction in a cruiser. When the police car spun around in a U-turn, I gunned our Austin Mini and sped around the nearest corner into a convenient underground driveway, where I extinguished our headlights. After a short spell, when we thought it was safe, we came roaring back out again, turned the corner and almost rammed the same police car, once again traveling in the opposite direction. This time the chase was definitely on. We took no more chances. Before the officer could make another U-turn, we screeched around the first corner we came to and leaped clear of the car while it was still in motion. Dodging and vaulting through the backyards and over the fences of a residential section, we kept running until we reached a set of railroad tracks.

By now it was early morning. Discovering an old Triumph motorcycle, I picked the ignition and we went our merry way around the deserted streets from one end of Galt to the other, trying to find the main road out. As Steve was in control, I just happened to glance behind me to see a cruiser chasing us. Indicating to Steve that we had company, he skidded into a gravel driveway and crashed into a tree stump, knocking both of us off the bike. We split up after that, but a few blocks from the scene we made contact the way we always did whenever we were separated in a chase — by whistling. Finding each other, we also lucked upon a car, which we hot-wired, then headed back to Toronto.

In the city of London we suffered a temporary setback in transportation one night until we came across a white 1970 Ford Torino. Driving to Woodstock, I was quite surprised by its speed. The majority of cars we had driven weren't capable of exceeding 110 miles an hour. Racing along the 401, I drew Steve's attention to the speedometer — the needle was well past the 120 mile-an-hour mark.

Exiting off the 401 at Birdsalls, we accidentally came upon just what we'd been looking for — a sports car for Steve. This one was a purple 1968 MGB, and Steve wanted it badly. However, we encountered one small problem: the door was locked and no amount of lock-picking seemed to do any good. As I squeezed my arm between the window and the doorjamb in an attempt to reach the inside lock button, the window shattered. I asked Steve if he still wanted the car and he nodded, so I hot-wired it and he was off. Trying to catch him in the heavier Torino on the gravel road caused my car to tango from side to side, threatening to knock me into the ditch. Blaring the horn or flashing the lights had no effect on Steve. Finally he turned onto a paved road and I overtook him, cutting in front and almost running him off the road. He had been in such a state of joy driving the sports car that he hadn't even been aware I was chasing him.

On the way to Owen Sound sometime later, by way of back roads, Steve was impressed with how well the MGB handled and offered to let me drive to see for myself. Traveling down the gravel road, which had a lot of hills, dips, twists and turns, I started to build up speed, with all four wheels leaving the ground. Steve had a death grip on the dashboard, trying to talk me into slowing down, saying, "Mick, I know this road. There's a lot of turns and bends in it. You'd better slow down."

That just made me go faster and faster, and I laughed each time the car bounced over a hill. Then Steve started to curse, which made me laugh even harder. One second we were airborne and the next we were skidding down the road sideways. We must have slid for about 150 feet, because for the longest time I was just sitting there looking past Steve to the oncoming rush of gravel roadway, waiting for the car to flip over. But it never did. Instead, it slammed into a dirt embankment halfway down the hill.

We couldn't get the car started again, so we thought we'd better hide it, not wanting to attract any more police attention than we had to. We decided to push the car over the huge embankment and into the river. When we were finished, we walked up the road to visit his mother. Steve's mother and sister were always after him to give himself up and do his time, but his invariable reply was "I'll do my time some other time."

One night in Kitchener Steve sported a 1969 MG Austin and I had a 1970 Austin Mini. In true demolition derby spirit we chased each other up and down and around streets, across lawns and through hedges. After a time we thought we'd better leave the residential neighborhood before the police tried to join in, so we went to a nearby golf course and continued our derby there.

Now Steve had the Austin Mini and I had the MG. First he drove over a grove of small pines. Then, starting from the outside and working his way to the center, he knocked them over like ten-pins and got stuck in the middle. I came along, saw him in distress, butted him out and roared off again. Then he ambushed me from behind a hedge, ramming me into a sand trap on the side of a slight hill and leaving me stuck. I went looking for him and found him sitting on top of a knoll with all four wheels off the ground. We rocked his car off, but before Steve could jump in and put the brakes on, the Mini rolled down the hill and crashed into a tree.

Reclaiming his car, we drove over to my car, but couldn't push it out of the sand trap no matter how hard we tried, so we flipped it over onto its roof, then back again onto all four tires. As I climbed back into the car, I noticed that the windshield was now level with my forehead, so I had to be careful to duck before I hit anything.

Then Steve became stuck running up a row of steel guard posts, so I had to punch him out of there also. Steve's car was pretty battered by then and I was concerned that he wouldn't be able to open the door and run if the police suddenly appeared upon the scene, which we expected any moment, especially with all the roaring, crashing and banging around we were doing. So we ripped both his doors off.

Something must have been seriously damaged when we flipped my car over, because it started to smoke so much I couldn't see where I was going, causing me to run right into a concrete fountain. I hopped into Steve's car, and crashed into a few more trees before becoming bogged down in another sand trap.

Now in need of transportation, we walked up the road until we came across another Austin Mini. Steve's uncle was in the hospital, so Steve thought he wouldn't mind too much if we went out to his place in the country just outside of Elsinore and stayed there for a few days. We drove out in the Austin, parked in the garage and let ourselves in.

We weren't there for more than fifteen minutes when we started shooting up the backyard with his uncle's .22 Cooey. I returned inside and was looking for more shells when Steve came waltzing in the front door, back from the neighbor's house, carrying a great big .45 revolver with an eight-inch octagonal barrel. We raced across the road to break into his uncle's next-door neighbor's house, as well.

After turning the stereo on, we found a .270 Winchester rifle, which we definitely had to try out. Steve chambered a cartridge and was waving it around as if he wanted to fire it but wasn't sure where, so I opened the sliding glass balcony doors. Kaboom! Steve fired it off inside the house! We were stunned. It almost deafened us, so we took it outside and shot off a few rounds over an apple tree.

Back inside the house again, not being able to find the proper shells for the .45, we used .38s. The only problem with that was if we didn't point the gun skyward, the shell would fall right out of the barrel onto the floor. After firing a few rounds, we had to pry the expanded shell casing out. I was trying to wrench one out, thinking the gun was empty, when I pulled the trigger. It went off and the bullet hit the balcony's wooden railing, bounced off, dropped to the deck and spun around like a bottle top. After we fired a few more rounds from a shotgun we found, we raced back over to Steve's uncle's house.

Steve had a touch of the flu and went to bed, so I went back over to the neighbor's place. The .270 had a scope on it, so I started doing a little target shooting, using his uncle's doghouse as a target, I didn't think the dog was inside, because as soon as Steve and I had started playing with the guns, it had taken off across the field in a hurry. When I got bored with the doghouse, I shot at the chimney, too, but missed. Putting the gun back, I ran back over to his uncle's to find Steve crouching behind the refrigerator in his underwear. He thought I'd been right outside the house with the gun!

Later that day we took his uncle's .22 out again and were target shooting, using his next-door neighbor's driveway post as a target, when all of a sudden we heard a loud boom. The neighbor had come home and taken a shot at us! We took off out of there in a hurry and headed back to Toronto.

We parked the Mini in the driveway behind our apartment building and woke up the next morning to find it gone. I was outraged.

The police or some other thief had stolen it. I didn't know what the world was coming to. Even stolen cars weren't safe anymore. It didn't take us long to replace it with a 1969 Ford Mustang, though.

I'd forgotten how well Mustangs cornered and was demonstrating its ability to Steve, so I wasn't really paying attention to his discomfort. Finally Steve said, "Okay, Mick, it corners real good. Now let's go back to the apartment." I was going faster each time and coming closer to the parked cars on Steve's side, so when I went around the block for the third time, Steve started to swear. "You son of a bitch," he said. "If you smash my knee . . ." He had water on the knee from a recent bike accident. I started to laugh and almost sideswiped a car. I went back to the apartment only after I saw an officer in a cruiser. He had been sitting there parked beside a doughnut shop the whole time, just watching me.

In the early hours one morning, Steve and I picked up a 1969 Chrysler 300 from the sleepy little town of Shelburne. The owner wasn't using it, so we thought we might as well. We drove it to Primrose Service Station and Garage to fill it up. Mr. Primrose was asleep, so we helped ourselves. While I filled in for the gas jockey, Steve mentioned something about paying him and went off in search of the cash register. I heard the sound of distant rumbling growing steadily louder by the second. Not being able to find the register, Steve had come up with a 400-pound safe with convenient castors instead.

It was quite a chore getting the safe into the car. Finally, after a lot of shoving, pushing, pulling, grumbling and sweating, we managed to heave it into the trunk. I threw a handful of loose tools on top of the safe and Steve hopped in behind the wheel. Just then I noticed the garage owner's car, a 1967 Ford LTD with the keys in it, and although we didn't need it and it wasn't very new, I didn't want to insult the owner by not taking it. So I hopped inside and Steve and I raced each other out into the country.

We parked on a seldom-used bush road, smashed open the safe and found $1,000 dollars. To celebrate our newfound wealth, we decided to engage in a little bit of demolition derby. As we put our crash helmets on and climbed inside our cars, Steve threw a short-handled sledgehammer at my windshield, spiderwebbing it and impairing my vision. That was against derby rules, so I protested loudly. But my complaint fell on deaf ears.

We drove our cars out into a field and brought them into starting position. Steve was sponsored by Ford and I was sponsored by Chrysler. Around and around we circled, sideswiping each other until Steve suffered engine trouble. Now was my chance. I mercilessly sideswiped him. Still his car refused to start as he desperately turned the engine over, hollering for me to hold on until he got it going. But this was war; no quarter would be given. I sideswiped him again, then rammed him from the rear. Just as I was about to deliver the coup de grace, his car started and the battle raged anew.

His trunk was crunched and my front end was crumpled, then my old war horse, having dealt a number of punishing blows, started wheezing and coughing and ground to a halt. Slowly I pulled myself from the saddle. As I looked into the car's big, pain-filled headlights a sadness swept over me. I couldn't let her suffer. With a heavy hand and heart, I gave her the ceremonial, merciful parting shot, then dived for Steve's car as he made a pass.

Clinging wide-eyed like a fainthearted Spider-Man spread-eagled across the hood of Steve's car, I held on for dear life and hollered for him to slow down. But it was too late. He was battle-crazed and continued to turn in ever-tightening circles, faster and faster. Almost rolling off, I finally managed to claw my way in through the passenger side window just seconds before he shot over a small rise and crashed right on top of a pile of boulders.

Taking off our helmets, we weren't impressed. The cars had lasted a disappointing thirty minutes. Ford tough, Chrysler reliability — nonsense! The little sports cars had sustained increasingly more damage and had lasted twice as long. We determined never to allow Ford or Chrysler to sponsor either of us in any of our derbies again. We left the cars smoking and hissing in the middle of the field, wondering what the farmer would think when he came across our little presents and how surprised he'd be. If he was shrewd, he wouldn't have to worry about car parts for a long, long time to come.

Boyle's IGA in Walkerton wasn't really an easy place to break into. I leaped across a six-foot space between two brick walls and clung to the narrow window ledge while jimmying open the frame. One slip would plunge me twenty feet to the bricks and broken mortar blocks below. To make matters worse, the police station was only 100 yards away. Once inside, after sampling a few choice delicacies, Steve and I removed the weekly receipts, then headed down the street to ransack Len Schmidt Motors. Finding nothing of interest or value there, we left town and roamed north, breaking into MacDuff Motors in Brant Township as well as a number of other businesses along the way.

The car we were driving was a luxurious but conspicuous marine-blue two-door Mercury. We thought it best to at least, out of respect for the law, change the license plates, so we went from car to car until we found a pair that would lend a touch of respectability to our excessive speeding habits. We stole a pair of doctor's license plates.

Finding ourselves in the vicinity of Port Elgin one night and debating the car's rolling potential in proportion to its overextended design, we pulled into the Bayview Golf Club to put our theories into practice on the greens. Unfortunately we ended up stranding the car in a small ravine and had to abandon it. Not to be daunted, we walked over to the golf course driving range shack, fitted ourselves with a pair of gloves, selected a set of clubs and about five hundred balls and went out to the driving range to practice our swings.

After exhausting our supply of balls, we went across the road to a farm and saddled up two horses. As we were quietly leading the horses out of the barn, I heard a peculiar, recurring sucking noise. I stopped to see what it was but couldn't find anything wrong. I continued on and again heard the noise but couldn't determine the source. I gave Steve the reins and told him to walk the horse by me while I listened. I was shocked! There was a huge dog-eared piece of hide the size of a steak hanging from the horse's chest, exposing a gaping hole. It was a mess. The cavity was what had been making the sucking sound as the horse moved. I couldn't believe someone could leave an animal in that condition unattended. After I took the saddle off, I slowly led the injured horse back into the barn.

We still had one horse, though, and after examining it minutely to ensure it was sound, we rode it all over the golf course. When we were finished, we returned the horse and saddle and took the farmer's orange 1972 Plymouth Duster and drove up the road to the Hampton Golf and Country Clubhouse. While Steve busied himself making a coffee, I wandered into the liquor storage room. The walls were lined with every variety and brand of alcohol conceivable. I was a nondrinker largely due to the repugnant taste of alcohol in most liquors. This was my chance to find out if indeed there were any liquors I did like. I sampled the entire supply, taking a tiny taste from each. When I finished, I walked out of the room, obviously in a much better mood. I even discovered I liked champagne and dark rum. Returning to the car, I noticed Steve was even more anxious than usual to beat me to the driver's seat.

Steve didn't trust me to drive with him asleep, nor did I trust his driving while I slept. Therefore, if at all possible, we each tried to stay awake and keep an eye on the other. In the morning as we approached Guelph, I noticed Steve falling asleep at the wheel. I offered to drive, but he shook his head and said he'd be all right. I was nodding off a little myself, so when I woke to find him falling asleep a second time, I offered to drive again. But once more he declined. This time I insisted, so he conceded, conditional on reaching the city. I agreed.

The next thing I knew I awoke to our car sideswiping another vehicle, which was driving right along beside us down a four-lane road. Steve had fallen asleep. So there we were, both asleep, driving down the main street of Guelph in a hot car as if our fathers had half the city police force in their back pockets. The other car stopped immediately right in the middle of the road, and the driver jumped out to assess the damage as Steve executed a U-turn up over someone's lawn, through a flowerbed and headed back in the opposite direction.

Returning to Toronto, we packed our belongings and picked up a canary-yellow 1969 Plymouth Roadrunner with a 383 engine and Hurst shift. Our plan was to drive up to Hidden Lake and rent a cottage.

On the way to the lake Steve decided to see what the Roadrunner could do. By the time he reached 150 miles an hour, I could hear the Devil playing the fiddle, especially when he ran out of road and almost clipped a couple of cars trying to slow down. Steve could drive just about as well as I could, and although neither of us trusted the other's driving, we each thought our own skills were pretty hot, which was probably the best indication of both of our abilities. Even so, we were always game when either of us wanted to try out a new technique or test-drive a new car.

We hadn't brought any furniture with us for the cottage, so one night we went to Paisley to acquire some. After breaking into a variety store, a co-op, a farm equipment business and two garages, we found ourselves inside Burley and Son Equipment. I tried the single-digit technique on the safe and we successfully removed $500 dollars. Then we entered a furniture store and removed a cherry wood color television set, a stereo system and half a dozen porcelain statuettes, lamps and related items, putting them into a brand-new 1972 Pontiac Parisienne and a 1969 Chevy Malibu that we'd borrowed from J. S. Howe Motors just up the street. With both cars packed, back seats piled high and trunks overflowing, we drove all the way back to Hidden Lake unmolested.

After unloading the furniture, we raced to Toronto, rear-ending and sideswiping each other along the way. Cruising down Yonge Street in the congested traffic, keeping time with the beat of the music on the cars' radios, naturally we collided with each other occasionally. As we both turned into a parking lot, Steve attempted to parallel-park, but there just didn't seem to be enough room, largely due to the fact that I had him jammed up against another car. He simply gunned the engine, grinding his way up the side of the other car. The onlookers gave us more than the customary curious glances.

One night around 9:00 p.m., just outside Port Elgin on Highway 21, we stopped at a snack bar for refreshments. But we noticed a police cruiser paying us an inordinate amount of attention and decided to skip the refreshments. As we started to leave, the cop tried to pull us over. I asked Steve if he wanted to outrun him, and he said, "Sure." So I hit the gas, and we shot the five miles from Port Elgin to Southampton like a bolt of lightning. But just as I reached Southampton, a pedestrian angled right out into the street. I yanked hard on the steering wheel and skidded straight for a pair of gasoline pumps. Somehow I managed to avoid the pumps, but swerved onto a patch of gravel.

Now we were doomed. The heavy Roadrunner, with its big 383 engine, had too much power. My tires just spun uselessly on the loose gravel until the cruiser was able to catch up to us. Still, I tried to lose him in a series of maneuvers but to no avail. Eventually he boxed us in with the assistance of a second cruiser. There was no exit, so I slammed on the brakes and the car slid sideways. With the oncoming cruiser almost crashing into us from the front and the pursuing cruiser nearly ramming us from behind, we leaped from the car, vaulted a nearby farmer's fence and sprinted across an open field. As I discarded my white turtleneck sweater to offer a less visible target, one police officer yelled after us, "Run, McArthur, you coward!" We thought that was pretty funny.

After we lost the Plymouth, we were still partial to Roadrunners, so we found another one in Proton. Naturally we brought it home. Janet, as well as one of my little sisters, was with us at the time. My little sister made the mistake of asking me if the car was fast. Well, I just had to show her how fast it really was. I roared up one gravel road, doing seventy miles an hour, then I slammed on the brakes and completed a 180-degree slide and roared back again. By the time I reached the end of the road, it was time to stop — so the stop sign said, anyway. But I was going so fast when I slammed on the brakes that we slid right across the highway and kept going. Luckily there was no traffic at the time.

I came up on an old milk truck on the highway, doing 110, and I was just about to pass, when an oncoming car suddenly appeared. No problem. I just pumped the brakes to slow down, but I couldn't stop. The car was going too fast. I hit the gas and passed the truck, somehow managing to squeeze through and get back in the right lane. After that, I took the car back and parked it. My little sister never uttered another word about speed.

Back in Walkerton again, after breaking into a dry cleaners, I took special pleasure in robbing a garage owned by a man who had at one time been our landlord. Although he had always been very quick to lecture me on the immorality of leading a dishonest life, with the odd personal threat injected to pique me, it never occurred to him to do anything constructive like offering me employment in any of his numerous enterprises.

It proved to be extra satisfying to discover his cash box hidden beneath the bottom filing cabinet drawer. After searching the drawer contents unsuccessfully, I heard a peculiar clink when I slid the drawer closed. Curiosity got the better of me, and sure enough, I got my prize after further investigation. Outsmarting particularly obnoxious and miserly businessmen was one of the many satisfactions of being a burglar.

Still having a few hours remaining until dawn, Steve and I trotted on over to a car dealership. After cutting the safe open with an oxyacetylene torch and relieving the owner of his funds, Steve went out to the lot to select a vehicle. I had to keep an eye on him because he was finicky when it came to choosing a car. He would sit in it to see if it was comfortable, make sure the radio worked, check the lights and signals, listen to the engine and even take it for a test drive. And all this before we even stole it.

As we were leaving town, we noticed the gas gauge was nearly empty. It occurred to us to lift some gas from a local gas bar, but since we had some money we decided it was wiser to keep driving and cop some along the way. Not long after we noticed a car following us. After turning a few corners to rule out coincidence, we knew that Dick Tracy was on our trail again. If the police were going to get involved, then an empty gas tank would take all the fun out of the chase. We stopped at a farm to buy some gas, all the while keeping an eye on our guardian angel, who had also stopped a quarter of a mile away in the middle of a side road. We waited for the farmer to investigate our arrival. It was daybreak and the cows were lowing, eager to be exploited and rid of the cumbersome weight of the milk that had accumulated overnight. We figured the farmer would appear any moment.

Steve, doing his customary snooping, had found the keys in the ignition of the farmer's car. We discussed the pros and cons of switching cars and throwing a curveball at Dick Tracy, but decided against it. Our car was newer. Finally we couldn't wait any longer to buy the gas, so we filled our gas tank and roared out of Bruce County, leaving Dick in a cloud of dust.

Sometime later we found ourselves in Kitchener, walking up a street late at night. Our attention was riveted on a 1965 Jaguar convertible parked in a driveway. "Take me, take me!" it cried. Upon further investigation, I found I was able to unlock the door, so we backed the Jag out of the driveway and rolled it down the street. But when I tried to start the engine, the battery proved dead. We left it and resumed walking up the street until we came upon a Jaguar dealership.

As I was about to pick the lock, Steve yanked the handle, pulling the door wide open! Someone must have been working late inside and would surely have noticed the door opening. We sprinted a short distance away and the door slammed shut with a loud bang. We waited, but no one came to investigate. Cautiously we returned and searched the garage, yelling, "Hello, is anyone here?" No one answered. The place was empty.

We looked all over for the cash box but found a big safe, instead. I examined a 1968 twelve-cylinder Jaguar XKE and started the engine. Then we lugged the safe over to the car and wrestled it into the back seat. Taking a few tools with us, we drove out into the countryside to open the safe. After a lot of work with a sledgehammer and a chisel, we finally peeled the outer skin off and broke the firebrick. But when we cut the inside wall, we found . . . nothing. As a testimony to our disapproval, we left the safe right where it was and hopped into the Jaguar to return to Hidden Lake.

Initially we were concerned something might be wrong with the car, since it had been in the garage, but its performance never even faltered once. Although it was an automatic, Steve maintained that it was a fast car. So I took it up to 130 miles an hour. As we approached a small village, I tried to slow down, but we passed through it at 100 miles an hour. Headlights immediately pulled out from a side street behind us. It could only be the police. I stomped on the accelerator. All of a sudden, before I knew it, there was a sharp curve up ahead. It was too late! We were going to go rocketing off the road like a shooting star, and there was nothing I could do about it. I went through the motions, anyway, yanking the steering wheel. The Jaguar clung to the asphalt like an impassioned lover, no tilt, no shudder, nothing, and we shot past the corner and were gone. I was amazed.

As soon as we reached Hidden Lake, Steve was so impressed with the Jag's handling ability that he had to race up and down the gravel road and around a ninety-degree turn, faster and faster each successive time. I wasn't the least bit concerned. I donned my motorcycle helmet and propped my feet up against the dashboard to await the inevitable. Sure enough he skidded out of control and crashed into the ditch, crumpling the front end and cracking the windshield.

Steve and I were driving past a new-car dealership in Kitchener, when I spotted a brand-new turquoise-and-white 1973 Mercury Cougar in the window. I whooped so loudly that Steve thought I'd seen the police. He glanced around in panic and looked as if he were about to make a run for it. We pulled right into the lot and parked the car. It didn't take us long to get into the dealership, and someone had been thoughtful enough to leave the keys in the ignition of the Cougar. So I switched license plates with those of another car, just to add a little extra confusion, then turned the radio on and drove right out of the showroom. As we passed a Datsun car dealership, Steve spotted a Datsun 280Z. He wanted it but couldn't find the keys, so we both took two big handfuls of keys and went over the entire lot, trying to find a match. Still, for some inexplicable reason our search proved fruitless, so we returned to the cottage with just the Cougar.

Steve had a near obsession with sports cars; consequently we traveled to Toronto to find him one. We cruised in and out of the parking lots and up and down the residential streets until he zeroed in on a dark green 1969 Alfa Romeo Spider convertible parked in the driveway at the front of the owner's house. Steve was really excited about this car.

I was unable to pick the ignition, so we hot-wired it. All the while we kept an eye on the living room picture window right above us, since it was only 8:00 p.m. and the lights were still on. We pushed the car out of the driveway and down the street, but there was about a foot of snow on the ground, which made progress difficult. Just then a passerby, thinking we were experiencing engine trouble, stopped and helped us push. When the Spider was well away from the owner's house, Steve climbed inside and started it. We thanked the gentleman for his help, and with me tailing Steve, we returned to Hidden Lake.

On Friday night I set off to visit a lost love in Galt in my Cougar and Steve decided to attend a family reunion in Owen Sound in his Spider. As we neared Owen Sound, I started to run out of gas, so I pulled into a service station to fill up. Steve failed to notice I was no longer with him but eventually did and waited for me a few miles up ahead at a side road. As I tried to catch up to him, I flew down a hill on Highway 21 at 120 miles an hour. Steve finally caught up to me when I slowed down at Owen Sound, then we parted company.

On my return trip, after having driven a considerable distance with a fair piece yet to go, I started to fall asleep at the wheel. So I pulled over and parked in a farmer's laneway to catch forty winks before resuming my journey. I awoke to find a cruiser parked behind me, blocking my exit, and a police officer heading toward me with his flashlight. I banged the door lock button down just as he started to flail away at the handle, frantically trying to open the door. Then I started the car and stomped on the gas pedal, lurching ahead, with him chasing me on foot. Silly boy. I crashed through the barnyard gate and into a field to put a little distance between me and my overly enthusiastic friend. Then I abandoned the car and proceeded on foot.

The police were patrolling the area heavily, but I managed to avoid them nonetheless. They would be expecting me to steal another car almost immediately, so three hours later and two miles up the road, I swiped a farmer's car and scrambled back to Hidden Lake. Once inside the cottage I was so tired I could hardly keep my eyes open to brush my teeth before going to bed. As soon as my head hit the pillow, the door crashed open. The police! It was Saturday, November 20, 1972, 4:30 a.m. I was arrested and charged with every crime from starting Louis Riel's rebellion to voting for Pierre Trudeau. Then I was thrown into the Walkerton Jail. Steve was caught shortly afterward and thrown in with me. The first thing he said was "A fine mess you got us into this time."

7

Hell-Bent for Prison

DURING THE COURSE OF AN INTERVIEW with a detective in the Walkerton Jail, I was asked certain potentially incriminating questions. I replied that I couldn't remember anything. With big brown sympathetic eyes, the detective asked me if I was reluctant because I felt so terrible about having committed the crimes. I looked at him to see if he was serious. He was! Where did they get these guys from? I wondered. Hell, I'd had the time of my life. But we'd been so busy breaking into places and stealing cars that we couldn't keep track of all the things we'd done.

There were well over 100 incidents that they knew of and over thirty police chases. The press had dubbed us folk heroes, the logic of which escaped me completely. It was also a popular misconception that I was the leader if not the instigator of our two-man crime wave. Not so. Steve was as independent as the wind and just as capricious and undiscriminating. He would steal anything from anyone at any time, and it didn't bother him one whit whatsoever. It was just that if we were going to do something I usually thought of a way of doing it properly. After all, if something is worth doing, it's worth doing right. We were about as dangerous as a pair of young otters. We didn't even consider ourselves criminals in the classic sense; we were just young, fun-loving and incredibly wild.

Through a series of negotiations with the Crown attorney, and after numerous remands, we finally reached a plea-bargain basis: three and a half years in exchange for guilty pleas on a number of break-and-enters, car thefts, joyrides and other related offenses, totaling 108 in all. I thought the sentence was excessive at the time, and although we had entered guilty pleas on all counts that very same day, and were both remanded in custody to the following day for sentencing, there were extenuating circumstances that we felt the court would be forced to consider prior to then — we were planning to break out that night.

We were imprisoned in cell block 3. The steel-barred corridor was braced by a solid, unlocked wooden door, which was left open. The guards' subtle form of punishment for minor infractions was to close the wooden door but surreptitiously peek through the peephole, all supposedly unknown to us. Every window in the corridor was enclosed with a structure of bars interlaced to form regularly spaced five-inch-square openings. The only exception was the washroom's six-by-twenty-six-inch oblong opening, which had been deemed too small to be provided with the involved lattice construction. Instead it was fortified with a single perpendicular bar, centered and supported by a horizontal midway crosspiece. The bars were monstrous, ancient things, relics of an era when everything was constructed to last forever. In the 106-year history of the jail, no prisoner had ever successfully cut his way out through the bars and escaped.

Having secured hacksaw blades from a source I'm not at liberty to disclose, Steve and I quietly tore thin strips of bed sheets and tied them together to form a cord. One end was held by the person sitting at the table, innocently reading a book, while the other end was tied to the person around the corner in the washroom, busily cutting the bar. In the event of the guard's appearance, the rope would simply be tugged sharply. This ruse allowed the guard always to have at least one of us in his sight, allaying any possible suspicions. Furthermore, we arranged to have the piped-in radio music tuned to the station with the most volume, thus disguising our activity.

At one point, while I was concentrating hard on cutting the bar, the metal protested loudly. At the same time I was horrified to hear a guard talking to Steve. He hadn't pulled the rope! I stopped cutting immediately, expecting a full complement of Her Majesty's best to come charging in. I was certain the guard had heard the distinctive back-and-forth rasp of the hacksaw blade, but I still tried to act as if nothing was wrong.

After flushing the toilet and washing my hands, I walked out of the washroom. Much to my astonishment, though, the conversation had come to an end and the guard had left without further ado. Apparently the rope had slipped out of Steve's hand!

Throughout our labor, we didn't have a hacksaw handle, so we were forced to work with the bare blade wrapped in cloth, which inflicted numerous cuts on our hands. Taking turns cutting and watching for the guard, we found the whole process took a lot longer than I had originally anticipated. As it turned out, we finished just moments before the guards were to lock us up in the cells for the night.

Steve went first. He tried to squeeze through, but couldn't. Grasping the bar, I broke off the two small wooden slats of the window frame, enlarging the escape hatch to eight by thirteen inches. Time was running out. The guards could enter the corridor at any moment and discover the missing bar, and we would be trapped. Steve tried again. I grew increasingly alarmed. Finally, after numerous pushes from me, Steve disappeared through the hole. Then I jammed myself in, cutting my ribs on the bar's sharp edge, and struggled through to the sweet air of freedom outside.

Earlier I had discovered a convenient water pipe running up the outside wall of the jailhouse. We lost no time in taking advantage of it. Steve scaled the pipe first, then I followed. When we got to the top of the dividing wall adjoining the perimeter wall, we picked our way along the peaked green roof. After what seemed an eternity, we finally reached the outer wall. Our plan was to jump down, but one dizzying look at the forbidding sidewalk below quickly changed our minds. Instead, we scrambled over to a lower porch roof and swung to the ground. We had made it! It was April 24, 1973, barely six months after our capture.

Not wasting any time, we discarded our white jail T-shirts and walked away quickly, bobbing and weaving through the back streets, laneways and alleys until we reached the polluted Saugeen River. We followed the river until we came to a house next to a shallow canal. A large white Styrofoam boat was attached to the rear of the house's prefabricated garage. It was perfect! We could sail right out of Walkerton and arrive in Paisley, eighteen miles away, before morning.

Cautiously we released the boat from its bindings, but the Styrofoam screeched violently against the corrugated fiberglass wall of the garage. The owner, whom we could see quite clearly in the house's kitchen, heard the noise and came storming outside. Anticipating an immediate call to the police department, we dashed up the canal and spirited away another boat, a heavy wooden thing of highly questionable seaworthiness. We dragged it back down the canal, retracing our steps, very much aware of the possibility that at any moment the police might burst upon the scene. This latest endeavor also caused considerable noise as we attempted to pass by the house of the owner of the first boat. Of course the irate boat owner was waiting for us. We exchanged a number of harsh words, which ended in his threat to report the whole incident to the police. And, as if to substantiate his warning, he went inside his house to do exactly that.

Now the cat was out of the bag, so we decided to turn our slight misfortune to our advantage. Quickly dragging the boat toward the river, we splashed water into it and, with a mighty shove, launched it out into open water. Then we splashed our way back up the canal and headed overland out of town. Later we learned that the boat owner had indeed phoned the police, who recovered the wooden boat a considerable distance downstream. Eventually the entire Walkerton OPP detachment exhausted the remainder of the evening, searching the densely wooded riverbanks and surrounding area for us.

Covering as much ground as physically possible, we ran along Highway 9 toward Mildmay and concealed ourselves in some woods in order to catch a few winks. The next day, as dusk gave way to darkness, we resumed our journey until we came across a lone highway diner, which was closed for the night. We broke in and proceeded to look for food, but could only come up with a large ham in the refrigerator. While Steve prepared himself a coffee, I set about warming the ham. Devouring as much as we possibly could, we left the diner and continued on up the highway into Mildmay. Eventually we were able to find a 1970 Ford station wagon with the keys still in the ignition, and before long we were back in Galt.

When we reached the Galt city limits, I parked the station wagon in a wooded lot and drifted off to sleep. Well past daybreak I awoke to unfamiliar noises. Still half asleep, I stepped out of the car to check the source of the noise. Out of nowhere charged a huge horse ridden by what had to be a man possessed. Caught out in the open like peasants pursued by a Cossack, Steve and I abandoned the car and dived into the thick woods, managing to lose the Cossack as well as one of my shoes.

Barely a mile from the scene, we noticed a low-flying, single-engine aircraft circling overhead. Obviously it hadn't taken the police long to link the stolen car with our jailbreak. We kept constantly on the move, barely staying ahead of the ever-vigilant plane. And, as if we didn't have enough problems, we could hear police dogs baying in the distance. The forces of the law were definitely closing in.

We grew weaker by the mile, nearing exhaustion. My feet were killing me now that I was shoeless. But we plunged on through the woods nevertheless. Finally we stumbled out of the trees into a vast field, discovering a farmer fast asleep in his truck. We couldn't turn back. To the left and right were nothing but open fields. We had only one decent chance. With the police dogs only minutes behind us now, we slipped up on the farmer and shot past the truck in an all-out, last-ditch effort for the highway, a quarter mile away. A short distance from our goal we froze, spotting a police officer on a motorcycle, his face turned in our direction. My heart sank. He had to spot us; it was impossible for him not to. We were barely 100 yards away in a newly sown field, frozen like half-naked statues in flight. He cruised slowly by, his eyes glued to the circling plane a short distance beyond us, then drove up the road. I couldn't believe my eyes!

We streaked across the road and into the farmyard. Parked in the driveway was a car, the keys still in the ignition. What luck! I jumped inside and turned the engine over, but it wouldn't start. I wondered if the farmer had heard the engine cranking over. He was probably loading his shotgun right now, I thought. Just then the police dog team broke into the clearing, while the plane banked for a return sweep. Still the car wouldn't start! Then Steve jumped in and the engine came to life with a roar. I slammed the shift into gear and hit the gas. A woman came flying out of nowhere, waving her arms in front of the car. If I slammed on the brakes, the car would slide on the loose gravel and hit her, so I yanked hard on the steering wheel, swerved and shot out of the driveway. We were on the road again.

After leaving the farmyard, we motored down the road for twenty precarious miles, changing directions several times. Finally, our nerves shot, we came upon a secluded sand pit, where we parked the car. We were just outside of Guelph now. It was time to lie low for a bit.

By mid-afternoon the sun was beating down unmercifully and I decided, since I was wearing little clothing anyway, that I might as well occupy the time sunbathing. All of a sudden, while I was relaxing on the side of a sand dune, I heard a terrific roaring noise. Startled, I looked up just in time to see a dirt bike fly right over me. Steve and I scrambled for the car, but when I turned the ignition, nothing happened. Steve had been playing with the radio and had run down the battery. The first dirt bike was joined by a second. It wouldn't take long for the two guys to put the latest new bulletins together with our situation, resulting in the police. Now it was every man for himself. Steve took off in one direction and I headed in the other.

Failing to locate Steve before sundown, I happened upon an unoccupied hobby farm. The owners were still at work. I spent an uncomfortable night sleeping in the barn hayloft, and the next morning I easily picked the ancient lock on the side door of the house, finding, to my surprise, no less than twenty-two cats of all colors, sizes, shapes and breeds. I was outnumbered! However, in short order I scared up a pair of jeans, a shirt and shoes, had breakfast and went to bed, setting the alarm clock so that I would wake up before the owners got back from work. The following day I returned to the house again, this time to have lunch and alter the jeans on the sewing machine, since they were one size too large. Then I phoned around to locate Steve. He was at his mother's. I told him where I was and he said he'd come and meet me. As soon as I hung up, the owner's eleven-year-old son came trudging up the road on his way home from school. Hurrying back to the barn, I heard the pop of small arms fire fifteen minutes later. Cautiously peeking through a knothole in a barn board, I spied the owner's son at the back of the house with his father's .22 rifle. He was practicing his marksmanship on just about everything in sight. I knew what was coming next, but I just had to wait around to see it. As the boy lifted the rifle, I hesitated. But when he aimed, I was certain. Just as he fired at the barn, I dived behind the largest post I could find to wait for him to run out of ammunition. He must have collected his allowance quite recently, because after fifteen minutes I didn't wait around any longer to see just how good a little boy Johnny had been the past week.

Shortly after, I stole a gold 1972 Yamaha 650. Steve came to meet me in a car he'd stolen. We liked the bike better, so we ditched the car. The bike had a windshield, luggage rack and engine guards. Even though a major manhunt for us was in effect, Steve wanted to go to Owen Sound. He had an idea how to get there, so we raced down gravel roads all night long until we finally reached the outskirts of our destination at dawn.

By now we were becoming quite adept on the motorcycle, or so we thought. We could change seating positions while traveling down the road at thirty miles an hour. I would stand up, bring my left leg over the seat, balancing on the right foot peg, while Steve slid up, taking the controls as I swung in behind. After a while we were even able to do it without losing control and crashing into a ditch. We were enjoying ourselves so much that when Steve came upon what appeared to be a good bike-climbing hill, he swerved toward it without a second thought. However, the bike wasn't designed for climbing hills. After tumbling down the slopes a number of times, we continued on down the road. By now the luggage rack was rattling, so we discarded it.

Though we were just outside the Sound, we seemed to be doing a considerable amount of traveling without really getting anywhere, so Steve decided upon a more direct route — the railroad tracks. That worked fine until the shoulder discontinued and we tried to ride down the middle of the tracks. Every time Steve hit a railroad tie the bike would jerk, causing him to twist the throttle and hit the next tie even harder until we both wound up in the ditch. After numerous attempts, the windshield split, so we removed it, threw it into the ditch and headed back to the road, bending the engine guards flush with the engine in the process.

Eventually we reached Steve's brother's house. He was away for the day at work, so we went inside and made ourselves a late lunch.

As we were about to leave, it occurred to Steve that we might be stopped by the police if we didn't have helmets. In lieu of real motorcycle headgear, we used two thin white plastic child's play helmets, which looked like miniature British pith helmets. When we got under way, it started to rain — hard. There we were, riding all over the road at ten miles an hour, with me holding both our little helmets on, since Steve had to control the throttle with one hand and wipe rain out of his face with the other. And we thought we were inconspicuous!

The rain finally ended, so we turned onto a seldom-used cart track. Speeding up the side of a steep hill, we almost reached the crest before the front wheel caught in a deep rut. We went flying over the bike, with me landing on top of Steve's head. I thought that was quite amusing, but he failed to see the humor in it. Yet he was determined to conquer the hill, so I moved a safe distance to the side of the track as he returned to the bottom. Four times and three head-over-heel flights later, he reached the top and we continued on into the city. We didn't stop at his mother's place, figuring it was too dangerous, but we did ride by, hooting and waving at his sister.

Steve knew of a cottage retreat on the other side of Owen Sound, so without our little helmets, which had failed to survive the last stunt, we dashed through the back streets to our new destination. Leaving the motorcycle parked a short distance from the retreat, we were observed by a concerned citizen, which prompted us to run back to the bike. Unfortunately it wouldn't start, so we resumed our journey on foot as darkness began to descend.

Finding another bike, this time a chopper, we pushed it quietly out of the owner's backyard. I climbed on and started it just as a car appeared. Panicking, I roared down the hill without Steve. I couldn't find the headlight switch, so I ran right smack into a ditch. As the car stopped, I decided to remain temporarily on foot and beat a hasty retreat back up the hill to Steve.

Soon enough we came upon another cottage area in Sydenham Township. Choosing a decent-looking cottage, we let ourselves in and stayed the night. The next day the owner came by and caught us napping. When I gave him a cock-and-bull story about my mother owning the cottage next to it and claimed we had entered the wrong cottage by mistake, he asked me her name. "Mrs. McArthur," I replied. That confused him for a moment, since his name was McArthur, also.

He threatened to call the police. I seconded the motion, insisting that it was he and not I who was the intruder. All the while I sidled toward the back window in anticipation of Steve's not-so-subtle exit. We vaulted out the window, and as the man chased us he yelled, "Stop or I'll shoot!"

Not believing he had a gun, yet not taking any chances, either, I yelled back, "Don't shoot. I'll stop!" Then I made a beeline straight for the nearest clump of trees. For a time we sat on a hill and watched police cars speed by, wondering if the law would put dogs on our trail again. As darkness fell, we walked up the road, stole a car, abandoned it in Toronto and purchased two tickets on the first bus heading north.

Sudbury was a miner's paradise. We walked unconcernedly down a sidewalk and into the various fragrances and aromas of Gilbert's bustling IGA supermarket, overflowing with produce. Purchasing a snack, we spotted a well-stacked safe. While we ate, we figured out a way to enrich our lives a little more. Outside the supermarket we found a tombstone engraver's shop and noted a pair of oxyacetylene tanks, filing their location away for future reference.

At nightfall we scouted the neighborhood garages and sheds, looking for an ax and some rope. That task completed, we stole a truck and headed back to the supermarket. When we got there, we left the truck in the deserted parking lot and used a drain pipe to climb to the pebbled rooftop.

While Steve acted as sentry, I chopped a hole in the roof. Then, using the rope, we lowered ourselves to the floor. Dodging from aisle to aisle, we ducked into the rear storage room and pushed a large flatbed cart to the front of the supermarket.

Steve jammed the cart against the base of the seven-foot safe, while I braced my back against the wall, straining to topple the metallic behemoth. It fell with a loud crunch onto the cart, shattering the axles. Returning from the storage room with a second cart, we transferred the safe onto it, then rolled it to the rear delivery doors.

While I stayed with the safe, Steve fetched the truck and drove it up to the loading dock, then got out and helped me load the safe.

Next we drove to the tombstone engraver's and picked up the oxyacetylene tanks, a sledgehammer, a hacksaw and a number of chisels. Our inventory complete, we headed out into the countryside and found a nice, secluded logging road.

The safe was divided into two compartments, a smaller, more secure round door on top and a larger firebox compartment connected below. I cut the outer steel layer from the top with the oxyacetylene torch, knowing that was where the large bills would be. Shattering the concrete encasement with the sledgehammer, I exposed the inner shell below. Then I attempted to cut the corner weld on the shell. But the composition of the metal dissipated the heat too rapidly, making it impossible. After draining the tanks dry, I used the sledgehammer to crack the weld but accomplished nothing more than rounding off the corner. Next I broke three chisels, trying to break through. Finally, in a desperate attempt, I resorted to cutting the shell with a hand-held hacksaw blade. It penetrated the metal like a hot knife slicing through butter.

At long last, after beating, baking, prying and gouging the safe for five hours straight, I was able to cut a small hole just large enough to see inside. And there was my prize — a price stamper! A goddamn price stamper! I cursed and swore and ranted and raved. I threw and kicked everything I could lay my hands on or feet to. I did everything but turn myself inside out.

Steve had appeared occasionally to check on my progress. Now, after spending the entire night in the truck, wet and shivering from the cold, he was out in a flash to see what all the fuss was about. Taking the last chisel, he began to work on the firebox, and in about twenty minutes, with my assistance, the safe was opened, revealing $11, 500. We were jubilant. Clutching two bags of money, we walked to the highway and eventually flagged down a Toronto-bound bus.

Back in the big city we separated. Steve returned to London and my sister Janet, while I went on to Vancouver. One week later, as I was making a phone call, who should I see across the street but Janet! She and Steve, plus my younger sister, had a hotel room just a short distance up the street. I had bought a brand-new white 1973 Triumph TR6 convertible, and with no license, insurance or identification whatsoever, we raced all over the city for the next two weeks, never even so much as being stopped once by the police. Discovering we were short of funds, Steve and I flew back to Toronto to retrieve the $2,000 in coins we'd hidden from the safe job in Sudbury. We also picked up Bill, my younger sister's boyfriend from London.

When we hooked up with Bill, we decided to hit the A & P supermarket in Woodstock prior to our return trip to British Columbia. After stealing a black 1967 Kawasaki 900 cc motorcycle, the three of us straddled it and cruised around the neighborhood, trying to locate a second bike. While we were doing this, Steve thought he saw a police cruiser approach. He yanked the throttle to full speed, and the big bike lunged forward, nearly knocking me off.

The motorcycle accelerated to sixty miles an hour in a matter of seconds. But when Steve slammed on the brakes to turn a corner, the machine screamed out of control and we shot right into someone's backyard and crashed into a fence. Instantly picking ourselves up, we left the motorcycle behind and hotfooted it through the backyard, leaping over fences and hedges. Shortly thereafter, in an Austin Mini, we headed out to Woodstock.

After chopping a hole through the roof of the A & P supermarket, we lowered ourselves to the floor with a rope. We were going to hoist up the safe, but we couldn't budge it. It was secured to, and beneath, another larger safe, and anchored to the wall. There was no way to dislodge and transport the two safes. And peeling them inside the supermarket was out of the question. In frustration I threw a potato, which accidentally hit Steve. Then Bill threw a steak at me. The next thing I knew I was in the middle of a full-scale food fight, with an occasional watermelon flying through the air. By the time we left the supermarket, it looked like a disaster area.

While exchanging cash in a bank in Sault Sainte Marie, Steve and Bill were apprehended. I managed to elude the police but was promptly captured by the RCMP when I returned to our motel room in Vancouver. They had been tipped off by the motel phone operator and were waiting for me. As soon as I walked into the room, they hustled right in behind me. I was arrested and returned to Walkerton to face charges stemming from our crime spree plus the jailbreak. We were convicted and sentenced to a term of three years and three months, then transported to Sudbury, where we were convicted of the IGA safe job and sentenced to a further two years and three months consecutive, giving each of us an aggregate prison term of five years and six months. We had jumped from the frying pan into the fire. And we weren't content to get just a few years in prison — we had to get a real asshole full of time. Still, we weren't finished yet.

8

I "Got" the Sheriff

IN THE SUDBURY JAIL, STEVE AND I WERE confined in a cell block with two older convicts, both of whom had previously served sentences in federal penitentiaries. After the initial few days of exchanging viewpoints, I broached the subject of escape. They enthusiastically endorsed the idea.

We had two sets of bars to go through. First we had to cut through the ones in the cell block to break out into the corridor. Then we had to cut through the bars in the window in the corridor to get outside. One convict named Gary Blacklock had a sympathetic supporter outside who would attach hacksaw blades to a long copper line torn from the radio cable. All we had to do was pull it in from our third-story window.

Steve and I were both keyed up with anticipation of the scheduled drop. The line was lowered at the appointed time — exactly 5:30 p.m. The tug signaling the completion of the drop was felt and we quickly reeled our "catch" in.

I was so excited that I could barely contain myself. The circumstances were perfect. The guards made their rounds only four times a day and always on schedule. As well, the bars were only an inch in diameter. We had discussed the escape logistics down to the most minute detail, so you can well imagine my surprise when all that came up on the wire was a packet containing amphetamines and a syringe.

The two older cons were as happy and excited as a couple of expectant newlyweds on their wedding night. They never even mentioned the absence of the hacksaw blades. Instead they shot up and spent the next fifteen minutes running around like a couple of chickens with their heads chopped off.

I was filled with utter loathing. I couldn't believe it. Here were two men who had a choice between their freedom and a few fleeting minutes of euphoria, and they chose to get high. It was beyond my comprehension. If a man didn't possess his freedom, his choice of destinies, what remained?

Back then I didn't realize that they were typical of the majority of contemporary federal penitentiary convicts. The last I was to ever hear of Gary Blacklock would be a few years later. Late one night in his cell he came face-to-face with the realization of his insignificance in the vast scheme of things and hung himself.

Unable to develop the proper opportunity to escape, one day Steve and I found ourselves being transported in an unmarked sheriff's car nonstop to the Kingston Penitentiary. I wasn't very pleased at all with the three-and-a-half-year sentence we'd received in Walkerton. Now, with a total sentence of five and a half years, I was even more determined never to reach Kingston. Although I didn't quite know how I was going to escape, I did know that if an opportunity presented itself, I would be long gone.

Sitting in the back of the sheriff's car, manacled, shackled in leg irons, I noticed that the law officers had judiciously covered the back seat with a heavy cotton blanket to protect it from the constant wear and tear. I suspected the blanket had just recently been dry-cleaned, noting the laundry tag still fastened to it with, of all things, a tiny safety pin. That was the break I'd been looking for. I now knew we'd never reach Kingston.

However, one small but potentially dangerous problem still remained. We suspected that the sheriffs might be toting or have access to guns. A choice had to be made between someone possibly being shot and the use of force on our part. To avoid gunplay and still make good our escape, we thought it best to overpower the sheriffs while keeping violence held to a minimum. Using knowing looks and hand signals, we formulated a plan of action. We would knock the sheriff in the passenger seat unconscious and then subdue the driver before he had a chance to draw a weapon or retrieve one from his satchel or glove compartment.

Quietly I picked the locks on our manacles and leg irons with the safety pin. Steve and I chatted and laughed occasionally to appear relaxed and cheerful. The sheriffs never even bothered to check on us once. They just took it for granted that we were enjoying the ride.

We waited for the most opportune moment. Near Whitby, as the driver was engrossed in negotiating a cloverleaf entrance ramp to Highway 400 at a decreased speed, we pounced. With a leg iron cuff and chain wrapped around his hand, Steve struck one sheriff over the head, while I hovered above the driver in preparation to wrestle his gun away from him with Steve's assistance. But we were mistaken; neither sheriff carried a weapon. As well, Steve failed to knock anyone out.

Nevertheless, as soon as the violence erupted, the driver slammed on his brakes and dived out of the car, which was an unexpected twist for me. I'd been primed for a life-and-death struggle over a gun, then quite suddenly no one was there. I quickly got into the driver's seat while Steve seized the other sheriff by the shoulders and pulled him into the back seat. All I caught sight of out of the corner of my eye were his two legs flailing the air as we roared away.

In a few seconds our positions had been reversed. Now we were driving the sheriff's car down the highway and one of our captors had become *our* captive! However, we soon let him go and drove to a small rural airport, where we abandoned the vehicle. It was July 10, 1973, only two months, two weeks and two days since our escape from the Walkerton Jail.

We quickly changed our clothes and traveled cross-country, avoiding all residences and businesses, reaching Whitby by twilight. Never once did we encounter the police or even the slightest pursuit situation, although we were pursued by one hound dog, which was so overjoyed at having found someone who was friendly that we couldn't get rid of it.

Knowing that it was best to leave the general area as soon as possible, we prowled around, looking for a means of transportation.

Finally we located a car with keys in the ignition. As I waited casually for Steve to return, he had entered a nearby house that had its doors unlocked. I was wondering what the hell he was up to now, when all of a sudden the lights came on and he came flying out of the house, swinging off the front porch screen door with one hand while slopping an open quart of milk around in the other. His feet never once touched the ground. Taking it for granted that he had encountered an extremely violent and capable male homeowner, I dropped into a crouch, ready to flee for my life. With all the breaking into homes and businesses we had done, it forever haunted us that one day someone would blast us into eternity with a shotgun. Now I figured *today* was that day! As soon as Steve neared, I bolted, but he stopped me. Apparently he had been rooting around in the refrigerator in the dark when the owner, a little old white-haired lady, switched the kitchen light on. As we hightailed it out of there, I couldn't stop myself from chuckling over Steve's late-night encounter.

After driving to London, we parked the car in a large apartment building lot and walked the remaining dozen or so blocks to a friend's house. A few days later I thought it best to move the car from the immediate area, drive it across to the far side of the city and abandon it there. I walked back to the parking lot and cautiously passed by the car in an attempt to detect if it was under surveillance. Uncovering nothing unusual or any suspicious-looking characters in the immediate area, I turned sharply toward the car at a brisk pace, slipped inside, started the engine and quickly drove out of the lot and down the street.

Before I knew it, a London police cruiser, manned by a lone officer, miraculously appeared out of thin air, traveling at high speed toward me. I sped up the street, negotiated the first corner and found myself looking at a dead-end sign. Swerving into the nearest empty driveway, I slammed on the brakes, jumped out of the car and ran through the backyard just as the cruiser pulled up and a pudgy officer rolled out and began to chase me.

I vaulted through several backyards and turned north, ending up right back at the same street. It was an old trick I'd used effectively many times in previous chases. Usually the police were still busily trying to cut off the last-known direction of flight by the time I crossed back over, heading in the opposite direction. Now, just as I emerged from cover to sprint across the road, I ran straight into Pudgy. I hesitated for a moment to see what his reaction would be. He didn't make me wait long — he clawed for his gun. Quickly I retraced my steps back to the protection of the houses and scuttled out of Pudgy's reach as if someone had lit a torch under me. Eventually I hooked up with Steve again and we stole another car, slipped out of London and drove to Grey County.

Since it was now mid-July and very hot, Steve and I, both being sports-minded, stole a half-ton truck in Owen Sound, drove to the marina and helped ourselves to a kayak, paddles, snorkels, flippers, helmets and other related paraphernalia. We were going to do some white-water kayaking on a river Steve knew of from his childhood.

We arrived in the early morning, and I tended the gate leading to the river as Steve drove through. But as soon as I closed the gate and jumped onto the truck's tailgate, Steve roared off just as fast as he could go, bouncing crazily down the cart trail. I was all too familiar with Steve's driving habits, so I had already taken the precaution of wearing a crash helmet. Somehow I managed to land inside the box. As I was clawing my way to the front, feverishly hoping to reach it in time before Steve smashed into something, he slammed on the brakes. Sure enough, all the equipment, including the kayak and me, went rocketing up to the front of the box as the truck came to a dead stop. I hastily disengaged myself from the heap and jumped out before Steve had a chance to roar off again.

We unloaded the equipment and found Steve's boyhood river to be a sedate stream. Steve jumped back into the truck again and began tearing around, while I stepped behind the nearest tree to watch. When he became marooned on a huge stump, we rocked the truck off and away he went again. He was slamming the truck back and forth between whatever happened to be in his way at the time, when he backed into a large sugar maple and almost knocked himself out. When he hit the tree, he bounced around inside the cab as if he were an Indian rubber ball, then dropped out of sight. Soon enough, the cab door swung open and he staggered out, weak-kneed and wobbly. He put on the other helmet after that.

I climbed into the truck, braced my legs against the dashboard and we roared away again, bouncing across a nearly treeless field, when all of a sudden the hood flew up. We couldn't see where we were going now, but neither of us was stupid enough to stick our heads out the window just in case we sideswiped a tree. Finally we came to rest against a large pine tree. The front wheels were off the ground and the cab was filling up with smoke, so we walked back to the stream to experiment with the kayak.

Steve practiced a few maneuvers first, then I tried. Eventually, after a lot of trial and error, we were able to master righting the kayak after it tipped over. It was quite difficult to maintain balance. One second you were right side up, the next you were underwater, staring at some goggled-eyed fish. Then we decided to go upstream with the boat. Since it was a one-man kayak, we had to position ourselves back to back, which made for a tight fit. Being cautious, we practiced getting out on dry land first. As soon as we set off in the water, I began to rock the kayak.

"Mick, don't rock the boat," Steve pleaded with me. "I don't want to get my clothes wet. I'm sick."

I started to laugh, and the next thing I knew we were both upside down underwater. Steve was supposed to wait for me to squeeze out first, since his legs were longer than mine. But I was still laughing underwater and almost choked to death. Finally I managed to slip out, and no sooner had I done so, Steve followed. I was still laughing when we surfaced in about three and a half feet of water, and Steve didn't help matters much, either. He had a miserable look on his face as he stood there looking like a drowned rat. I laughed so hard that I had to hang on to the kayak to keep my balance. But the biggest joke of all would have been on us if we hadn't first practiced getting out of the kayak on dry land. We both would have drowned in less than four feet of water.

We left everything the way it was, waded across the stream, sloshed up the road, found a Volkswagen station wagon and drove to Toronto. After switching the Volkswagen in Toronto for a 1968 Barracuda, we arrived shortly after at Steve's cousin's in Kitchener at 4:00 a.m. and parked the car in the out-patient parking lot of a nearby hospital. We spent the remainder of the night as well as the following day there and planned to leave as soon as his cousin returned home from work at 5:30 p.m. Fifteen minutes after he came home, just as we were about to leave, two of his friends came by for a brief visit on motorcycles. Five minutes later the apartment was surrounded by the police. There was no way out. Apparently an inquisitive neighbor had mistaken the two bikers for us and called the police.

Four days after our escape from the sheriff's car we were arrested and transferred to the Whitby jail.

Two OPP detectives handcuffed us behind our backs and placed us in the back of an unmarked car. The handcuffs were so tight that my circulation was cut off. My hands began to swell, and I became nauseated. I brought the matter to the attention of the officer in the back, but he refused to loosen the cuffs, even though I advised him I was about to vomit. A few moments later I did just that, and his response was to try to stomp me into the floor of the car.

After reaching the Whitby police station, a detective fingerprinted me, then suddenly punched me in the stomach. He did it again, but I did my best to ignore him. I could tell by the excited leer on his face that he wanted to thrash the living daylights out of me but had to wait until I did something to give him the excuse. I realized then that there were some pretty twisted cops running around in the country.

All told we were given nearly nine years for petty car thefts, break-ins and prison escapes. I couldn't believe it! This wasn't justice. All we were doing was what was expected of us. Every time we did something crazy or wild or escaped, the public giggled their asses off because we made the police look foolish. Everyone cheered us on. And the newspapers, sensationalizing everything, spurned us on by painting us as heroes. It was all so obvious.

After we reached Kingston Penitentiary, Steve said to me, "You know, Mick, I don't belong in this place with these people. I'm not a criminal. I know I belong somewhere, but I don't belong here, not for what I did." And I felt the same way.

Not long after we were transferred to Millhaven Maximum Security Prison. My convict number was 9864 and Steve's was 9875. We had reached the big time.

9

Parole by Deception

THANKS TO THE MILL I RECEIVED FIRST-hand experience in the delights of being a prison convict. It was the craziest place I'd ever seen, a veritable menagerie. The big weight-lifting convicts weren't the ones to be leery of, as depicted in the movies. It was the crazy little ones, the psychotic killers who would slip up behind you in a crowd, while you were at the urinal or in the shower, and drive a knife through your heart before you had a chance to defend yourself. They had the most to prove.

The convicts from the Kingston Psychiatric Centre and Pene-tanguishene insane asylum, prior to being transferred down the cascading system to another penitentiary, first had to be filtered through the Mill. And a good many never made it. Being young, cute and slim, I knew I was in trouble right off the hop, so I started acting a little weird, and everyone stayed away from me. In the meantime I enrolled in the educational program and worked out in the gym during the evenings.

Six months after Steve and I were imprisoned in the Mill a violent windstorm erupted while we were walking outside in the main exercise yard. The wire clattered and the fences shook wildly. My eyes widened with excitement, anticipating a chance to escape. Steve took one terrified look at me and realized I was serious. Instead of running for the fence, he gumbooted back to his cell. It was around that time that Steve and I began drifting apart. He kept associating with known prison low-lifes, which I didn't approve of. I couldn't figure out why Steve was doing that. We were still the best of friends, but there was a dark side to him that I hadn't seen before.

One weekend I was outside exercising in the weight-lifting pit when a group of convicts decided to stage a demonstration in the yard. However, they found they didn't have the genuine support of the entire prison population. I overheard the leader of this little faction of left-wingers propose a bill ordering the beheading of anyone attempting to leave the yard. His party voiced a hearty round of approval for the proposal, the votes were cast, the bill was passed and he marched up the yard to the main gate, swinging a shovel menacingly.

I had nothing against a good old-fashioned riot now and again. They could promote long-term growth and progress if they were handled responsibly and were for a just cause. And I had nothing personal against the leader. He had never bad-mouthed my maw or dated my girl. And I didn't even mind a hearty, backwoods, eye-gouging, groin-kicking brawl on a Friday night. But if I was going to get my head smashed in, it would have to be for something I believed in and in a fight I had a chance to win or at least inflict as much damage upon my adversary as he did upon me. This affair wasn't for a good cause, and we had just about as much a chance of winning as teaching a hound dog how to square-dance. All it amounted to was just one person attempting to dictate his personal policy to 100 men, to coerce everyone's support by sheer, unmitigated threats of violence, with the assistance of his henchmen, who echoed his every word.

If the reason for the disturbance had been valid, it would have been recognized, accepted and supported by a large percentage of the prison population. That, in turn, would give the demonstration an air of respectability that would be taken seriously by the prison administration. But this revolt was supported by only a small portion of the penitentiary's inmates. Riot squads would soon be dispatched to crush the mob forthwith. When the warden finished reading the Riot Act over the public address system, I knew I had just enough time to finish my last weight-lifting set before all hell broke loose. As far as I was concerned, the only difference between the riot troops beating a tattoo on my head and me cracking my skull up against the concrete was that the guards wouldn't get any personal satisfaction out of having caused me the pain. And besides, if I was going to riot, I wanted to have a little say in the matter. My family background had instilled strong democratic feelings in me.

To prepare myself, I picked up a small iron weight-lifting bar, figuring it would do the trick. Then I walked up the yard toward the gate and stopped just before reaching the ringleader of the "riot." Sure enough, he was making good on his threats, stopping small groups of men from leaving the yard. Well, since this wasn't going to be a one-sided discussion, I discarded my jacket and pulled on my weight-lifting gloves.

"I'm leaving," I told him.

"No, you're not," he replied.

"Stop me," I said.

I knew that if he was going to do anything it would be now. I figured he had one swing with that shovel, and if he caught me in the head, I'd be in deep trouble. But if he missed, I'd be all over him like a cold pail of water. And he knew it.

As I watched him closely, I could see the little gears turning in his head. The tower guard opened his window and pointed a .308 FN rifle at us. Just then a nearby Holy Roller interceded in the spirit of brotherly love. I instructed him curtly not to get his tongue caught in a wringer, and split. The hardcase called for the support of his party, but they wanted no part of the action. At that point my opponent didn't know what to do. We had ourselves a Mexican standoff, and he knew if he didn't let me go, things were going to get a little messy. Either way, he was going to lose some face, so he stepped aside.

Even though no violence ensued, I was charged with a disciplinary offense. I lost sixty days "good time," which would have automatically been deducted from my sentence if I had been a good little boy. Some justice system!

It was around that period of time that I noticed a muscle-bound east coast con named Craig Weiss. He had a reputation for beating up younger cons who wouldn't go along with his perverted sexual practices. One day he began to make advances toward me on my way to the shower and even tried to persuade me to enter his cell. I didn't respond the way he expected and even became a little cocky.

Mark, another prisoner who later became my friend, advised Craig not to bother me if he knew what was good for him. Mark was right. Had Craig tried a number on me he would have been a very sorry boy. I had some pretty wild friends, and the "in" thing in the Mill was, and still is, to kill someone. They would have butchered, quartered and hung up old Craig like a hog being dressed for market. Craig, needless to say, took Mark's advice and switched targets, and one week later he beat up some other young kid. It would be many years later when Craig would realize his full potential as a stoolie, turning informer against a number of other convicts in a Millhaven murder to save his own bacon.

After fourteen months I was transferred to Collins Bay Penitentiary and Steve went to Warkworth Institution. If you didn't transfer from the Mill to an institution with a lower security classification, you got nothing — no parole, no temporary absences, nothing. I wanted out, so I transferred as soon as possible. At first the guards watched me closely for any peculiar or suspicious behavior patterns that might indicate I was about to escape, but I maintained a low profile and their vigilance waned. I remained there for two years and was employed in the audiovisual department run by Saint Lawrence College, which was under contract with the federal government to provide educational services to the prison.

One day I received a notice that I had been sued by the Sudbury IGA to the tune of $11,500 for the safe job in 1973. I couldn't believe it. Who in their right mind would sue a burglar? I had no substantial bank account, real estate or investments. My car had been seized and impounded by the Vancouver police and a $2,400 bill was outstanding. When I looked into the matter, I discovered my wages could be garnished if I was ever employed in any legitimate position, so I declared personal bankruptcy to thwart them.

By now I had three and a half years completed on my sentence, well over the one-sixth day parole and one-third full parole eligibility dates. So I began the process of applying for parole. Repeatedly I applied for day and full parole, temporary absences and transfers to a minimum-security penitentiary, and every time I was vetoed. The only excuse the National Parole Board would offer to justify their denials was "We feel uncomfortable granting you a parole at this time." I had explained to the prison classification officers and parole board members that although I entertained no doubts that I was capable of escaping from Collins Bay, I wanted to obtain my freedom the right way and for the correct reason — on parole and gainfully employed. It was no dice. I had had enough of their nonsense. I had been a model prisoner and was set to go straight. I deserved a parole and I was determined to see to it that I received one — no matter how!

Collins Bay Penitentiary opened in 1937. With its bright red peaked roofs it looked more like a fairy-tale castle than a prison. It was surrounded by a concrete wall twenty-five feet high and two and a half feet thick. Each corner was secured by a thirty-five-foot-high concrete tower, which was topped by a searchlight and manned by a guard with a .308 assault rifle. The exterior perimeter of the wall was patrolled by a roving vehicle with a guard armed with a .38 revolver. The interior was patrolled by two guards on foot from two separate guard posts stationed on either side of the yard. All towers, guard posts and the vehicle were within immediate contact with a central control room as well as one another via portable two-way radios.

My second-story cell window was caged in a framework of seven horizontal rectangular antistress steel-reinforced concrete beams set behind a sliding glass window. In the thirty-nine-year history of the prison no one had ever broken out through those windows. Cell block 4 was the most secure wing in the penitentiary.

My equipment included a three-band radio, which was contraband, but I had doctored it to look like a legitimate two-band radio. I also had a miniature wireless microphone that could be tuned to any FM station on my radio. By monitoring the UHF on the three-band radio, I had isolated the penitentiary's security frequency, thus determining the identification numbers of each tower, guard post and vehicle, plus the time schedules, routes and shift changes.

I double-checked my information with surveillance and research whenever possible. Since I was on the opposite side of the building from one foot patrol guardhouse and would need someone to transmit the guard's erratic and unpredictable comings and goings to me,

I picked Mark. We experimented with various frequencies on the FM band until we located one that was free of broadcasts. Then we accessed an undisturbed carrier wave.

It was Tuesday, December 21, 1976, 9:15 p.m. All the preparations were completed. The guard on range patrol had just completed his hourly cell check, and the outside foot patroller had recently begun the routine that would carry him to the distant side of the yard. I flicked the light off, concealing the cell in near darkness, then dismantled the aluminum prefabricated window frame with a screwdriver head I had fashioned out of a spike. Earlier I had drilled a hole in the end of a mop handle, using a handmade drill and nail. Now I threaded two straightened wire hangers through the hole and fastened the mop handle to the top concrete beam of the window. Tightening a weight bar collar on the bottom of the handle, I slid a round cast-iron fifty-pound York weight, which I had smuggled into the cell beneath a floor polisher, up the mop handle, tightening a second collar snugly beneath it and centering the weight with the bottom concrete beam of the window. I now had a giant pendulum. I walked down to the first-floor office to check on the guards. Sure enough, they were all sitting around a table, playing cards. I slipped back up to the cell and slid the solid cell door shut, bracing it so no one could get in. Then I blocked the tiny observation window so no one could see in. I wrapped my winter coat around the bottom beam and zipped it up. Since the framework of beams was prelaid concrete fitted into the wall, I was concerned that too-vigorous a blow with my improvised sledgehammer might deposit the entire structure prematurely into the guard's path directly below my window. Bringing the pendulum back, I gave it a forceful but measured swing. Much to my dismay, the heavy weight rebounded, nearly striking me. Immediately I rushed to the cell door and peered through the crack, fully expecting to see a horde of guards racing up the corridor. But it was quiet.

I checked the beam for damage. It was unscathed. Incredible! Once more I swung the pendulum, this time with all my strength, then ran to the door again. No guards. I returned to the beam, only to find there was still no damage. I brought a chair over to the window, stepped up on it and swung. Still nothing.

Feeling confident by now that the noise of my work hadn't been overheard, and perplexed by the seeming invulnerability of the beam, I swung the pendulum repeatedly. After each successive swing, I checked for damage, but none was visible.

A little frustrated, I walked over to the door to see if the coast was clear. The sight of two guards not more than twenty feet away, questioning a prisoner, hit me like a slap across the face! I was amazed they hadn't heard my demolition work.

After waiting for them to leave, I decided to give it one final, tremendous swing, then go back to the drawing board. Climbing onto the chair again, I lifted my battering ram as high as possible, then leaned into the swing with all my might. Miraculously something gave. The concrete beam had completely shattered, exposing a half-inch ribbed reinforcement bar. Unknown to me, the beam had been breaking up inside after each concussion, resulting in its total disintegration on my last blow.

Hastily I disassembled the pendulum and unzipped the coat, pulling in the concrete fragments. But my heart jumped when I heard the crunch of the guard's footsteps on the icy path below. Exposed by a shaft of light from the exterior night-lights, I peered down to see if he was looking up in my direction, but he wasn't.

Time stood still as he went down the alley to punch the clock. In panic I quickly grabbed a dull gray piece of cardboard, fashioned in the exact likeness of the beam, and placed it over the reinforcement bar. Frantically I tried to tie it on before he returned. His crisp metal punch key rang out like a rifle shot, piercing my eardrums. There wasn't enough time! I held it on with one hand, drawing back into the darkness of the cell. Would he notice? If he detected the breach, my only alternative — my only chance — would be to dive out of the window and make a run for it. I didn't relish that thought. A struggle would probably ensue, and shots would definitely be fired. If the guards in the towers didn't get me, the guard in the vehicle would have a better chance.

I tensed, ready to plunge at the first sound of recognition. But the guard didn't look up. Then the wind caught the end of the cardboard, threatening to tear it away. Closing my eyes, I grabbed it with two hands and held my breath. The guard's footsteps faltered for a second, then he was gone. Breathing a deep sigh of relief, I rapidly tied the cardboard on and placed a half-dozen wet socks out to dry over it. Then I reassembled the window and began to wait.

At 11:00 p.m. the guards, both inside and out, finished doing their rounds. My three-band radio, which was tuned to the penitentiary frequency, came alive. "Collins Bay 5733791, report."

The patrol car, guard posts and towers responded. "Number 1 clear. Number 7 clear. Number 8 clear." And so on.

At 11:20 the radio spoke again: "Collins Bay 5733791, the count is clear. The count is clear." All towers would now be unmanned except for number 13, which controlled the back entrance sally port, plus numbers 7 and 8 guardhouses and unit number 1, the patrol car.

Soon I could hear the low, steady monotonous tone of Mark's voice over the FM frequency, telling me, "No one is home. No one is home." That meant that the guard wasn't at his post. I waited for the midnight rounds to be made, giving the guards plenty of time to vacate the towers.

Midnight came and went, but no rounds were made, inside or out. At 12:15, still no rounds. Where were they? Then the half hour passed. It must be a trap! I had no choice now. I couldn't repair the concrete. If it was a trap, the spotlight beams and possibly bullets would begin flying the moment my feet touched the ground. There would be nothing I could do. I would be in a dead-end alley, and the only escape would be to run toward the ambush.

Silently I slipped out of the window and dropped to the ground. Padding quietly along the wall to the corner, I peered around. The guardhouse was empty. As I darted behind a pile of sand, I fully expected a shout or a bullet. But all I heard was the lonely howl of the wind over the wall. Wasting no time, I scanned the yard for foot patrols. Nothing. If the guard in tower number 13 was inexperienced or nervous, he would begin firing immediately when he spotted me. If he was a veteran and smart, he would wait for a slower, more visible target.

I ran like hell for the ten-foot tennis court fence and vaulted over it onto the frozen asphalt below. It had rained earlier in the day, but at nightfall the temperature had dropped to freezing. If there was any ice on the pipe running up the wall, I would be in big trouble.

Holding my breath, I grasped the pipe — it was cold but dry. Not needing my gloves, I threw them onto the ground and clambered up into the blinding lights, silhouetted against the dark sky, expecting a bullet in my back any moment.

When I got to the top, I swung over and dropped to the icy bank below. My eyes darted about for the patrol car. Nothing so far. Running through the nearby farm camp's parking lot, I headed across the grounds and into the darkness, expecting with every breath to hear the hue and cry of pursuit. I had damaged one of the floodlights when I had swung over the wall, so it wouldn't take long for the patrol car to realize something was amiss. Then the prison officials would notify the police and the chase would be on once again.

The penitentiary was surrounded by Bath Road and a commercial district ahead of me, Little Cataraqui Creek and swampland to the right, King Street and Collins Bay to the rear and vast acres of farmland to the left. I made a long, semicircular detour to the left, which was the lengthiest, least expected, but most open route, hoping to circumvent any attempt to cut off my escape. Then I came to a rude halt when I encountered a wide ditch. My only clear avenue of flight was cut off! Was it a moat to stop escapees? I wondered, glancing around for an alternative course. But there was none. Tentatively I placed one foot on the ice in hopes of soft-shoeing it across, but it cracked. Lying down spread-eagled, I tried to distribute my weight evenly over the ice and inch my way across. It cracked some more.

Losing time and patience, I decided that the ditch couldn't be more than a few feet deep. So, running back a number of yards in order to build up enough speed to jump, I charged recklessly ahead, launching myself high into the air and landing right in the middle of the ditch — up to my ankles! Grateful that no one had been around to witness my ridiculous performance, I jumped out of the ditch, cut across the field and headed down the railroad tracks leading into Kingston.

It was bitterly cold out, and my tennis shoes quickly turned to lumps of ice. But as long as I continued running, dressed only in my long johns, which blended in nicely with the snow, I could generate enough body heat. Hours later, after almost being run over by an express train that had shot out of nowhere, I reached the far side of the city.

The fierce wind had taken its toll on me, though. I was beginning to stumble and fall with increasing frequency. As I picked myself up for the umpteenth time, an old shed loomed into view. When I reached it, I staggered inside and searched for something, anything, to warm me up. All I could find was a dirty old quilt, but I was in seventh heaven, anyway.

After a brief rest, I set off down the tracks with renewed determination. Eventually I reached the home of a loyal family member and spent a few days recuperating in bed. Once again I had regained my freedom.

After I was fully recovered, I decided my best course was to get back to nature. So I purchased the necessary camping gear and set out into the woods on the outskirts of Galt, even though the time of year wasn't particularly conducive to outdoor activity. Still, winter camping did prove to be an enlightening experience to me, what with the glittering snow, the fresh air, the lonely whistle of the wind through the trees and the challenge of braving the elements. After a week of such enlightenment, though, I'd had enough. The Stone Age routine might have been just fine for cavemen, but I was freezing my ass off. What I needed was an instrument of modern-day technology, say a shotgun, then I could rob someone and rent an apartment.

That evening I broke into a Canadian Tire store and relieved the premises of a semiautomatic shotgun, shells and a hacksaw. I left just as a cruiser responded to the silent alarm. Making a hasty departure through the snow, I soon had numerous pursuers.

Three hours later they were still chasing me and I was still running through knee-high snow. Every which way I went I ran into a cruiser or an officer on foot. There must have been a whole detachment out there. One detective even started shooting at me. Eventually the circle began to contract and I dived under a nearby truck, hoping to be overlooked as the ring of police tightened. But it wasn't meant to be. They surrounded me, and the detective with the spastic trigger finger ordered me out from beneath the vehicle. With no other alternative apparent, I did as I was told.

As I got to my feet, the overzealous detective advanced on me, his gun raised. Cornered but not cowed, I met him head-on, issuing a challenge as I stepped toward him. Caught off guard by my belligerence, the detective lowered his gun and let the uniforms handcuff me, smiling when the constables granted me a few love taps to speed me on my way into the back seat of a cruiser.

When I arrived at the police station, a blond officer built like a brick wall began the usual barrage of insults. Now, I might be a thief, but a man has his pride. I threw down the gauntlet. With the other officers eager to see me slammed around a bit, we were escorted into a comparatively empty interrogation room. My handcuffs were removed and the battle began.

Besides being very large, Blondie was also quite strong and well versed in wrestling techniques. Still, I bounced my fists off his head a number of times just to let him know I was still in contention. He wasn't a vicious fighter, just hard to hurt. Unfortunately, just as we were getting to know each other better, a sergeant nonchalantly strolled into the room and called time. Soon after I was transported to the Kitchener Jail.

10

April Fools' in February

IMMEDIATELY UPON MY ARRIVAL AT THE Kitchener Jail, the authorities sectioned off cell block 1 and converted it into super maximum security for me and four other "problems." We were locked up for twenty-three hours a day in a cell behind two sets of bars. For the remaining hour of the day we "exercised" in handcuffs and leg irons in a separate special yard. We weren't permitted to have any contact whatsoever, neither physically nor verbally, with any other prisoner in the entire jail.

I wrote a letter to the provincial ombudsman's office, citing cruel and unusual treatment. An investigation followed, which resulted in our release from the cells. Henceforth, we were confined to the cell block for the duration of the day. That left me with just one set of bars as well as an eighteen-foot wall to contend with. Of course I was going to escape.

The day the warden had to let us out of the cells he told me, "Now don't do anything foolish." I just looked at him with the same amount of respect he had shown me. I wasn't forgetting the twenty-three hour lockup, or the time I had spent in the hole. For him April 1 would come early.

The four other "problems" in my predicament were a motley bunch. Benny Way was a young man with a short history of petty

thefts. Jimmy Knight, about twenty-five years old, had been imprisoned for a minor crime and seemed genial enough. Philip Andrews
was a bank robber with a fourteen-year prison term who had just
returned from a thirty-day psychiatric assessment at Pene-
tanguishene. The fourth gentleman was a local yokel who seemed
decent enough.

After obtaining hacksaw blades, again by a method I can't reveal,
I began plotting my strategy. Initially the escape plot was devised to
include only Andrews and me, but Benny began to whine about not
being allowed to come, so I changed my plans and included him,
too. Two days later Benny started having misgivings, so I excluded
him and again altered the plans. The next day he changed his mind
again, and that was when I lost patience. After I let him have a piece
of my mind, he decided he was going, after all.

By this time I didn't trust Benny. I had an uneasy feeling about
him, so whenever any guard entered the cell block I made sure
Andrews or I was right beside him. The local yokel, for his part,
decided he didn't want any connection to the escape, so, after
making a quick judgment call, I consented to his arranging to change
cell blocks. Knight wanted no part of the break, also, but wanted to
hang around for the entertainment.

The guards on duty on cell block 1 had strict orders from the
warden to check the cell block every hour on the hour without fail.
They were required to enter the time, the status of each round and
their signature in the jail logbook and were accompanied by another
guard at all times. Every time a guard and his escort entered the
corridor, we all sang a few verses of the song "Me and My Shadow"
in four-part harmony, then burst out laughing at them. After five
consecutive days and nights of this treatment, the guards had had
enough. They wouldn't come into the cell block anymore. Soon all
they would do is pop their heads around the corner, but we would
catch them and break out in the song again. Finally they closed the
heavy wooden cell block door and gave up checking altogether. It
was a shame, too, because with all the practice we were getting we
were beginning to sound like a professional barbershop quartet.

The warden's super maximum cell block security had evolved
into the easiest area in the entire jail to escape from by virtue of

possessing one structural defect that no other cell block had — direct access to a window. And the closing of the door had, in effect, soundproofed the cell block.

The Kitchener Jail featured the same monstrous bars as the Walkerton Jail. We began cutting one of the bars and watching for guards in shifts. After two hours everyone was pretty tired, but we had succeeded in severing a bar. All that remained now were the steel clamps holding the screen. We had to finish the job that night and escape, or else risk our work being discovered. I spurred the others on with words of encouragement, but it was too late. I could hear the guards coming to lock us up. In a desperate attempt to salvage what was left of our chance for liberty, I jammed the bar back into place and attempted to cram it with soap. Without warning it slipped and fell to the concrete floor with a dreadful clang. Grabbing it quickly, I jammed it back into place and again crammed it with soap. This time I was successful. After hastily pasting a couple of matching paint peelings over the cuts, I closed the window and waited . . .

Within moments the guards entered the cell block. After locking us up in the cells, one guard, an ex-OPP officer, proceeded to do something no other guard had ever done in the past. He casually walked over to the window and opened it. Then he began yanking on the bars. My heart nearly stopped. When I opened my eyes, though, he merely closed the window and walked out. I couldn't believe what had just happened. How he had managed to miss that bar I can't explain. The vibration alone from his pulling should have knocked it loose. We all agreed we had just witnessed a miracle. After reliving that experience a dozen times in my mind, I finally fell into a fitful sleep.

The following day seemed to last forever but proved uneventful. That night I tied everyone's sheets together, rapidly cut the clamps and removed the screen. Benny squeezed out first, and I threw him the rope. As I wriggled through the window, he shouldered the rope and hustled over to the wall. I bounded through the snow behind him and we paused for a moment.

Using my body as a ladder, Benny climbed onto my shoulders and placed his feet in my hands. Then I boosted him to the top of the wall. When I turned around, though, I saw that Philip was stuck in the window. I ran back and pulled him out, tearing his shirt and gouging his side. Philip and I then hot-footed back to the wall, where Benny lowered the rope. I pulled myself to the top and was rewarded with a commanding view of the Kitchener police station parking lot.

Philip grabbed the rope and started pulling himself up, but fell before he could reach the top. He tried again, but without success. By this time I could hear the guards' voices in the office above us, then a hush. Had they heard us? How long would it be till a police officer emerged from the station and spotted us profiled on the wall like gargoyles? I whispered to Philip that we would haul him up on the rope. As we got him to the top, I reached out to grab him, but he couldn't hold on to the rope any longer and plummeted to the ground.

In an escape it's every man for himself, and the longer we screwed around the slimmer our chances were to escape. Even Philip pleaded with us to leave him. But I couldn't.

Quickly I fashioned a noose and threw it down to him, telling him to put it around his waist. I was determined to succeed this time. Painfully we hauled him up again, got him near the top, and then he started slipping once more. This time I lunged and grabbed him, and now all three of us were on the wall.

Without hesitating another moment, I ran along the top of the wall, jumped down and waited for the others. They seemed to take forever. One prisoner in the holding tank inside the jail heard the noise and yelled to the other prisoners that there was something happening outside. I whispered for him to remain quiet just as my colleagues came along the wall. Benny jumped down into a snow-bank, and Philip hit a sheet of ice. His legs flew out from under him and he struck his head violently on the ground, stunning himself. We helped him up, then began to walk as inconspicuously as possible across the street. The night was brisk and clear. The streets were deserted. It was Tuesday, February 22, 1977, 6:30 p.m., sixty-three days after my escape from Collins Bay.

As we walked, Philip's limp got more pronounced. He was exhausted, dazed and hurt, and his feet were so banged up that we had to half carry him up the street. Nearing exhaustion ourselves, we paused to rest and I noticed a car following us. Philip, sensing the precariousness of our situation, urged us to leave him. Admitting sadly that we couldn't help him anymore, Benny and I left Philip behind a nearby house and made good our escape.

A later investigation into the jailbreak would reveal that Philip had phoned a taxi from the house and was consequently arrested. At the exact time his call was registered at the cab company, the guard on duty had made an entry in the jail logbook to the effect: "7:00 p.m., checked cell block 1, all in order."

For our part, we moved silently, easily now, loping through back streets and alleys, shunning the police as well as traffic and pedestrians. Eventually we followed a rail line out of Kitchener until we came across a Mercedes dealership that appeared to be closed for the evening. We gained entrance through a rear window and selected a car, but before we left, I searched for and located the dealership cash box and proceeded to open it with a screwdriver. As I was doing that, an attractive young lady casually walked by and noticed me in the dark office prying the box open. She smiled, said, "Hi," and just kept right on walking, never even breaking her stride or composure. I bolted for the garage, flew past the Mercedes, noticed Benny talking with a gentleman and dived out the window. I waited to lend assistance when he followed me, but he never did. He just remained there, discussing the purchase price of the Mercedes with the gentleman. Alone now, I continued on down the tracks, cold and tired but free.

On the outskirts of Kitchener I stole a car and drove to Toronto, where I purchased a one-way ticket to Quebec City, getting off in Montreal instead. After three and a half years inside, I was determined to go straight, get a job and stay out of prison. I rented a cheap apartment for a little over $100 a month, and for the next two weeks I rose at seven each morning to solicit every local business and company for employment of any kind — manual labor, dish washing, janitorial work, anything. My search proved fruitless, however. Despite the frustration, though, my determination remained undaunted. In the end, I went to the Metropolitan Labour Supply Centre and found work for $3.50 an hour, the minimum wage there. Work was work, the way I looked at it.

The first day, I woke up at 5:00 a.m. and arrived at the center at six, even though it didn't open until seven. Jobs were dispensed on a first-come, first-serve basis, or to those who had families to support or were most in need. Since I was new and needed the money immediately, I was shown preferential treatment for the first few days. The work was heavy manual labor, which I loathe because of the utter mindlessness of it. But it was my ticket to a free life, so I persevered. Even so, all too soon the work dwindled and I joined the ranks of the hopeful unemployed. Every day we arrived at 6:00 a.m. and waited for the center to open. Every day we would end up sitting around until 6:00 p.m. for nothing. I wouldn't even leave for lunch. I didn't want to miss a work opportunity, plus I couldn't afford to go to lunch, anyway.

Eventually I had to move into an eighty-dollar-a-month room, even though I saved every penny I could. Still the work continued to diminish, and finally it disappeared altogether. I had to do something. I was now in worse financial condition than when I first arrived in Montreal. Inevitably I began thinking in terms of crime again.

I had one pair of used work boots, thoughtfully provided by my sister-in-law. When I originally tried them on, they were a perfect fit, exactly what I needed. However, after one short month they had begun to cut into my Achilles tendon. At first I could almost reach noon before starting to limp; finally I couldn't walk more than half a block before I was hobbling the entire six blocks to the center. The pain was just excruciating. I couldn't believe one measly pair of boots could be responsible for so much agony. I tried wearing them every which way. I laced them up. I unlaced them. I tried stretching, beating and even cutting them, but to no avail. If I'd had a gun at the time, I'm sure I would have shot them full of holes.

One night, on the way home from the center, I gave up in disgust. I marched into a Hudson's Bay store and exchanged the boots for a pair of tennis shoes. As I was leaving, I pocketed a work hat, and the store security nailed me. Just outside the store an Oriental security guard placed his hand on my shoulder from behind and flashed his identification, saying, "Bay security." Sure, I thought, I'll just give him the brushoff and test out my new tennis shoes. The brushoff was as far as I got. The next thing I knew I was unceremoniously on my way to the pavement with a well-placed side kick to the cranium to ensure I arrived there on time. Now I was riled. He had cut my eyebrow. But there were two security guards on the scene by now, and the second one looked even meaner than Bruce Lee. I figured discretion was the better part of valor, and the security guards marched me back into the department store.

If I could have gotten Mr. Lee by himself, I'd have tuned him up a little before making good my escape. I had brushed up on my boxing and endurance training with the punching and speed bags prior to my escape from Collins Bay. My hands were quick and I could hit hard enough to split a canvas heavy bag with one crack.

With revenge in mind, I feigned a need to go to the washroom. Bruce was quite willing to escort me by himself. I could sense he wanted to give me a free introductory lesson into the art of self-defense. But the other guard caught the play and wasn't buying any of it.

While I was waiting in the security room for the police to arrive, I knew no one would realize who I was until after my fingerprints had been verified by the Canadian Police Information Checks. When that happened, all hell would break loose. But before such an unfortunate event could occur, I was determined to make a run for it when I was escorted outside to a police cruiser.

Two cops responded to the security guards' request for help, and I was charged under an alias. Incredibly enough they believed every single word I said when I told them I had never been involved with the police before. All ready to set a new world record for the outdoor 100-yard dash, I couldn't believe what I heard next. They told me I could go! But I had to sign an agreement to report to the police for fingerprinting in a week and make a court appearance within ten days. Furthermore, I had to promise not to leave town in the meantime. I looked straight into one officer's big baby blue eyes and promised him with all the false sincerity I could muster. Then I waltzed right out of police custody with my new tennis shoes and returned to my room. They kept the hat.

I intended to delay the inevitable for six days at the most. I wasn't about to report to anywhere and get my little pinkies printed. I wasn't crazy. But two days after the Bay incident, as I was about to leave my room, I noticed two gentlemen in detective garb about to enter the rooming house. I hastily returned to my room, gathered a few personal items together and departed via my window and the rear fire escape.

I had given legitimate enterprise a good, hard, honest try, but I guess it just wasn't meant to be. If being honest meant living in poverty, then I wanted no part of it. I had grown up poor, and it just sickened me. I was determined to rise above my upbringing. And there was no way in this goddamn world I was ever going to live in poverty again. I'd rather die with a gun in my hand than starve in the streets. I might be a thief, but I'd die before becoming a beggar. The lousy break concerning the whole affair was that if I had been able to secure steady employment, even at minimum wage, I'm sure I'd still be slaving away there today, such was my determination to remain free.

11

If You Snooze You Lose

MICHAEL CAMERON WAS ONE OF THE best fraud artists in Canada. Aside from being one of the most amiable persons I had ever met on the wrong side of a penitentiary wall, he was also highly intelligent. Michael was five feet nine inches tall, blond and handsome. He was a long-distance runner, and looked as if he belonged on a beach in California rather than in a federal prison for bouncing checks. We had become friends in Collins Bay Penitentiary and he was an inspiration to me.

Eventually, finding myself in Saskatchewan, after my close call in Montreal, I thought I'd pay Michael a visit in Prince Albert penitentiary, where he had been transferred. Realizing there was a good chance that I might end up back in prison myself, I assumed an alias affiliated with a religious group that regularly visited Collins Bay and entered Prince Albert Maximum Security Prison. Needless to say, Michael was quite surprised and happy to see me.

"I'm glad you didn't forget me," he told me, then asked me what I was doing in this area of Canada.

"I want you out," I said to him.

Thus it was settled. We began to plot his escape. Michael had a friend named Rodney, and it was arranged for me to stay at Rodney's farm, where I spent one of the most enjoyable summers of my life.

The one thing I appreciated the most about the prairies was the flat land. You could see clearly for twenty miles. You didn't get that hemmed-in feeling prevalent in Ontario, due to the trees, or in British Columbia, with the mountains. There was nothing but wide-open spaces. Rodney's wife had a moped, which I frequently used to tour the long prairie back roads and fields of golden-yellow wheat.

I came to know Rodney well, and although he had no knowledge of the true nature of my stay, we got along as if we were brothers. We did all the things I'd missed in prison. We water-skied, went to horse shows and generally just had a great time. The tension and frustration I had built up from years behind bars seemed to evaporate like a mid-morning prairie dew, and I almost forgot that I had ever been in prison. I didn't think, not even for a minute, that I was ever going to return.

I couldn't continue to visit Michael on a regular basis in the guise of a religious friend on vacation from Ontario, so we needed a liaison, someone who could be trusted, who wouldn't be suspected by prison security and who had a vested interest in Michael's release. That was where Michael's girlfriend, Jessica, came into the picture. She was gorgeous, with long auburn hair, dark eyes, high cheekbones, a regal nose, full lips and long legs that ran all the way up to her shoulders.

The first time I met her she thought I was a police officer, since I had that same clean-cut look and businesslike manner. Initially we planned for Michael to arrange for a trip to the hospital, where I would then take custody of him from his unsuspecting escorts. Jessica was in agreement with Michael's jailbreak at first, but as soon as I assured her that I would effect Michael's freedom even if it meant a guard or two might get a little shot up, her composure disappeared. The next day she left, returning to Nanaimo, British Columbia.

One week later I received a message from Michael, telling me that the break was off and that it wasn't Jessica's fault. But I read between the lines and knew Jessica was our weak link. I didn't know exactly what the problem was, but I was determined to find out, even if it cost me my freedom. I walked back into Prince Albert Prison to visit Michael, sincerely hoping I didn't encounter a guard who had been transferred from Collins Bay to Prince Albert.

Sure enough, I found out that Jessica wanted no part of the blood-and-guts routine, even if it meant Michael would have to serve his entire fourteen-year prison term. There I was trying to break him out, and my biggest hurdle was his girlfriend. She was much closer to Michael than I was; she was his girlfriend and I was just his friend. It seemed to me she should have been a little more enthusiastic about setting him free than I was. We still needed her as our contact, so Michael and I decided to entice her back with a watered-down version of the escape — no violence and no gunplay. Her fears allayed, she agreed to visit Michael every two weeks to relay my instructions.

For three consecutive days and nights I concealed myself in the brush and woods around the prison with a pair of binoculars to survey, take notes, draw sketches and snap photographs with a telescopic lens. I prowled closer only at night to investigate certain almost imperceptible peculiarities. Quite soon I was able to determine the schedules, routes, practices, equipment and capabilities of the interior foot patrols, exterior patrol vehicles, guard towers and perimeter security fortifications.

The main outside exercise yard was surrounded by two galvanized chain-link fences fourteen feet high, spaced eighteen feet apart, topped with strands of barbed wire and rolls of concertina, guarded by two towers twenty-five feet high and manned by two correctional officers with assault rifles. The far end was protected by a twenty-five-foot steel-reinforced concrete wall. It was two feet thick and overseen by two thirty-five-foot towers capped with two searchlights and under surveillance by two additional guards with assault rifles. The entire penitentiary was patrolled by two roving vehicles, each containing a guard armed with an assault rifle. All security personnel were equipped with penitentiary band two-way radios. I attempted to pinpoint the weakest, easiest, exploitable link in the chain of security, and I soon found it. During evening exercise period for the main prison population, all towers were manned. However, during work hours, only one tower was manned at the near end of the yard. The only problem was that we had no way of determining which tower would be occupied, since they alternated unpredictably, or so it seemed at first.

With additional data, cross-checking and further surveillance, Michael and I assembled a tentatively predetermined routine and decided to take our chances on the tower nearest to the paved road passing by the penitentiary, since it would be unmanned on the day scheduled for the escape. In the event our prediction was incorrect, alternative measures would be put into effect. The only prisoners permitted into the yard during the day were the gymnasium recreation work crew, so Michael immediately arranged a job change.

I began assembling the equipment essential for the prison break: one vehicle, one on-road motorcycle, one off-road motorcycle, two handguns, one high-powered rifle, two walkie-talkies and one wrench. After I'd given each item the proper amount of preparation and testing, everything was set. Michael was ready, the day was tomorrow, and I even thought the plan might work. We'd need one hell of a lot of luck and we'd have to catch them sleeping.

That evening I parked the car fourteen miles away and hid the dirt bike just across the road from the prison, camouflaging it in some trees at the foot of a hill. Now the fun part began. I had to deposit a walkie-talkie and a handgun in a prairie dog burrow ninety feet inside the exercise yard. Michael wanted the pistol as insurance in the escape, and even though I didn't think there was a need for it, he insisted on having it.

The prison guards changed shifts shortly after 11:00 p.m. By 3:00 a.m. the majority of the tower and patrol vehicle guards had expended most of their excess energy and were beginning to settle down to the boredom of their routines. Dressed entirely in camouflage fatigues and makeup, I glassed the penitentiary grounds carefully for patrolling vehicles or guards. All was motionless. Then I belly-crawled from the far side of the road, through a culvert and a ditch and then over to the fence.

The night was dark and warm, with a faint breeze. Carefully, with the wrench, I removed the nuts, bolts and clamps holding the rod that interlaced the chain-links to the post on the first fence. Everything was going smoothly so far. The patrols seemed to have deserted the area. Cocking my ears, I listened for telltale sounds. All I heard, though, was the familiar sigh of the wind in the trees.

I squeezed smoothly through the first fence and began to remove the nuts on the second one. Suddenly I detected an odd rustling sound coming from my left. It sounded like a terrific wind whooshing through the trees, but there were no trees to the left and the wind was barely a whisper. And then I knew what it was. The patrol truck was gliding toward me with its lights out not fifty yards away!

Desperately I dived for the first fence, wriggled through and streaked for the culvert. But the patrol truck was coming on too fast. I'd never make it! With no choice I hit the dirt, hugged the ground and hoped the guard wouldn't spot me. Then the patrol truck whirled on by, paying me no heed as it continued on down the fence line. A close call indeed!

Returning to the second fence, I determined this time to keep a sharp ear out for any approaching patrol. Quickly I removed the nuts and bolts and crawled through, making my way stealthily to the gopher hole. All of a sudden I was bathed in glaring light. I spun around quickly and rolled toward the fence out of sight. The tower guard was merely playing with the searchlight, so I continued on. Then I heard the hiss of the patrol truck tires on the compressed dirt surface of the road. Almost at the burrow now, I hesitated, calculating whether to stay where I was or make a dash for the ditch. If I stayed and was spotted, I'd be mistaken for an escaping prisoner and shot on sight. If I left, only a few seconds of spent energy and an unpromising opportunity would be lost, but the prison break wouldn't be compromised. I chose the ditch. Dashing frantically back through both fences, I made it to the ditch with seconds to spare.

I was beginning to get the timing down, feeling confident now with my mad dashes. For the third time that night I entered the yard. Finally I succeeded in depositing the walkie-talkie and pistol in the hole. Covering them with loose dirt and grass, I slipped out of the yard, reset the fence and replaced the clamps to appear secure yet yield to pressure. Returning to my hotel room to catch a much-needed forty winks, I woke early enough to set off once again to reconnoiter the prison prior to morning light.

From my observation post in the brush, I scrutinized the interior of the crucial tower minutely. We had guessed accurately. The tower was empty. Excitement stirred within me. At exactly 7:00 a.m. I was prepared and in position to assist Michael in his break. Then eight o'clock arrived, but there was no movement in the yard. Nine o'clock passed and still no movement. Something was definitely wrong. Were the altered clamps discovered and our escape plan destroyed?

For the entire day and long into the night, I remained secreted beneath the shrubbery, waiting and watching, but to no avail. The prison seemed lifeless. Neither prisoners nor guards appeared. At 11:00 p.m. I emerged from hiding to examine the fence and ascertain if any repairs had been performed, but my handiwork hadn't been disturbed.

In bed later that evening I couldn't sleep. I was filled with despair and bewilderment over the uncertainty of our situation. Early the next morning I telephoned the penitentiary under the pretext of inquiring into the visiting schedule for the day. I was informed that although there had been a minor disturbance the day before, which had resulted in the prison remaining closed to the public for the duration of the day, things were expected to revert to normal presently.

With renewed hope I returned. At 7:30 a.m. I concealed the on-road motorcycle in the heavy bush a mile from the penitentiary, then removed the off-road motorcycle from hiding and placed it in readiness. At 7:45 I probed the observation tower with the binoculars. Lightning had struck twice in the same place. It remained vacant. At 8:00 a.m. I was primed for Michael's bid for freedom. This time there was movement in the yard. I could see the work detail moving about their assigned tasks like little green toy convicts, and I knew Michael was among them. Soon enough he came strolling nonchalantly down the path with a wheelbarrow full of sand and a shovel, intent upon filling in the gopher hole. Through the binoculars, I observed him recovering the walkie-talkie and the 9 mm gun. Immediately I jumped up and tore down the hill to warm up the bike. The engine started on the first kick. I revved it for a few minutes, then shut it off and raced back up the hill, ducking behind a derelict pipe. All the while I was attuned to the three-beep signal on my walkie-talkie, indicating Michael would be moving into escape position.

The beeps never came, not that morning. Instead, at 11:00 a.m., everyone disappeared inside for lunch. At 1:00 p.m. they reappeared and resumed work. Again I flew down the hill, kicking the motorcycle to life, then raced up again, just in time to see the patrol truck drive up and park right beside the unmanned tower for two long, agonizing hours. Running out of time and opportunity, I camouflaged my face in preparation to belly-crawl through the culvert, underneath the truck and pop up on the driver's side, getting the drop on him. Just as I was about to start through the culvert, the 3:00 p.m. shift change arrived and he left. Thank goodness!

Suddenly I was startled to hear three loud, measured beeps. I acknowledged enthusiastically by returning the signal. For the third time that day I ripped down the hill to the bike, but this time with a definite sense of certainty and exhilaration. Racing back up to the top, I dived behind the pipe and leveled the 30-30 rifle, anticipating the need to fire a discouraging round over any tower guard's head if shots erupted.

Soon Michael casually appeared again, his attention seemingly focused upon clipping the grass hemming the interior of the fence. As he slowly neared the breached section of the fence, he seemed to linger unnecessarily, almost hesitantly. My thoughts screamed out to him, "Now, Michael. Now!"

After a few endless moments, he slipped through the fences and came trotting across the road, as if he were out for a Sunday jog in the park. We greeted each other enthusiastically but tersely. Rushing down the hill, we quickly mounted the dirt bike and roared away. But we didn't get far. The bike just sputtered and died. Hastily starting it again, we roared away for the second time, and once more the bike shut down.

There we were right out in the middle of a penitentiary field, a couple of sitting ducks on a motorcycle with a 30-30 carbine in full view of any patrol truck or motorist who happened by. If the patrol truck spotted us, there would be no friendly greeting and offer of assistance. We would get our asses shot at in short order. Eventually the bike wouldn't even start at all, so we just left it and began running across the never-ending prairie field to the secondary motorcycle a mile away.

As we cut across the field, we were bellowed at by a farmer who wanted to know exactly what the hell we thought we were doing on his property. Since he was some distance away, I hollered that we had been out hunting but had lost our hound and asked if he had seen it. He replied that he hadn't, but if he did he would be sure to shoot it. We continued across the field and vanished into the bush as I caught sight of the farmer hurrying toward us.

Since we were somewhat disoriented, having entered the bushes from an unfamiliar angle, it took a few frenzied moments of search-ing to finally locate the camouflaged motorcycle. We grabbed it and pushed it out into the open. I leaped on, and was in the process of starting the bike, when the farmer suddenly charged blindly through the bushes like an enraged bull. Attired in black rubber boots, blue denim overalls and scowl, he was armed with a pair of menacing meat hooks.

The bike roared to life, and I stomped it into gear and jerked the throttle. The rear tire spun, spitting up soggy leaves, twigs and dirt. I lunged forward just as the farmer grabbed the handlebars, jerking the motorcycle off balance. Throwing my weight to one side, I strained to prevent it from toppling. Michael stepped back and chambered a shell into the carbine as if he were John Wayne, but as he did so, the chambered shell ejected out of the gun, somersaulted and landed on the ground. I prayed the farmer hadn't noticed it.

"We're leaving," Michael warned. "We don't want any trouble, so just stand back."

The farmer seemed uncertain what to do and watched us as we mounted the motorcycle and sped away.

The farmer's unexpected challenge had seriously jeopardized our timetable. The road passing by the prison was seven miles in length, terminating in a dead end with only one exit, which was Macdowall Road, also seven miles in length. It ended up in the tiny village of Macdowall, where our escape vehicle was parked.

Figuring we had a few minutes before the farmer reached his phone to notify the police, who would instantly launch into action with roadblocks and helicopter patrols, I sped down the gravel back road at ninety miles an hour, expecting at every bend to lose control, crash and fly headlong into the trees lining the ditch. To conceal the 30-30 from the view of passing motorists, Michael positioned it between us, with the butt resting on the seat and the barrel aimed skyward.

Somehow we made it to the exit, which greatly surprised me. Advancing to a ninety-degree left turn, I slowed and negotiated it successfully. Turning into the first right-hand cart track, I negotiated it somewhat less successfully. As a matter of fact, the bike spun out from under us, the gun exploded and we were both thrown ass over end into the ditch. When we picked ourselves up, Michael asked excitedly, "Are you hit? Are you hit?" I thought the answer to that was self-evident. I would hardly be picking myself up off the ground with half my skull blown away.

Pushing the bike down the track and off into the bush, we meticulously concealed it beneath some bushes and ran back to the entrance, carefully obliterating the tire tracks and any telltale signs. Then we crossed over to the far side of Macdowall Road and, to our horror, observed an RCMP cruiser arrive, speeding from the opposite direction of Macdowall. It skidded to a halt not far from us. The officer jumped out and raced down the track, disappearing into the forest. We prepared ourselves to flee if he emerged with the motorcycle or exhibited any signs indicating he had discovered it. Then, just as suddenly, he reappeared, raced back to the car, leaped inside and roared away again. This same act was repeated a second time by two officers five minutes later. Lingering long enough to determine the motorcycle hadn't been detected, we began running swiftly cross-country, restricting ourselves to the prairie bush and steering clear of farmhouses whenever possible.

The afternoon was hot and humid, and we found the going difficult as we kept on the move throughout the remainder of the day and well into the evening. After stopping for a drink of water, I became violently sick, weak and light-headed. The water I'd drunk had been contaminated slough water. Shortly afterward we came upon a set of railroad tracks, which offered us an option of left or right. Michael insisted left would guide us south, away from Prince Albert, while right would take us north toward Prince Albert. I maintained the opposite, but being sick and not trusting my sense of direction, I didn't have the strength to argue. Hoping he was right, we turned left.

All through the long, dreary night we followed the tracks as I reeled from side to side like a drunken sailor, taking frequent rests and fighting off the urge to slip into sleep. As the warm glow of a late-summer Saskatchewan morning dawned on us, so did the guard towers of Prince Albert Maximum Security Prison. We had taken the wrong direction! Now we were definitely in trouble. Everyone and his dog would be out looking for us.

I started constructing a good defense for court. Insanity. Yes, that was it! Insanity! They should believe that, given our present location.

Michael could say he was Henry Hudson and I was his retarded son John and we were still trying to find the northwest passage to Cathay. That way we would only have to spend ten years in an insane asylum instead of twenty years in prison.

Shaking our heads, we scrambled off the tracks. Barely a quarter of a mile from the prison, still on penitentiary property, we concealed ourselves beneath bundles of cut straw for the entire day, miraculously without incident. The itching of the straw almost drove me nuts.

Reversing direction at nightfall, we followed the tracks for a number of miles, switching to back roads until we finally reached Macdowall. It was predestined — we had been everywhere else! Changing clothes, we drove to the village of Vanscoy and boarded a bus for Calgary. When we got there, we registered in a motel and set about replenishing our exhausted physical reserves.

In the middle of the night I was fast asleep in an adjoining room, when Michael came in and woke me up, whispering that someone had tried to gain entrance to the room but had been discouraged by the chain lock. Shortly afterward he had heard a brief scuffle outside, followed by silence. We waited. Someone knocked on the door.

"Who is it?" Michael asked.

"The police" came the reply. "Is everything all right in there?"

"Yes, fine, thank you," Michael answered.

"Okay, just checking. Sorry to disturb you."

A few minutes passed, then we heard someone knocking again.

"Who is it?" Michael asked.

"The police. Did anyone gain entrance to your room?"

"No, the door was locked and chained," Michael replied.

"Okay. Sorry to trouble you again."

A short time later someone knocked for the third time.

"Who is it?" Michael asked wearily.

"The police. We have a problem and we'd like to speak with you for a moment."

I returned to the adjoining room, leaving the door slightly ajar, climbed into bed and feigned sleep, all the while clasping a 9 mm pistol under my pillow. Michael opened the door. Two Calgary police detectives clad in dark suits introduced themselves, entered the room, sat down and related their problem. They had a burglary suspect in custody whom they had observed attempting to enter various rooms, including Michael's. But upon being apprehended, the man had insisted he had been invited into the rooms.

"Did you invite him into your room?" they asked Michael.

"No," Michael said.

"In that case, would you be willing to testify to that effect in court?"

"Sure," Michael said nonchalantly.

He then went on to tell them that all they had to do was notify him when he had to make his court appearance and he would make the necessary arrangements with his company. He told them he was a Massey-Ferguson district manager and traveled through Calgary every second Friday.

"Do you have a business card?" one of the cops asked.

"No," Michael replied. "I lost my wallet earlier today, but I can give you the necessary information to contact me."

Michael then proceeded to dictate to them an alias complete with name, address, phone number and head office, which they dutifully put down in their little black notebooks. In turn, he asked for one of their business cards so he could contact them if the need arose. The detectives obliged.

During the entire confidence game, I remained silent and tense, anticipating an outbreak of violence at any moment. How the detectives failed to recognize Michael mystified me. His picture had been splashed across the front page of newspapers all across the country. Later, after the cops had left, we realized that one of them had been sitting right next to an open flight bag containing the second gun. We spent the remainder of the night at the motel, then caught the first bus to Vancouver in the morning.

After that, Michael and I split up. He went to the United States with his lady and remained there for two years until he was arrested by the American authorities and deported back to Canada. Meanwhile I went back to Ontario as a prelude to my new career robbing banks.

12

The Shooting of Officer McNeil

WHILE IN COLLINS BAY I HAD READ AN interesting article in a popular magazine concerning Dr. James P. Randolph, a renowned cosmetic surgeon in Toronto. All his operations were performed in an operating room adjacent to his Royal York Hotel office on Front Street. Following an average four-hour operation, the patient walked out under his own power, requiring no hospitalization whatsoever. The particular aspect of his practice that caught my attention most was that he accepted no patients under any health care plans. His services were strictly cash and carry. When I got back to Ontario, I went to Toronto and made an appointment with the good doctor under an alias. After a few close-up photos and payment of $1,000 by certified check, I was asked to come back again in a week for the operation.

It occurred to me that I might get a little more than I bargained for upon my return. If I talked under the anesthetic, I might even get arrested. However, seven days later on a Friday afternoon at one o'clock I walked back into Dr. Randolph's private hospital. Relieved of my clothing and personal possessions, and dressed in a cute little gown, I envisioned the newspaper headlines reading: ESCAPED

CONVICT MICKY McARTHUR ARRESTED DRESSED IN GOWN
AT VANITY CLINIC!

Ushered into the preoperating room, I was injected in the butt with
a tranquilizer by a reassuring nurse. All Dr. Randolph's staff were
pleasantly efficient and cheerful. Lying on the bed and waiting for
the drug to take effect, I could hear the soft laughter of the nurses
across the room, which soothed my nerves somewhat, though the
gown still bothered me. If I was arrested, I hoped they at least would
let me put my pants back on. Then a mask was gently placed over
my face and I was asked to count down from 100. The last number I
remember reaching was ninety-four.

I awoke four hours later, feeling slightly nauseated but fit, and was
escorted by two attentive nurses to the elevator and down to a
waiting taxi below. The cotton batting in my nose was uncomfortable
and forced me to breathe through my mouth, making swallowing
difficult, but a week later I returned to have it and the tiny cast
carefully removed, and for the first time I was able to see the new
me. Although my nose was still partially swollen and it would take
some time for the skin to settle and conform to the correct shape,
there was a definite change in my facial appearance, or so I thought.

With my new face as insurance against any arrest, I found myself
once again in Saskatchewan, but not coincidentally so. The little
prairie town of Hague wasn't far from Rodney's farm, and I had
wanted to rob its bank the very first time I'd seen it. It had been love
at first sight. After stealing a luxury car with out-of-province plates
in Saskatoon, I drove without incident to Hague the night prior to
the upcoming event, camping out in the vehicle for the evening.

As the rising sun warmed the chilly November morning, I donned
a three-piece suit, disguise and gloves and checked my pistol, not
that I seriously thought I'd have to use it. Then I drove at a leisurely
pace into Hague and parked in the community lot, making sure I had
an unobstructed view of the bank. At 9:00 a.m. the manager arrived,
accompanied by a female assistant.

At ten o'clock I watched the unhurried activity in the main street.
An ancient dark green Dodge pickup loaded with lumber rolled to
a stop nearby. A middle-aged gray-haired gentleman slowly descended, lifted a long white pine plank and hauled it away as the
staccato noise of hammering resounded in the background. Two

elderly ladies, each with large flowered handbags, chatted amiably on the sidewalk.

At exactly 11:15 a.m. I sauntered into the bank, flicking the lock button as I closed the door, continued on over to the end of the counter, where I was greeted by a cute young teller.

"May I help you?" she asked cheerfully.

Unzipping my satchel and producing the gun, I politely replied, "Yes, this is a robbery." Expecting her to cooperate, or at least remain motionless, she did neither. Instead she uttered a sharp little shriek and ran around the corner into the washroom. "Get back here!" I ordered gruffly, but she ignored me.

Now I was standing in the middle of an empty bank, holding a gun, with no one to rob. In an attempt to regain control of the situation, I stepped briskly into the manager's office and ordered him to bring the teller out of the washroom. The manager called out to her, his arms frozen to his sides, and eventually she reappeared, a timid look on her face.

Realizing by now that she was quite inexperienced, I assured her that she was in no actual danger, and she seemed to calm down considerably. In a pleasant voice I instructed her to open the safe and tills and deposit the money in the satchel. All the while I kept my eye on the manager, who seemed to have been stricken with rigor mortis.

Then I heard a customer try to gain entrance to the bank, find the door locked and depart. A second customer arrived and attempted to gain entrance but finally left, too. Then a third customer, a middle-aged gentleman, began knocking persistently on the door. I instructed the girl to tell him we were closed due to an audit. But he insisted he had an appointment with the manager at noon. Here I was trying to rob a bank and I found myself competing with a customer for service. Following my instructions again, the teller let the gentleman in and ushered him into the office, where I greeted him with the gun and asked him to sit down, which he did with great haste. Informing him of the situation, I asked for his cooperation, which he readily agreed to give.

By the time I finished handcuffing everyone, they were much more at ease. Then, as I was about to leave, the businessman told me his handcuffs were too tight. I loosened them and remarked offhandedly that I should leave soon, since I'd been in the bank for close to twenty minutes now. At the same time I wondered what I was going to do with the dinky Browning automatic when the police paid us the social call I expected any moment.

I asked the customer if he was more comfortable now and he replied yes and thanked me. We were getting along better than some families do, but I suspect my little peacemaker might have had something to do with that. Finally, retrieving the satchel, I left the bank and made my getaway.

I drove down Highway 11 in a southerly direction, observing the speed limit, but when I got far enough away from Hague, I turned right at the first gravel road and sped up, then turned right again at the first dirt road. Now I was traveling in a northerly direction, circumventing the town completely. Cutting across a newly harvested wheat field, I drove in the tractor tire marks, concealed my car in a grove of trees and waited for nightfall or the police.

After considering the car's position and finding it lacking, I decided to move it to a better position of concealment, only to have it get stuck in an exposed area. Frantically jamming rocks, debris and decaying boards beneath the wheels, I only succeeded in digging myself in deeper. I didn't have a shovel, and attempting to dig with an old plank proved to be futile. Realizing a police airplane or helicopter might appear on the horizon any moment, I had to think of something or abandon the car in a hurry.

Taking out the jack, I raised the rear end of one side, filled in the hole with rocks and dirt, then lowered the car, repeating the procedure on the other side. Just as a low-flying single-engine plane swooped over the area, I moved the car and camouflaged it. Listening to the local radio station, I found out that my license plate number had been recorded. By pure chance, near a grain elevator, I found a pair of discarded Saskatchewan license plates and exchanged them for my originals. As darkness slowly descended, I reappeared from the grove of trees and drove to Saskatoon without difficulty.

As I cruised up the main Saskatoon street on a busy Friday night, a police cruiser suddenly appeared in my rearview mirror, approaching fast. I tensed, ready to crank the steering wheel and hit the gas at the first flash of the dome light, but the cruiser passed me and accelerated into the night in response to some other emergency. After carefully examining the interior of the car for any telltale signs of my occupancy and removing the license plates, I left it in Saskatoon and boarded a bus for Regina.

The following morning, well rested, I rose and walked across the street to a respectable-looking restaurant and ordered breakfast. As I was waiting for my bacon and eggs to arrive, I sensed something unsettling about the establishment, particularly the customers. They all seemed to be homogeneous in dress, stature, facial aspect and mannerisms. Nevertheless, breakfast arrived and I busied myself with my meal, dismissing my earlier concerns as the paranoid after-effects of the robbery. When a police cruiser arrived and two officers entered for breakfast, I put it down to a coincidence. But when they began chatting cordially with two other gentlemen I had previously categorized as businessmen, it suddenly dawned on me. For all intents and purposes, I might as well have been sitting in the middle of a police department. The restaurant I had selected to dine in was also favored by the police, and as I casually looked around, there were no less than seven detectives! No one seemed to be paying me the slightest bit of attention. Even so, I cut short my meal and returned to my motel. After calling a taxi, I caught the first bus leaving the city and resumed my journey eastward.

When I got to Toronto after a long, arduous but uneventful bus ride, I flagged a cab and told the driver to take me to the Westbury Hotel. As I got out of the cab to pay the driver, he said to me, strangely, "Stay out of trouble now." Then I noticed a gentleman in a dark suit with his arms folded across his chest, watching me from behind the plate glass hotel frontage. As I turned toward the doorway and entered the lobby of the hotel, he positioned himself slightly out of view. I sensed something was wrong. Shrugging, I registered, checked my room, then quickly returned to the lobby. The mysterious stranger was nowhere to be seen.

Determined to find out who my shadow was, I asked the registration clerk if he had noticed the man in the lobby. The clerk failed to even acknowledge his existence let alone his identity. That cinched it for me. Either he was the hotel detective or I was under surveillance. Wasting no time, I returned to my room, gathered my possessions and exited through the rear door. Shortly after, I registered in a second hotel under a different alias, this time without any problems. Just to be sure, though, I carried my Browning automatic with me at all times.

Michael Cameron had schooled me in the art of fraud, and I was impressed with the ease with which one could obtain expensive jewelry and merchandise with virtually no risk of immediate arrest. I was eager to put my newly acquired criminal technique to the test. Over the next few days I purchased or constructed the necessary equipment, opened a checking account under the pseudonym of Richard Emmitt Sutter III and visited every expensive jewelry store on Yonge Street downtown, examining diamond rings and Rolex watches and leaving a substantial cash deposit each time with a promise to return on Thursday or Friday with the balance in a certified check. Success of the fraud depended on the merchants being unable to verify the authenticity of the check due to the bank being closed.

On Friday, November 11, 1977, at 5:00 p.m., I walked out of my hotel room dressed in a dark blue three-piece suit with black leather topcoat. The first establishment on my list was Gold's Jewelers, which I entered and, following the usual small talk, stated my business, handing the saleswoman the counterfeit certified check, which she declined to accept, asking that I return on Monday. When I asked what the problem was, she replied that she had no way to confirm that the check was genuine. Then she said she would get the manager's approval, and off she walked with my check to his office. Realizing something was amiss when she failed to return within a reasonable period of time, I walked into the manager's office to retrieve the check and was advised that the authorities had been notified.

Leaving the store, as well as the check, I walked rapidly up the street, around the first corner and caught a cab, seating myself in the front seat beside the driver. Just as the cab pulled away, a uniformed police officer came flying across the street and sprawled right across my side of the hood, his hat toppling to the ground. I was caught! The driver slammed on his brakes. I was trapped in the car and there was no way out. Then the constable scooped up his hat and dashed up the street again.

Immediately returning to the hotel, I changed into a light blue three-piece suit and telephoned the remaining businesses on my list. I told each one that I was returning their phone calls concerning a complication with my purchases. Those who indicated anything peculiar in their responses, however slight, I automatically deleted from the list. Then I walked to Chapman Brothers Jewelers, the first store on my list. Upon entering the store, I noticed a beefy young salesman I hadn't seen before, possibly the jeweler's son or even store security. All the sales personnel on my earlier visit had been middle-aged gentlemen. Another salesman approached, but I indicated I would wait for the person I'd dealt with earlier.

In my peripheral vision I saw a fourth salesman nod at the linebacker masquerading as a salesman. Something was wrong. As I moved casually along the glass display counter toward the entrance, viewing the jewelry, the beefy salesman had by now moved just as casually out from behind the counter and was peering indifferently out the front door. Walking directly toward the door, I tried to leave, but he engaged me in a conversation regarding the weather. Politely ending our talk, I expressed concern about my illegally parked car just a short distance away and said I'd better rescue it. The pseudo-salesman dismissed my concerns as unwarranted, explaining that the meter patrols weren't exceedingly vigilant in the area, then he started talking about sports.

For the second time I politely ended the conversation, reaffirming my earlier concern and desire to leave, all the time wondering just how far this talkative hulk was going to press the issue. Casually I unzipped my satchel, which contained the Browning. As if he hadn't heard me, the linebacker continued yammering away about the latest football news. Finally I told him I was leaving, and started toward the door. Staring at me, he asked if I had any identification, which I thought peculiar. I was pretty certain now that I was dealing with store security, so I replied "Yes, right here," and showed him my gun while shielding it from the view of everyone else in the store. Then I said, "Move away from the door." He hesitated, so I repeated my order twice more.

Then the unexpected happened. He lunged, arms outstretched, as if he intended to grapple with me for the gun. Startled by such a foolish act, I leaped backward hastily, firing the gun at the floor near his feet to halt his advance. The bullet went through his kneecap, ricocheted off the hardwood doorframe behind him, reversed direction and flew past me, hitting the safe twenty feet behind me and chipping off some paint. I had almost been shot by my own bullet!

At that point the security guard became plainclothes Constable Brian McNeil, Fraud Squad, Metropolitan Toronto Police, and my gun turned into a joke. The retainer sleeve had fallen off, and the recoil spring had popped out and was hanging extended four inches beyond the end of the barrel, bouncing up and down. The only sequence missing in this slapstick comedy was the sound of the spring going *boing*.

The shot had startled the officer, and he reeled backward momentarily, then drew his revolver and aimed at me. Everything seemed to move in slow motion. I tensed, waiting for the bullet, but it never came. I was arrested, charged with attempted murder, taken into custody and interrogated Gestapo-style for six hours.

All they wanted was my name, just my name, so I gave them a choice of three and they gave me the washing machine treatment, permanent press cycle. A cloth hand towel was folded lengthwise and wrapped around my head, much like a bandanna, held by a knot twisted at the back and rotated from side to side like a washing machine, causing disorientation, nausea and loss of balance. I could actually hear my brains sloshing around inside my head. I went from standing up to sitting down, to kneeling, then onto hands and knees; eventually I was lying spread-eagled on the floor.

Midway through the interrogation, I suddenly became angered by their lowbrow methods, substituting brute force for investigative intelligence. In an attempt to discourage them, I feigned laughter and boasted, "I can take this all night long." Well, that had the same effect as if I had tried to shove a sharp stick up their asses. They practiced their George Chuvalo impersonations on me, using me as the heavy bag, until they finally exhausted themselves.

When an inspector entered the room and said, "I don't think you'd tell the truth to save your soul," I knew I had won a small victory. Actually, it wasn't my soul I was attempting to save, just my hide! I had informed them I was a reporter from the *Winnipeg Tribune*, concluding they would cease their destructive impulses in fear of the power of the press. If they had known I was an escaped convict from a federal penitentiary, it would have been a free-for-all.

Following my rather untimely arrest, detectives saturated the surrounding area of Chapman Brothers Jewelers in search of my nonexistent car and suspected accomplice. Through the process of elimination, checking each registry of every major hotel in the downtown area, they eventually found my "office," discovering a uniform complete with Sam Browne belt and Mountie hat; a psychology book; and a novel entitled *Where the Money Was* by Willie Sutton, American author and bank robber extraordinaire. No doubt this cache of goodies stoked their already crackling fires.

The interview ended when one of my sparring partners said, "Don't come back to Toronto when you get out, or we'll blow you away." I appreciated the warning. Actually, I was quite content to get away with just the washing machine and boxing routine. The Metropolitan Toronto Police Department was infamous for its interrogative techniques, which included a vast repertoire: a free boat ride down at Cherry Beach, where you were hung over the side by your legs; suspension by your ankles from a high-rise window; being catapulted in a chair down a flight of concrete stairs; repeated thumpings over the head with a Toronto telephone directory; the application of a cattle prod to your testicles; surgery on your scrotum with a jackknife; or the puncturing of your eardrums with a pen. All these wonders were practiced in the name of speech therapy and designed to loosen your vocal cords. Having shot a police officer, I was convinced I'd receive all of the above standbys plus a few of the more modern methods they were probably itching to try out.

After my interrogation, I was transported to the Don Jail, registered under the alias of Ronald George Irwin and placed in solitary confinement. My cell was a seven-by-twelve-by-fifteen-foot concrete box. It contained a single steel bed two and a half feet wide and six and a half feet long, constructed of boiler plate, which was perforated every two and a half inches by two-inch squares and welded to the top of four steel posts embedded in the floor. There was no mattress.

The floor was bare concrete that sloped inward toward a hole four inches in diameter. The hole was my toilet, which flushed on its own every five minutes day and night. There was no sink. A fifteen-watt night-light shone twenty-four hours a day and was protected by an unbreakable sheet of Plexiglas. There were two steel doors six feet high, three feet wide and two and a half inches thick. The interior door was fitted with a five-by-eight-inch tempered glass observation window and a three-inch meal slot at the bottom. The exterior door had no window and no space. Both doors were lever-locked from the outside.

The meal was a four-inch-square bean cake two inches thick, a combination of compressed precooked ingredients that smelled and tasted like ordure, and one cup of tea. My prison garb was a baby doll, a multi-ply canvas bag cross-stitched every two inches. It was tear-proof, with three holes for the head and arms. I had no socks or shoes. At 11:00 p.m. a six-by-three-foot canvas blanket was thrown under the door. At 7:00 a.m. it was taken away.

I was locked inside the cell for twenty-four hours a day and allowed no exercise, no contact with other prisoners and no books, except the Bible, which was taken away at night to prevent it from being used as a pillow. I was allowed to write two censored letters a week. Most of the time I slept. When I was awake I sat huddled on my bed with my arms, legs and head curled inside the baby doll to preserve heat. Whereas every other prisoner was escorted by a single guard, including those on trial for murder, my movement anywhere outside the cell featured two senior officers, "white shirts," in hopes of preventing another one of my disappearing acts.

Officer McNeil showed up in court about sixty pounds lighter. They had had to replace his kneecap with a plastic one. The bullet shattered the top half and cracked the bottom half. It missed his artery by a few millimeters. He permanently lost forty percent of the strength of his right leg, and it would always ache in damp weather. The police department gave him a bravery citation. I didn't feel too good about shooting the officer, but I didn't agree with the citation at all. There had been no need for him to try to disarm me. He could have just let me go. They would have arrested me later on another job, or while I was sleeping in bed eventually, anyway. But he'd wanted to play hero. The bottom line is, when a man has a gun, you do what he wants, because even a six-year-old kid with a dinky .22-caliber pistol can take your life. It has nothing to do with being a coward or a hero. It's just plain common sense.

One day on the way to court I was roughed up a bit by three police officers as well as two correctional officers from the jail. It all began in the basement of the jail in preparation for a court appearance. One officer, flanked by his two colleagues, started searching my clothing and began to purposely drop each article onto the floor.

"What the hell are you doing?" I asked angrily.

"Pick them up," the cop ordered.

As I reached down to comply, I was kicked in the face. Right, I thought, all I'll get out of this is a few bruises. As I stepped in, I gave my opponent a snappy left uppercut to the chops. He staggered back and covered up, then I followed in with two more quick uppercuts. But that was the last thing I can remember, because his partners practiced their drumming technique on my skull with their billy clubs.

I woke up thirty feet later down the hallway, still fighting, but now I was handcuffed and shackled. One officer was sitting on my chest, smashing me in the face with a pair of handcuffs wrapped around his fist brass-knuckles style. And while a guard held me by the hair, the other officers pinned my arms and legs, allowing another guard to kick me in the ribs with his steel-toed work boots. The pain was overwhelming. When I get a beating, I keep my mouth shut, but the pain was so incredible this time that I screamed. Actually, the blows didn't hurt half as much as the knowledge that I had let them know they had caused me to cry out. My shirt was so drenched in my own blood that they tore it from my body before they took me to court. Later from the hospital bed I could still recall Michael's assertion: "You'll never get caught inside."

13

Ground Through
the Mill

I WAS TRANSFERRED TO MILLHAVEN AND
arrived right on the heels of an investigation into a group of rogue
guards known as the "Millhaven Mafia." A special Commons subcommittee studying violence in the federal prison system was investigating allegations of intimidation of staff by staff, harassment of
prisoners and the blackmailing of the administration. Staff cars were
damaged in the parking lot and guards who didn't toe the union line
were beaten up. But it was difficult to obtain evidence against the
"Mafia" because the victims refused to identify their attackers.

Prisoners' allegations of group assaults by a ten-guard "goon
squad" were substantiated through consistent patterns of complaints against the same guards. The administration was black-
mailed by the guards' refusal to work overtime and threat to take
sick leave if their union demands weren't met. They had an overtime
"racket" functioning, whereby they incited the 350 prisoners to riot
in order to collect overtime. Guards, reportedly, damaged or appro-
priated institutional equipment, drank and slept on duty and acted
insubordinately to senior authorities. The situation was described as
"law enforcement verging upon a state of lawlessness," and an

undercover investigation to uncover offenders or a crime commission was proposed.

The conditions were blamed on a complete loss of authority over the guards by the prison director, Bob Conley, Millhaven's third warden. It was common knowledge that one previous warden, Raymond Brewster, had to carry a gun and hire a bodyguard. After he was run off the road on the way home from work, his bodyguard, a man named Clement, went down to the local Legion, a watering hole patronized by many guards, and knocked out the three perpetrators.

Millhaven operates under the team concept, which means that CX8 staff and lower are in uniform. CX denotes the category of correctional officer. The warden is the chief administrator and his basic function is to protect society, then to assure the safety and security of the prisoners. The assistant warden of socialization is next, and he controls prisoner case management and programs. On par with the AW Soc. is the assistant warden of security, who is responsible for the internal and external security of the prison. There are five other assistant wardens in charge of finance, technical services, administration, industries, and education and training.

Staff higher than a CX8 are out of uniform. Immediately junior to the assistant wardens is the senior CX8, the shift supervisor, who is in charge of staff deployment and inmate movement in the eight-hour period between 8:00 a.m. and 4:00 p.m. Next in line is the internal preventive security officer, whose role encompasses intelligence and investigations. After the IPSO are the CX6s or keepers, squad leaders who supervise the prison and certain posts between the hours of 4:00 p.m. and 8:00 a.m. Next are the CX4s or junior first line supervisors in charge of the living units. At the bottom of the heap are the line staff or basic guards stationed at various security positions throughout the prison. All told it is a very neat, nicely regimented setup with all the qualities necessary for a well-run, well-regulated prison. But don't bet on it.

There is a Guard Code that is pronounced, separate and often at odds with the official penitentiary Code of Discipline. It is a traditional, clear and marked set of rules, principles and directions governing the comportment and ideology of a guard. The Guard Code became firmly entrenched in the Mill in 1971 when the building was first opened at a cost of $18 million. The nucleus of the correctional staff was first formed by a clique of a dozen or so officers who had transferred from other institutions. These men socialized together, lived in the same area and, in some cases, had joined the service together. If one of the officers belonging to the clique was injured in a confrontation with a prisoner, it was quite common for the other officers to abandon their posts and give the responsible prisoner a beating in retaliation.

The power of the code is demonstrated in the following actual case. One CX4 officer reported another officer on his shift to the keeper for sleeping on duty and demanded a replacement. The keeper said, "I want you to think about what you're doing. I'll send you a replacement, but I want to make sure you know what you're doing." The CX4 had grown up in the military. He believed that if it was necessary to take action against his subordinates to get a job done, he should do so. He believed in doing his job and everyone else doing theirs.

The derelict officer's shift was terminated and he was replaced and sent home. The code demanded that the other officers seek retribution. The CX4 found a piece of cheese in his mailbox, and his car, which had been parked in the penitentiary parking lot, had its windows soaped. He was put on the "grease," meaning no one would talk to him, and had to eat alone in the mess hall for three months. And he constantly had to repeat orders to the subordinates on his shift, while the same men readily performed their duties unbidden for any other CX4.

The message was clear: "Play ball." The guards resented his being promoted ahead of the other officers because of his military training. During Christmas and New Year's Eve, when the guards could usually expect trouble from the prisoners, an incompetent CX4 would be taken out of his living unit supervisory position and replaced with the competent CX4. The living unit officers resented it.

The pressure was so strong that the CX4 seriously contemplated quitting his job. The prisoners were a problem, but an expected problem. They came with the turf like bad drainage on a piece of low-lying land. But he hadn't expected a problem from his peers, and it was the biggest problem of all. He couldn't retaliate in kind because the Code of Discipline forbade it, and if he did, he would just be playing right into their hands. When he saw the wrongdoing of another officer he was supposed to ignore it and keep his mouth shut. He believed he was supposed to take action or see that action was taken against the officer, but the code commanded that he didn't dare and that he look the other way. He couldn't grant a favor to a prisoner because he would hear about it from his peers. He was under extraordinary peer pressure to demonstrate that he wasn't a "con lover."

The code pervades the entire correctional system and requires an officer to know what his peers are thinking twenty-four hours a day. A guard has to be careful not to breach one Code of Discipline regulation, however minor, or it will be used against him as a means of enforcing the real code, the Guard Code. That code has survived the Commons subcommittee investigation, the transfer of certain undesirable officers, the undermining of the union's power and a new administration, and it still exists. It is undocumented, evasive and subtle, but it is there just the same.

The guards are typically viewed by the prisoners as automatons, turnkeys, men in uniform representing authority who tend prisoners, basically stereotyped as apathetic and callous. But there is another aspect, a less cynical perspective. Guards are the frontline staff separating prisoners from freedom. They suffer the invective, degradation and physical abuse of the prisoners.

A case in point. One CX2 was monitoring the meal line during lunch when a usually quiet and reserved prisoner who had been locked up for an extended period of time smashed him in the face with a tray holding a cup of boiling hot coffee. The CX2 had been standing there with his head turned, talking to another guard, and never saw it coming. He turned his head just as the tray hit him full in the face. The CX2 received first-degree burns to his face and neck, four stitches to close the cut in the corner of his eye and had to have the back of his eyeballs turned and scraped to remove the burnt tissue that would have built up and eventually caused blindness.

The officer couldn't understand it. He'd always tried to treat prisoners fairly. In one suicide attempt he had even defied the Guard Code and saved a prisoner's life. On that occasion the prisoner had been so intent on taking his own life, on mutilating himself irretrievably, that he had carved out a strip of flesh in his forearm two inches wide right down to the bone, vein and all. It was midwinter and the roads were snowbound. The ambulance couldn't possibly arrive from nearby Kingston and return in time to save the prisoner's life. The other guards had given up on him. They had fulfilled all the duties and obligations of their job descriptions and nothing more was required. The prisoner was considered dead. It was just a matter of a short waiting period before the exact time of death could be recorded.

The CX2 thought otherwise. Revolting against the prevailing attitude, he threw the prisoner over his shoulder, carried him to his own car and, soaked in blood, drove to the hospital himself, thereby saving the man's life. This was the same guard who received the meal tray in the face. After the tray-hurtling prisoner was taken to the hole and booted around by the goon squad, he was internally charged and appeared in disciplinary court. All the injured CX2 wanted to know was "Why me?" It was revealed that the prisoner had predetermined he was going to attack someone, and he wasn't very discriminating about who it happened to be. All he said was "I'm just sorry it had to be you."

On this sojourn in the Mill I learned the printing trade and took an interest in criminology and penology. Through my studies and daily contact with the concealed schemings of my fellow convicts, I began to perceive a distinct and eccentric thought process in the convict mind.

The classic convict seems rational enough during personal interviews with the prison administration or during social functions, but behind that facade lurks the split personality of a Dr. Jekyll and Mr. Hyde. His most deadly weapons are intelligence and charm. He is distinctly and perceptively aware of any injustice pertaining to his own immediate existence, yet unconscious of anyone else outside his own concern. He fully expects the authorities to play by the rules and is shocked and infuriated when they don't, even though he himself, as a criminal, plays by no rules whatsoever. The criminal is extremely sensitive to his own distress, misery and dystopian existence but dispassionate about his victim, who, once out of sight, usually dead, is therefore out of mind. In short, the convict is generally incapable of feeling genuine guilt. He wallows in a state of self-commiseration, assuming the role of the hapless victim. "Poor me, I have twenty years" are the words that spring to his lips as he completely ignores the fact that someone else's life has been taken or someone else's person has been violated. He categorically refuses to recognize his own accountability for his actions, attributing his misfortunes not to himself but to uncontrollable factors and other individuals, often society as a whole, whose norms he tenaciously refuses to accept.

The convict is full of compassion, concern and fidelity for those he feels an emotional bond with but lethargic, flint-hearted and ruthless to those he believes are his antagonists, regardless of familial affiliation. He is at war with the world and distrusts all square johns, appraising them as either goofs, assholes or working stiffs, notwithstanding that he himself possesses no close friends except for a near total dependency upon a spouse or lover. The convicted criminal is morally insane and considers any other convict to be a decent individual if he is "solid" and displays sensitivity toward other prisoners regardless of the hideousness of their crimes or future premeditations.

The inmate is torn between two worlds: the well-being of the safe, correct society and the instantaneous rewards of the precarious criminal underworld. He craves just one more chance. He perpetually theorizes he could successfully accomplish that one financially colossal job. The convict is like a sprinter primed to explode out of the starting blocks at the first crack of the pistol — directly into the concrete wall he fails to see ten feet in front of him. Punishment does not alter his behavior but rather compels him toward obsessiveness. His most serious misconception is apparent in his overestimation of his own intelligence and devaluation of others', irrespective of his own low education and lack of learning skills. Convicts are ultimately fatalists: successful criminals who commit infamous crimes remain unknowns; unsuccessful criminals have a fatal hunger for recognition and a propensity toward vaunting, confidentially, their undetected felonies.

One of the most frequent games the convict plays is I'm More Dangerous Than You Are. He boasts about killing this person, that person or a whole group of people. It is an elaborate version of the child's game My Father Can Beat Up Your Father. But it is merely a psychological defense created by fear, and only succeeds in intensifying and perpetuating the paranoia in others.

The most prominent characteristic of the convict is that he lies almost incessantly about everything, and anything, from the crimes he commits and how he committed them, to the money he's accumulated and is now hoarding in his fictitious safe deposit box, to the mundane little fabrications and manipulations applied to satisfy his diverse everyday wants, needs and desires. He attempts to speak nonchalantly about his prison term, but his real feelings are betrayed by his bitter "I don't give a fuck." The only defense he has against the pain is to fake being proud of his crime, proud of being a failure.

Convicts purport to have a deep prejudice against any form of authority, including the police, correctional officers, judges, parole officers and politicians, all of whom sustain the convict's pseudo-superiority complex, which in actuality is a defense mechanism for miscreants. The convict is chronically antisocial, violent and abused, with a poor consistency in work behavior attributed to a low esteem for labor. He is devoid of veneration for life, therefore equivalently indifferent to his own death. He is cognizant of the difference between right and wrong but consistently accepts his acts through complex justifications and rationalizations, with only an occasional attack of conscience. These characteristics are all symptomatic of psychological disorders rather than lapses in learned social mores, and in this respect the conventional penal system is archaically inadequate.

The majority of convicts are dangerous. Their crimes quite clearly indicate this. But their crimes aren't committed in a state of robotic mindlessness. It is usually the opposite. An emotional thought evolves into a spontaneous, impulsive, frenzied act, with no preconceived principled barrier interceding. It is interesting to note what the alleged leading minds of the country, namely our government, does with these emotional misfits, for indeed they are misfits, not even able or stable enough to fit within themselves. These individuals are herded together like so many diseased cattle into a barn where everyone is afflicted with communicable diseases of the mind and soul. They are thrust into this environment, which twists, churns, contorts and tortures their already distorted minds, and then they are released into the soft underbelly of society once again. Back in society they are supposedly "rehabilitated" and have learned some abstract lesson in the charnel house they were formerly incarcerated in.

If you wanted to turn a dog into a killer, what would you do? You'd lock it up and beat it and starve it and torture it. And if you were really twisted, you would lock it up with other dogs that were beaten and starved and tortured, so that they could rip and tear one another apart. And in the end you'd have a killer dog. And not only would it be a killer, it would be an experienced killer, filled with bitterness, hatred and viciousness toward every other living creature. So what is the difference between a man and a dog? A man can think. Wonderful! So what you have in the end is a thinking killer. That sums up our judicial system. That is how the CSC, Correctional Service Canada, and our penitentiaries work. They produce killers. Sure you protect society, while they are in prison. But the moment they are released, someone pays a price, a price for all the hell and torture they went through. All convicts do in prison is sit and think of all the people who put them there, and what they will do to them when they get out.

Studies conducted on recidivism rates have firmly established the fact that sixty-eight percent of all prisoners in federal prisons are recidivists incarcerated for increasingly violent crimes. And the shame of it all is that it all comes down to economics. The government refuses to invest the necessary funds, resources and personnel to effectively combat and correct the social disease of criminal behavior through behavior modification and psychological programs. The common criminal mind could be cured. Crime is a learned behavior. Politicians refuse to recognize the problem because for them the problem doesn't exist. It is the proletariat, the common folk, the business communities, that suffer the wrath of the convict. Extremely rare is the case where a criminal has killed a politician, and those who do never see daylight again.

Put simply, as long as people ignore the real nature of criminal behavior, they will continue to be beaten, robbed, raped and murdered. As long as the penal system remains the way it is, it will manufacture, activate and release walking time bombs, the Clifford Olsens and Henry Lucases of tomorrow, who will march out into society and detonate with tragic results.

In the Mill I met a rare personality named Richard Christopher Brooks, the Job of the Underworld. Arrested and convicted of bank robbery at the age of twenty-eight, he lost his company, house, savings and wife.

That in itself wasn't significant; it was the way in which he lost them. After Richard was honorably discharged from the Royal Canadian Air Force he launched his own company with the money he had managed to save. Initially the company was successful and enabled him to purchase a luxurious house in which he resided with his new bride. He was deeply in love and thought the sun rose in the morning with his wife. Then fate struck. He began experiencing financial difficulties with his company, and his bank refused to lend assistance in the form of a loan or any other financial arrangement. After exploring every other potential avenue available without success, he was on the verge of losing everything he had worked his entire life for.

He decided to rob a bank. He was arrested, convicted of bank robbery and received a twenty-two-year sentence. His wife continued to visit him faithfully while he was in the penitentiary but constantly indicated a need for financial assistance, which he readily provided, selling his company, depositing the money into a savings account and dutifully doling out the funds upon her request until the account was finally drained.

Then one day, still in need of money, she asked him to sign the house over in her name for the purpose of a sale. He agreed. After all, she was his wife. They had exchanged wedding vows before God and man. To love and honor for better or worse and all that.

Then fate, still hungry, struck a second blow. Richard received news that his wife was living in his house with the police officer who was responsible for ensuring he went to prison with the twenty-two-year sentence. Shortly after, she filed for divorce and married the cop. Yes, sir, Richard Brooks, the modern-day Job.

Richard lost his mind for a while, but he snapped out of it eventually. One would think after an experience such as his that a man would either go permanently insane or become bitter to the core concerning life. But Richard did neither. His tribulations didn't change him one iota. He still had a heart of gold and helped others in need many times without their bidding or knowledge. He was still loyal to friends and family alike to a fault. He still had the heart of a lion. But the one quality that set him apart and above the crowd, after all the hell and betrayal he'd experienced, was that he still had a little twinkle in his eye after fifteen years in the slammer. They hadn't beaten him down yet and they never would.

It was through Richard that I became involved with the Juvenile Awareness Program, STYNG. The Save the Youth Now Group was essentially a group of men, specifically a group of convicted criminals, mostly lifers or with aggregate sentences of ten years or more, who made themselves readily available to inform youthful offenders about the cruel realities of a criminal lifestyle or career.

The background of the youths varied, but many came from broken homes, had committed minor offenses or had done time in training schools. They were all between the ages of thirteen and eighteen and had tendencies toward repeated criminal acts such as theft, break-and-enters or joyriding. The program was coordinated by the STYNG executive with area parole and probation services. Youths were only referred to STYNG after authorities had exhausted all conventional methods of rehabilitation — expulsion from school, curfews, probation and short jail terms.

The Juvenile Awareness Program was multifaceted. There was an adult program with a public education aspect for persons who had no involvement with crime but wanted to become aware of what was going on in prison. The soft-core program was for youngsters who had had minor involvement with the law. The hard-core, intense, three-hour confrontation program was for juveniles who had serious encounters with the police for such crimes as armed robbery, break-and-enters and assault. The emphasis was not to scare them, but to present them with reality. They were given honest, vivid information about prison life, and it was hoped that the candid revelations would be powerful enough to steer offenders away from a life of crime. Youths were taken on a tour of the prison, including solitary confinement. They were locked in a cell for short periods and given rap sessions. They saw how prisoners lived and suffered the loneliness and stress of a tightly controlled maximum-security penitentiary. The whole program was designed to stop teenage delinquents from idolizing prisoners and their way of life and was considered to be a significant object lesson for youths who were on the borderline of criminal involvement. STYNG was one of the most positive, dynamic programs ever implemented in the Canadian penitentiary system.

Initially I was involved in the group for one reason and one reason only. Anyone in STYNG was going places. That meant transfers from maximum-security level to medium-security level. In STYNG was where you found the elite of the criminal subculture, the shakers and the movers. The most intelligent criminals had long ago come to the realization that jail was a purgatory that twisted the soul. Besides, there was no money in prison. The real money was out there on the streets.

I was involved in the program from its beginnings in January 1979. The founder and original chairman was Ronald Lauzon, a highly intelligent and smooth individual. When the six initial members abandoned the group, objecting to its increased involvement with the government, it fell flat on its face. Richard Brooks, Fred Cadeddu, Roger Jackson and I picked it up and became the four pillars on which it was to rest and reach its zenith. Richard assumed the position of chairman, Fred undertook the role of co-chairman, Roger was program coordinator and I became secretary and audiovisual technician.

Although we had various criminal records, extending from murder to bank robbery, and had come together for different reasons, our dedication grew as our involvement expanded. Soon we shared the essence of the program, believed in it wholeheartedly and had a burning desire, a need, to help young offenders. Every single word spoken to each kid came straight form the heart. There wasn't a liar or bullshitter among the entire group. Every man had committed the crimes he claimed, the way he claimed and for the reasons he gave. In talking to those kids it was like a self-examination of your entire life, dragging the long-forgotten or suppressed, kicking and screaming, up from the murky depths of the past and throwing it down on the floor for everyone, including you, to see.

A lot of men didn't like what they saw and more than one tough guy walked away at the end of a session just wanting to be alone for a while, including me, although I was neither tough nor brutal. I saw men with multiple murders to their credit, and I don't mean two or three, I mean six and twelve murders, reach out a verbal hand and touch a kid to try to get — to make — him understand what he was getting himself into. I saw a man pull his shirt off to show a torso that looked like a painter's nightmare, with dozens upon dozens of deep, ragged slash marks and gouges, and then ask the kid, "Now why did I do this?"

Yes, we believed in the program with all our hearts and souls. And it was a success. We had the solid, dedicated support of the Millhaven administration, specifically Henry Neufeld, the warden. We had widespread television and radio coverage. It was a going concern right up until the mismanagement of the program by the Ministry of Community and Social Services.

Prior to the ministry's involvement our supply of youths stemmed from independent sources within various social services. We finally consented to a verbal agreement requested by a representative of the ministry sent to Millhaven, and the STYNG program was officially endorsed as a pilot project in August 1979. The agreement specified that 100 juvenile offenders between fourteen and eighteen would be carefully chosen from two training schools — Champlain in Alfred, Ontario, and Brookside in Cobourg, Ontario. They would be referred by officials of the Ontario Ministry of Correctional Services. They would then be split into two groups of fifty. The experimental group of youthful offenders was to be sent through the program, eight boys per group on a regular basis, and follow-up reports were to be done at various intervals over the next one-year period with the initial evaluation made after six months. A second group, with matching family and social backgrounds and offense histories, would adhere to normal training school procedures, without the benefit of the program, and were to have follow-ups conducted simultaneously with the experimental group. The reports would then be compared and any significant behavioral differences noted to determine the validity of the program. The pilot was formally launched in September 1979. We were eager for the study to be conducted; we knew the program had a positive effect.

Prior to the ministry's involvement we had had a steady and at times overwhelming supply of youths, but when we consented to the contract, it gave the ministry, in effect, direct, recognized controlling interest in the flow of youths from various social services. Once the ministry had social services under its thumb once again, it failed to honor the contract. The number of youths diminished to a trickle and the program collapsed.

In March 1979 there was a bizarre escape attempt from the Mill involving a prisoner from Salem, Ohio. Dennis Dale Hunter, twenty-nine, had been sentenced to seventeen years for armed robberies and attempted murder in Vancouver and Winnipeg. He was so desperate to escape from the Mill that he punctured his own eyes. He planned to flee from the ambulance en route to the hospital with the aid of his wife, Samantha. Initially he alleged that he was attacked from behind by another prisoner, but the escape failed because the police had been tipped off ahead of time. Doctors were unable to restore sight in one eye and could only save two percent of the vision after repairing the other eye. Later Dennis and his wife pleaded guilty to the charge of conspiring to escape by force.

The price some men place upon their liberty can never be understood by anyone outside the context of a prison environment, but Dennis's desperation impressed everybody. Eventually he was transferred out of Millhaven and deported to the United States, but he never received a medical parole as a consequence. What harm could a blind man do? Sadly Dennis traded a seventeen-year prison of sight for a permanent prison of darkness.

I was the prison photographer at the Mill, and one day Moe, an affable robber, asked me if I'd take a few pictures of his artwork in his cell to send home to his mother. I said sure; after all, that was my job. He asked me if I'd take a picture or two of him while I was there. I agreed. Then he asked me if I would mind taking a couple of nude shots of him to send to his girlfriend. I wasn't too crazy about snapping pictures of him in the buff. Besides, I didn't think they would get by the prison security censors. Finally he confessed to what he really wanted — an affair. He said that he was very discreet and that he didn't become involved with just anyone. In short, he was very selective.

So how do you say no to such a hilarious proposal, without hurting the guy's feelings? You pass the buck, that's how. I told him that although I appreciated his offer, I was already involved with a lady on the street who was faithful, and my morals made cheating impossible. He tried to talk me into being unfaithful, but I stuck to my guns. One week later I saw him sitting at a table in the common room, watching television beside another con, an ugly little gnome of a man. They were both clean-shaven, happy, smiling and glowing like a couple of lovebirds.

From time to time I used a little less subtle approach to parry sexual overtures, particularly when they came from violence-prone convicts. Those advances usually began when someone whom you knew by name but never associated with sat down uninvited beside you and engaged you in conversation about anything and everything from your crime to the correct time until eventually they came to the ulterior subject, your feelings about sex and what your reaction would be if one sunny morning someone slipped between your sheets while you were sleeping, or late one quiet night stepped naked into the shower while you were there. I would calmly explain that although I didn't mind homosexuals, providing they never involved me in their routines, if approached in the cell I would be justified in stabbing him in self-defense because the location would obviously substantiate that it was he and not I who was the aggressor. And the shower would be the perfect place, because the water would wash all the blood from my hands. At that point the conversation would dry up and the person would take his leave.

There was only one way to discourage mentally unbalanced homosexuals in prison, and that was to act considerably more unbalanced than they were. I figured that even if they guessed I was bluffing, for anyone even to talk like that he would have to be half-crazy just for starters. But the funny thing was there was more fact than fiction to the matter. When a person did something wrong or something you didn't like, you asked him very politely and very respectfully to quit. And when he didn't, you stabbed the shit out of him. You didn't argue or fight with him or ask him twice. You just stabbed him. That was the way it was done.

Sex was a serious problem, or rather the lack of it. After a number of years without the company of women, some men become so sexually frustrated they lose the innate ability to differentiate between a woman and a man as a sexual object. Men who have never previously participated in a homosexual experience become homosexuals freely and willingly. The basic arrangement usually consists of two persons, one of whom is a dominant personality while the other is obsequious. The former becomes the "old man" and the latter becomes the "old lady." There have even been cases where two men have fallen in love or in "lust" with each other and a mock marriage relationship is embarked upon, but those are infrequent occurrences. There were no "marriages" in the Mill while I was there; most of the couples I knew were living in sin!

There was no shortage of partners for the homosexual who was gay prior to his imprisonment and continued to be so afterward. Customarily sexual activity was very discreet, and unless one was quite perceptive and knew the indications, the telltale signs were difficult to detect. It was only those prisoners with the strongest characters and personal values who survived the tangled web of prison perversion. Some convicts attempted to coerce sexual compliance from other prisoners, and that was usually when the aggressor found himself a quart or two short of blood. The Boys didn't take too kindly to sexual perverts, especially forceful ones.

Tony was a professional armed courier robber and self-admitted homosexual. Previously he had had sexual intercourse with only one woman in his life, and he hadn't liked it, so he reverted to men. Tony approached me very openly, honestly and sincerely, like a gentleman.

"You're a good-looking man, Mike," he said. "I'd like to take care of you. You wouldn't have to do anything for me. I'd just take care of you, and I'm good at what I do."

I talked to him straight. "Tony," I said, "it just isn't my bag. I like women too much."

He told me that if I ever changed my mind to let him know, and that was the end of it. He never approached me again and he never tried any soft talk or pressure tactics, either. And he was still a gentleman afterward. Even though Tony was a true-blue homosexual, he had more class than ninety percent of the convicts I've known.

A substantial number of men went the homosexual route in the Mill, but I knew that no matter how long the authorities kept me caged behind bars, I'd never break. I'd never turn homosexual, because no matter how feminine a man might appear to be, for me he could never compare to a woman, and I found any attempt at such not only ridiculous but repulsive. I loved women, not only individually but as a separate gender. They held the answers to my being, the truths of the earth and the mysteries in the stars, and I was totally enchanted by them. When I think of women, I think of comfort and warmth. When I think of men, I think of fighting. How a man can ever possibly provide the comfort and warmth, the essence of a woman, is beyond the realm of my imagination. And the day I find myself sexually desiring a man will be the day I die on the fence in broad daylight, trying for my freedom.

By now I'd had enough experience and familiarity with the Mill to evaluate the hierarchy of the prison subculture. In other words, the who's who in the zoo. There was a status scale within the Mill whereby all convicts could be identified according to category.

The highest-ranking convicts were those who had led a successful criminal career within society, made a substantial amount of money and proven themselves to be quite capable in the rough-and-tumble existence of prison life. They included high-caliber professional bank robbers and armored car or armed courier robbers, about five percent of the total prison population. These persons were employed in the highest-paying, cushiest, white-collar positions within the prison, such as the servery, canteen, clerk's office or enrolled with the educational faculty. They had the highest morals, self-respect and personal dignity and always conducted themselves as gentlemen. They had attained fame and fortune and would neither kill, maim nor injure another individual for status. Nor would they sacrifice their personal principles for financial or material gain. Rarely did they associate with the lower criminal echelon.

Next in ranking were the advanced-level international drug smugglers, those who had netted considerable sums of money, a million dollars or more, in drug deals. They had a reputation for being quite capable in prison, but generally this wasn't the case. Highly intelligent, they were usually first offenders, offspring of normal upbringings who resorted to smuggling in a one-time get-rich-quick scheme that netted a fifteen-to-twenty-year term, after which they didn't reoffend. Smugglers, contrary to their crimes, didn't become involved in the prison black market drug scene either as distributors or on a personal level. These gentlemen comprised about one percent of the populace.

Then came the expert fraud artists, who had acquired an ample quantity of money. These prisoners were usually very intelligent and inclined toward nonviolence. However, they were not above utilizing the talents of the prison fighters for personal protection. They were smooth talkers, had pleasant personalities, were witty, very presentable and rarely received severe sentences due to the nonviolence of their crimes. Fraud artists made up four percent of the prison body.

Coming directly after the fraud boys were the professional killers, who had multiple murders to their credit. They totaled two percent of the population. Killing someone was easier and required less skill and intelligence than robbing a bank vault or escort service, smuggling drugs from one country to another or committing large-scale fraud. Furthermore, the dividends were far less, approximating $10,000 to $15,000 per hit. Killers and murderers were dead inside. They seldom smiled and never laughed, suffering from advanced psychopathic disorders. Habitually loners, they were quiet and reserved and usually slight of stature. They walked very unassumingly, almost gently, and were always exceptionally considerate and respectful to everyone since they were all too keenly aware of how vulnerable a man could be and the ease with which a life could be taken.

One percent of the denizens were superior embezzlers who had bilked their victims for a great deal of money, property or material worth. These persons weren't very competent in fending for themselves in prison. In society they were criminals masquerading as straight johns, but in prison they were straight johns masquerading as criminals. They were unscrupulous businessmen who rapaciously stepped over the fine line between legitimacy and illegality. Anyone who worked for a living was considered to be a "straight john." They were usually middle-aged, docile family men. Most embezzlers never reach the penitentiary, since they use the "talents" of lawyers to manipulate the court system or exploit the flaw in the judicial system that usually deems their crimes civil suits.

Convicted and unconvicted murderers who posed as potential

prison killers represented a large twenty percent of the prison inhab-
itants and stood sixth in line. They were the classic emotionally
unbalanced convict best known to the public. These persons were
status seekers due in large part to a lack of success in their criminal
careers, resulting from ambition hampered by a low IQ, lack of
education, immaturity and well-developed physical attributes. They
were extremely dangerous and out of control. And like a car careen-
ing down the road after having sideswiped a tree, they usually hurt
a lot of innocent bystanders along the way. Murderers legislatively
opposed capital punishment but penally they supported it, put it
into effect and enforced it. Once a murderer killed a person in prison
he was respected and feared by the other convicts. They culled their
victims very carefully like wolves singling out weak or enfeebled
calves, avoiding anyone who was as capable of homicide as they
were. They were responsible for the largest percentage of prison
deaths by far. Everyone makes mistakes in life; it's part of the
maturing process. Killers were no different from anyone else; they
made mistakes also, except their mistakes were counted in bodies.
Most convicted murderers serving life sentences had the attitude
"After the first one the rest are free."

Three percent were cop killers and guard killers, who were
granted a higher status than run-of-the-mill murderers but not as
high as hit men. The reason for this was that cop and guard killings
were usually a consequence of circumstances gone awry rather than
a direct result of deliberate planning. Usually they were committed
by dime-a-dozen robbers or thieves who had launched their bid for
status, and their prison sentences in the "big time," with one impulsive act.

Prison fighters or brawlers were next in line and accounted for ten
percent of the group. They were usually in excellent physical shape
and engaged in either boxing or weight lifting. They were a surly lot,
always posturing and acting tough. They strutted around with ex-
aggerated movements of their shoulders and expansion of their
chests, symbolically warning "Don't fuck with me. I'm bad." They
all belonged to the Apple under the Arm gang. In reality most weight
lifters couldn't fight their way out of a wet paper bag; they just
thought they could. The fighters usually had noses that roamed all
over their faces, deep scars, lower jaws that could be easily dislocated

by the owners and no front teeth, all of them sacrificed in battles over the years. Fighters avoided killers at all costs. Generally fighters didn't kill and killers didn't fight. But after a number of years in prison, fighters, out of curiosity, graduated into killers. They wanted to know what it felt like to kill someone.

Prison drug dealers enjoyed a higher than normal privilege regardless of the category of their crimes, excluding rapists, informers and molesters, owing to Meyer Lansky's law of supply and demand and providing they continued to furnish the wants of the inmates. They remained incognito, supplying dope to the killers and brawlers, who then remained loyal to them, depending upon the drug supply. The drug dealer was everyone's "buddy" and everyone was his "buddy," as long as everyone got his share. But if someone didn't get what he wanted or thought he had been short-changed, then all hell broke loose and the drug dealer usually got the bark beaten off him. All of a sudden he was a sleaze bag. Drug dealers usually served their entire sentences stoned. But the administration was always well aware of who the drug dealers were and extracted the difference when transfer or parole time rolled around. One of the biggest problems in the Mill was drugs. Not soft drugs, such as marijuana or hashish, which actually were conducive to the stability of the prison by curbing violence and easing tension and frustration, but the pills, acid and speed that were taken in large doses, causing extreme disorientation, depression and paranoia. When it came to the avid and questionable world of prison drugs, no one was ever right. Someone was either being ripped off or thought he was. As one old-timer aptly reflected, "With the 'new wave' generation of drug addicts permeating the prisons, everything has gone all to hell." Dealers claimed two percent of the prison.

The general prison population ranged in age from sixteen to eighty years and accounted for the ten percent convicted of a diverse range of crimes that included arms dealing, arson, assault, attempted murder, burglary, car theft, conspiracy, counterfeiting, extortion, forgery, hostage-taking, kidnapping, manslaughter, robbery and theft. These convicts were usually very sociable, unaggressive and compliant. Safecrackers might be included in the general population, but the "juicemen" of yesteryear were a dying breed. As for hijackers, pirates and terrorists, very few were in prison. And I have yet to meet anyone incarcerated for treason or espionage.

Straight johns were commonly in prison for murdering a wife, lover or some other family member. They weren't viewed as members of the criminal underworld per se. Despite this they were frequently treated with consideration and protected by the professional robbers from being taken advantage of by the murderers, brawlers and other predators. Straight johns behaved with a great deal of caution and attentiveness, taking great care not to offend anyone. They were quite conscious of the lethal nature of their enforced associates. Their former lifestyles had in no way prepared them for the abrupt shocks of a prison existence. They were psychologically closest to societal normalcy, suffered the greatest grief for their crimes and were subject to suicidal rather than homicidal tendencies within the initial period of their confinement. Johns made up five percent of the population.

Twenty percent were prison bisexuals or closet queens, who entertained one or more partners and typically avowed an intense dislike for sexual deviates of all natures, including homosexuals. One form of manipulation a bisexual used was to supply a young con with hallucinatory drugs or any other material or financial needs available. But he expected sexual permissiveness in return, and when his advances were rebuffed he used threats of violence. Frequently the young con would check himself into protective custody or would be beaten up or stabbed on some fictitious justification. His only other alternatives were suicide or sexual acquiescence. But the sleaziest play of all was when some naive sixteen- or seventeen-year-old kid who had informed for the police or testified against his co-accused entered the prison. Two or three bisexuals would have his police statement or trial transcripts sent in from the street through a lawyer, reveal the damning evidence to the kid and agree to keep it on ice, providing he let them have their way with him sexually.

Totaling two percent and next in line were the discriminating effeminate homosexuals, who attempted to keep their sexual preferences on a respectable standing by remaining faithful to one partner at one time. These persons, notwithstanding their feminine affectations, were often very dangerous individuals and not to be treated lightly. On the other hand, they could be very humane, thoughtful and sympathetic if they were treated with consideration. Their distinctive features were that they were usually encumbered with hands the size of a major league basketball player, feet that doubled as flippers and shoulders more befitting a star football receiver. They also had five o'clock shadows at one o'clock in the afternoon. But the physical contortions and performances they went through to appear feminine were quite amazing to watch.

One percent were village idiots and butts of practical jokes, harmless abuse and at times sexual harassment. They constantly lived in fear for their lives. The harder they tried to win friends, the more they were taken advantage of. In most cases the village idiots were used as gofers by the killers.

Lower on the scale were the young drug addicts, who would do anything for narcotics, including theft from other prisoners and sexual favors. They comprised seven percent of the inmates, occupied a relatively minor station and were often just a low grade of petty thief. It wasn't uncommon for them to exchange a $300 stereo or a $200 guitar for twenty dollars' worth of drugs. They begged, coerced or conned their parents, girlfriends or wives out of money, jewelry or other expensive items to support their habits.

Four percent and decreasing dramatically in value were the psychotic killers or "bugs" or "nutbars," who killed indiscriminately without provocation, justification or warning. They were called nutbars because they were nuts and usually wound up whacking someone over the head with a bar. These persons suffered the greatest degree of delusions of persecution compared to the normal convict. And it didn't take much to get one mechanically lurching toward you with a knife in his hand like a psycho in a slice-and-dice horror movie. An untimely, prolonged look, a five-dollar debt, an insult, an unsubstantiated rumor, anything at all would do. They were the most dangerous and unpredictable prisoners and were employed in low-paying menial cleaning posts.

The third from the last on the status scale, and at one time on par with the subordinate informers, were convicted rapists or "skin hounds." Known convicted hounds comprised one percent of the residents and were subject to the first sharp knife or blunt pipe that came along.

Informers, rats, pigeons, stoolies or canaries registered second from the bottom and claimed at best an ephemeral one percent. Once their perfidious traits were exposed they rarely survived more than twenty-four hours. They were looked upon as scum and hated with a passion that made them disposable. Many informers were kept out of circulation for a few years and secreted in protective custody in some other institution until the populations turned over. Then they were inconspicuously inserted back into the population where no one knew their past. In a number of cases this method proved to be successful. The unsuccessful cases were registered in the hospital if the recipient was lucky and in the coroner's office if he wasn't.

Inmates convicted of infanticide or child murder involving sexual abuse were judged by the entire population to be the amoeba, the most worthless, despicable beings in the entire prison. They constituted an ever-diminishing one percent of the count. There wasn't a lineup of other prisoners waiting to murder them, but they were killed on a first-come, first-serve basis, and there was always a plentiful number of convicts more than ready to serve as executioner. The intense revulsion felt by the public toward such individuals was magnified by prisoners to the extent that to murder one assumed the status of a privilege and honor.

I first became aware of the Convict Code in the Mill. The code is an unwritten but well-defined, distinct set of canons, regulations and guidelines governing the conduct, communication and philosophy of a convict. It originated with the establishment of the first Canadian prison in Kingston in 1835. The code commands that:

1) No convict shall force or coerce either physically, by use of threats, gestures or by any other means, any person to engage in the act of sex with him.
2) No convict shall interfere in the voluntary sexual arrangement between two other persons.
3) No convict shall act as an informer for the authorities regardless of the circumstances. When witness to another person committing a crime, a policy of nonintervention shall be adhered to.
4) No convict shall accuse, hound into protective custody, beat, stab or kill another person accused of being a rapist, informer or molester on hearsay alone without prior evidence of a trial transcript or witness.

5) No convict shall disseminate disparaging rumors about another person. When accused of being a rapist, informer or molester, the accused shall absolve his reputation by an act of violent retaliation.

6) No convict, once having authorized his own placement in protective custody, shall be permitted to revert to the general population.

7) No convict shall cheat, attempt to defraud or exploit any person engaged in cards, narcotics or any other business dealings.

8) Every convict shall assume a stance partial to a prisoner and against an officer in any altercation between a prisoner and a correctional officer, despite the circumstances, and shall give evidence to that effect if necessary.

9) Every convict, upon the murder of a rapist, informer or child molester, will testify in a court of law under oath in favor of the accused if required.

10) No convict shall bear witness against any person in a court of law notwithstanding the person's status or the motive and factors related to the occurrence.

11) No convict shall constrain or request another person to perform in accordance with the wishes or policies of a correctional officer or employee of the prison administration.

12) Every convict shall fight any other person on a one-to-one basis equally armed with the exception of a rapist, informer or molester.

13) No convict shall maintain eye contact with another convict, not an associate, for an unreasonable period of time.

14) Every convict shall observe August 10 as National Prison Justice Day with a twenty-four-hour fast and the wearing of a black armband.

15) Any protest or demonstration supported en masse will be endorsed in the name of solidarity by every convict regardless of individual ideology.

The code demands that every convict's moral precepts, expressions and deportment respect, preserve and promote the mores of the criminal subculture while disdaining, undermining and disintegrating the correctional subculture and prison administration. The punishment for failure to abet the code is exceedingly finite, ranging from being ostracized, burnt out, beaten, stabbed or murdered, depending upon who is meting out the penalty. There exists no definite minimum or maximum sentence for an offense. But there is a paradox: every prisoner has skeletons in his convict closet. There has never been a person born "solid" with a complete sense of prison values who at one time or another hasn't to some degree breached the Convict Code. And like a lot of people, prisoners are self-accusing and introspective. Those who are quick to denounce and condemn others unjustly and viciously in the name of solidarity in order to inexpensively boost their own status often have the largest skeletons in their closets and are in the greatest need of redemption. It's a funny world, but it seems that the people who are the most immoral are the most judgmental. It seems that being judgmental lends security to one's own sense of self-worth. Solidarity — the last refuge of the unscrupulous.

14

A Little Dab'll Do Ya

A SHORT TIME AFTER I GOT TO THE MILL, I met a woman through my sister Janet. Linda Fockler was a hairstylist from Kingston, Ontario, and she was also my sister's best friend. Janet took her into the hairstyling business after Linda was abandoned, along with her three-year-old daughter, by a common-law husband. Janet had fifteen years of experience as a hairstylist. She was top of the line and taught Linda everything she knew.

Linda was twenty-seven, of Sardinian descent, five feet four inches tall and had black hair, blue eyes and olive skin. After the first week of visits, she came to see me and said, "I love you . . . well?"

I told her I loved her, too; after all, what's a man supposed to say when a woman makes such an impassioned declaration?

"Let's get married," she then said.

I told her I thought it was a little premature and that we should wait until we knew each other better. The love affair lasted for over two years until my transfer to Collins Bay Penitentiary in 1980. We were engaged. I bought her an engagement ring, and she bought me a Maltese cross with a chain, which I always wore. We were going to be married just as soon as I was paroled.

Linda said all she wanted in life was for someone to love her and her little girl, Penny. She told me how her husband used to beat her up and cheat on her, and that he didn't give a damn about his daughter. My heart went out to her. All this woman wanted in life was a little piece of happiness for herself and her child, and all she'd ever gotten was misery and pain. I decided right then and there to put an end to my life of crime. My sole purpose in life was to be the best husband and father in the world, and the happiness of my family, Linda and Penny, was all that would matter to me. And it didn't make a bit of difference that I wasn't Penny's natural father. I believe if you honestly love a woman, you love her children, as well, with the same love and care you would give to your own children. That's the decision you make — to love unconditionally and completely.

I had the Hague bank robbery and Prince Albert prison break charges waived to the jurisdiction of Napanee, Ontario, where I pleaded guilty, taking the chance of receiving an additional ten-year sentence, even though I strongly doubted the police could prove that I had committed either of the offenses. I didn't want them hanging over my head after I settled down with my family. Through the plea-bargain process I received an additional two-year consecutive sentence. When I took the witness stand to speak on my behalf prior to sentencing, I told the judge straight out that I was finished with crime and intended to do my time, get out and support the woman who loved me, and her child. It was a pretty emotionally charged address, and half the women in the courtroom started to cry. My lawyer came over to me with tears in his eyes during recess and said that on a score of one to ten on addresses to the court I had scored a ten. He added that he thought I was pulling a flimflam, but I wasn't. I was never more serious and sincere about anything in my entire life. There was a big write-up in the *Kingston Whig-Standard* about it that ended with the question "Will she wait for the man she loves?" I was sure she would.

As a prisoner I was earning seven dollars a week, working as an apprentice in the print shop. I was the first person in the shop in the morning and the last one out at night. I had never held down a steady job for an extended period of time on the street before, so I had to learn how to work. It was a habit I knew I would have to acquire in order to take proper care of my family. To supplement my income, I took on the photography job as well as any other available employment opportunities within the prison, and I sent every cent home to

Linda. After all, I was a provider now, a husband and a father, if not in name, then at least in spirit. The only money I spent at the canteen was on postage stamps with which I sent her over two hundred letters steeped in love and adoration. Just to save money, I would make Linda romance cards out of the material I could obtain from the print shop supplies or other sources. Eventually I was able to make cards that were more beautiful than commercially bought ones. And with every card I sent to Linda I included a miniature duplicate for Penny. On Linda's birthday I splurged. I sent her pictures enlarged to poster size of her holding Penny as a baby.

I didn't spend any money on soap or shampoo. The doctor supplied me with those items after I concocted a story about my skin being allergic to the stringent cleansing agents in most consumer products. I never bought confectionaries, sweat suits or running shoes, as did the rest of the men, and I couldn't even afford the twenty-five-dollar Christmas bag. Every single cent I made I sent to Linda to help her support Penny — all $1,200. It wasn't much, but it was all that I had, and I felt guilty that I couldn't send more.

Linda owed her father $300. She had borrowed it from him years before when she had been in a difficult situation down in the States. I reimbursed him the 300 without his realizing it came from me. I figured that if she ever needed to borrow money from him again in another difficult time, he wouldn't refuse her.

Linda and I kissed during our visits, naturally, and we shared the intimate secrets of desire and whispered the tender words and touched each other caressingly as two persons in love do. She told me she loved me and cared for me and wanted to spend the rest of her life with me. I thought she was the most sensitive, caring, loving person. I thought she was so special and that I was so lucky to be blessed with her. We talked of the happy home we would share one day and we looked at real estate catalogs featuring various local houses and properties for sale. She wrote me love letters, telling me that all she wanted was to be my wife and the mother of my children. She told me she would never cheat on me because she wasn't that kind of a woman. Her upbringing had taught her to be honest, true-blue and faithful. And I believed every single word she said.

I was so devoted to becoming a decent, responsible, moral person that I wouldn't even treat another inmate or guard rudely or inconsiderately regardless of the instance. And if I even thought I'd hurt someone's feelings, even accidentally, I'd apologize without hesitation. I became a man who cared about others and was sensitive to their feelings and suffering. I never looked at another woman with desire, let alone talked to one. I wore my loyalty to Linda like a crown of thorns. My entire family knew her, and everyone was just as convinced as I was of the honesty and faithfulness she so adamantly professed.

Then one day, after I'd been transferred to Collins Bay again, my little sister Kathy came to visit me and told me she'd seen Linda the night before with another man. According to Kathy, Linda had had her hands all over him, mauling him in a bar in front of everyone. I didn't believe her, of course, so I asked my other younger sister Marilyn. She said it was true. Still doubtful, I phoned Linda, and she admitted it. I asked her why and how it could happen, and she attacked me in a tirade of vehement accusations, saying I didn't love her or want Penny, all of which I couldn't understand. It confused me because it came right out of left field. It didn't make any sense at all. It just wasn't true. Then I was struck with a very romantic yet tragic idea to win her back. I would attempt suicide. If I lived, she'd realize how much I loved her. It would make a difference and we would find the love we'd lost. And if I died, well, then I guess it wouldn't matter, would it?

It didn't hurt too much. I just slashed the two main brachial arteries in the crook of each arm with a double-edged razor and bled all over the floor until I passed out. It was really strange to stand there, opening and clenching my fists and watching the blood pour out of the arteries in my arms like miniature water faucets, all the while knowing I was taking my own life but not giving a damn. It was as if time stood still and I was watching everything dispassionately from a distance. Then I came to and crawled into bed, cradling a picture of Linda and Penny against my heart in my blood-soaked hands.

The next thing I knew I was on the floor again, so I figured I must have lost enough blood to make it a life-and-death struggle. I pressed the cell emergency alarm button, then passed out. I came to again as the guards were rushing me down the corridor to the hospital on the stretcher. My main concern was that if they ran through the barrier gates too fast, they would slam my arm against the steel grille.

In the prison hospital the doctor was absent, so the dentist tried to fit an intravenous line into my vein but couldn't because I had lost so much blood that my veins had all collapsed. On the way to the Hôtel Dieu Hospital in Kingston in the ambulance, I lost and regained consciousness a number of times. I can still vaguely remember an ambulance attendant forcing compressed oxygen into my lungs and blurting, "He's gone again!" every time I stopped breathing. Each time I started to slip out of existence, he would coax, "Come on, Mick, you can make it." And I remember thinking, Fuck it. I really wanted to die, to let go, to be carried away by the wave of defeat.

They got me to the hospital in time, pumped blood into my body and stitched up my arms without an anesthetic. Then my stomach rejected its last meal. Little did I know that the prison priest, Father Tardiff, was sitting right outside, ready to give me my last rites if I didn't make it. He had followed the ambulance all the way from the prison to the hospital in his car.

My mother, and Linda, too, arrived at the hospital within minutes. My sister blubbered all over me in the operating room, and I remember thinking in my semiconscious state that if I didn't die from loss of blood or heart failure, I'd surely drown in all the tears. But Linda never shed a tear, not one single tear. Instead she said she couldn't handle the scene and bade me goodbye. She was as cold and heartless as a bitter winter wind.

In the hospital room late that night I was going to put the final touches on my romantic theory by jumping out the sixth-floor window, but I was too weak. My ankles were shackled, and I thought I'd look pretty silly sprawled on the floor after a feeble attempt to jump over the four-foot windowsill, only to bounce off the plate glass window.

I was an emotional wreck after that. I still couldn't believe Linda could do what she'd done. One moment she was hugging and kissing me and the next she was driving a knife into my back. I just couldn't understand it. How could a person do that? How could a person become so filled with such cruel vindictiveness? And all I had to say to her was "What did I do wrong?" I couldn't even eat. Just the thought of her going to bed with another man made me want to vomit. I couldn't sleep and I was in a state of total depression. I remember walking outside in the huge exercise yard all alone in the rain because that way I wouldn't have to hide my feelings and no one would know the difference. And I knew the other prisoners wouldn't be able to understand why a supposedly hard-core convict was so depressed.

It was really strange. When I finally did get to sleep, I'd wake up in the morning with a deep, dark sense of gloom, and I wouldn't know why until I remembered what had happened. I just couldn't make it through the day. Each waking hour was like a bad dream, so I'd try to make it till noon. But I couldn't, so I'd try to make it until 10:30 a.m., coffee break. I developed an ulcer and had a constant throbbing headache that just wouldn't go away.

I knew I was pretty mixed up, so I phoned Linda a number of times and asked her if she would come to see me if only for a few moments. I just needed to talk to her to help me understand what had happened, but every time I phoned she said that she didn't want to talk to me, wouldn't come to see me and that I'd better not call again. Then she'd hang up on me. When I finally did manage to arrange a pass, I went to see her, but she wouldn't talk to me, and her father tried to pick a fight with me.

She had always assured me that if we ever did break up, she would at least come back to explain why, but she never did. It wasn't so much what she did, but the way she did it. Every time I cried out in pain or reached out my hand for help, she just gave the knife another twist. I thought I had met some cold, callous persons in prison, but up until Linda I'd never met anyone who didn't possess some form of pity deep down inside his or her heart. Linda didn't break my heart; she ground it up like so much hamburger. And it wasn't just that I had lost the love of my life. No, I had lost my whole family, because I really did care about her and Penny. I wanted only the best for them.

The worst thing a woman can do to a man in prison is develop that kind of a relationship with him and then betray it, because he's a drowning man in an ocean of misery and hopelessness, and she's his only straw. People walk in and out of your life, and with them each person takes a piece of your heart. And pretty soon all that's left of you is just bits and pieces, memories of what used to be.

I lost my mind there for a while. I don't remember the winter at all. I remember bits and pieces of the spring, and then the warm, beautiful sunlight of summer slowly, gently, coaxed me back into reality. I suffered permanent damage to the nerves of my arms. When I slashed my arteries, I also hit the ulnar nerves, so when I touched my matching two-inch scars together, it felt as if electric shocks were shooting down my arms to my wrists. To make matters worse my brachial arteries no longer functioned properly. Needless to say, my immune system took a while to recover and my short-term memory malfunctioned for a few months. Even after all that I still would have taken Linda and Penny back because I still loved them.

In 1981, after somehow managing to fumble my way through a one-year business machine repair course, I was transferred to Frontenac Minimum Security Institution adjacent to Collins Bay. At the farm annex there were neither bars on the exterior doors or windows, nor were there any cells, but rather two large dormitories that were separated by office dividers into individual sleeping quarters called cubicles. There were no locked doors within the building itself. Prisoners were considered extremely low security risks and their movements weren't restricted. The only exception to the rule was at night, when everyone was locked inside.

Everything seemed to progress well. I completed a temporary absence program and was employed by a printing firm in Kingston. Then, one night, a very large inmate, a biker by the name of Boucher, began prowling the cubicles at all hours of the night and day, armed with a heavy metal bar and a knife. He started breaking into lockers and stealing the personal possessions of other prisoners. After being caught by two prisoners, whom he feared would expose him, he began stalking them with his knife in a game of cat and mouse from one cubicle to the next.

But the two prisoners weren't so easily caught. John and Paul were on the Inmate Committee and took a dim view of Boucher, and after a hasty and informal meeting, it was agreed that the biker should be ejected from the house forthwith. James, the sergeant at arms, John and Paul approached Boucher with an ultimatum: "The front door, the back door or on the floor." His reply was to pull out the bar immediately and smash John over the head with it. Then all hell broke loose.

I was in my cubicle when I heard the ruckus and knew the debate had reached its climax. I knew and respected John and Paul, so I ran down to see what the status of the discussion was just in time to see John riding Boucher's back, his arms locked in a death grip around the roaring biker's neck. Paul, meanwhile, was banging Boucher over the head with a wooden bookcase, which shattered like a movie prop after the third whack. Then James, having wrestled the bar out of Boucher's hand, started smacking him over the head with it. After the second love tap, Boucher's eyes rolled back into his head momentarily, then he went down for the count.

Boucher went to the hospital at Collins Bay to receive medical attention. In the fracas James had been accidently cracked on the forehead with the bookcase by Paul. He required stitches to close the large gash, so he went to the hospital, as well. Both parties maintained they were injured in separate "accidents." Boucher's head swelled to the size of a pumpkin, and he almost died. Naturally the warden of the Camp, George Downing, treated the explanations skeptically, and he refused to transfer James back to Frontenac.

Everyone was upset, so a general assembly was called downstairs in the basement. After listening to everyone rant and rave, I addressed the men with one question: "Was everyone genuinely willing to carry through their threats if Downing refused to yield to pressure?" Everyone wholeheartedly agreed they would.

The next day John and Paul marched fearlessly into the warden's office. Waving the banner of righteousness and justice, John gave a full disclosure of the event. But Downing didn't want to know what had happened. He had an incident on his hands that contravened an act of Parliament, and his job was at stake. Downing would have to notify the regional director general's office, and an investigation would follow, complete with individual interviews.

Soon after, Downing's flunky called a meeting in the cafeteria to collect the names of those individuals intending to transfer back to Collins Bay, which was the prisoners' threat if James wasn't returned. The moment of truth had come. But only John, Paul, me and six other men out of a total of fifty-five called out their names. The rest remained as quiet and fearful as field mice in the shadow of a hawk. I was thoroughly disgusted and let the rest of the men know in no uncertain terms what utter contempt I felt for them. I barely knew

James — I'd said hello to him once or twice perhaps — but I respected him for what he had done. When the rest of the prisoners had needed him, he'd been there, but when he needed them, they forsook him. It wasn't right, nor was it honorable, not after having voluntarily given their word. Where I came from a man's word was his bond, and if your word was no good, you weren't worth spit.

We were transferred back to Collins Bay, where the administraiton recognized privately, if not officially, that I was right. Six weeks later I was transferred to Pittsburgh Farm Annex, a minimum-security institution just outside of Joyceville. However, since my transfer followed so closely after the Frontenac incident, the Pittsburgh warden refused to accept me. In the end, the regional director general had to issue a removal warrant, commanding the warden to take custody of me. At Pittsburgh I was employed in the horticultural department and elected chairman of the Inmate Committee, which I'm sure the warden had more than a few reservations about.

At about that time, fully disenchanted with the virtues of leading an honest life, I decided to change my fingerprints. Although the dactyloscopy authorities, and especially the police forensic investigators, led everyone, even their own people, to believe that it was impossible, I knew for a fact the opposite was true. I had been taught the method by an individual who did change his prints and successfully eluded the law. While at large for nine years he was arrested and fingerprinted six times, both in and out of Canada, for offenses ranging from bank robbery to attempted murder. Interpol computers always registered the response "Unknown," when requested to search for and locate a criminal record.

To change my prints it was necessary for me to research a few basic things about fingerprints and their applications in forensics. Fingerprints are classified according to ridge line patterns. These patterns are divided into three main groups, the arch, loop and whorl, which are further divided into eight subgroups, namely the plain arch, tented arch, radial loop, ulnar loop, plain whorl, central pocket loop, double loop and accidental whorl.

Ridge counting is the method employed to classify and file prints. The ridge count is the number of ridges between the core, the center of the fingerprint pattern, and the delta, the formation in front or near the center. The delta is a point on the first fork, a meeting of two ridges, an abrupt ridge ending, a dot, a piece of a ridge or any point upon the ridge at or nearest to the center of divergence of the type lines. It is the position used as the starting point for ridge counting.

Each ridge that crosses or touches an imaginary line drawn from the core to the delta is counted. Typically all digits are represented by a different count. While one right index finger may register a count of seven ridges, the left index finger may only register a count of three. A fingerprint point identification is based on twelve to fifteen distinctive characteristics, such as dots, bifurcations (Y-shaped forks), formations of islands (hollow circles and ovals), ridge endings, crevices, bending lines and comparatively short ridges. On the average a finger has thirty to forty such markings.

The police use an electronic processing system to evaluate finger and hand prints. The data on known persons is stored as formulas. For identification purposes, prints are compared with the data stored in the computer, which delivers a report of the specifics and formulas required to identify a given person.

Skin is basically an organ comprised of two parts. The outer layer of the skin is called the epidermis or cuticle, and the sensitive vascular portion of the skin below the epidermis is called the dermis or cutis. It is the vascular structure of the dermis that determines the subsequent shape of the epidermis.

Drano is basically composed of four parts. Fifty percent is small, various-sized white granules of sodium hydroxide, also known as caustic soda, while thirty-five percent is sodium nitrate. A variable percentage of Drano contains tiny grains of crystalline sodium chloride or salt, and the filler consists of silvery particles of aluminum. The most potent components of this commercial product are the smallest granules of caustic soda.

With a ten-power magnifying glass and an indelible fine-tip felt pen, I dotted the core and delta, as well as any outstanding groups of characteristics, on one of my fingertips — thirty dots total. Taking a double-edged razor blade, I snapped it in half lengthwise. Then I twisted one piece lengthwise again and broke it in half, which gave me one piece with a scalpellike edge on one end. Taking the edged piece, I carefully cut a straight line three-thirty-seconds of an inch through each dot right into the epidermis, but not into the dermis, which would draw a noticeable amount of blood. Using a pair of tweezers, I picked up a small pellet of caustic soda and inserted it into one cut. As soon as the caustic soda combined with my bodily fluids, a caustic reaction resulted that lasted approximately one minute. And, yes, it hurt. It hurt like hell. In fact, I nearly did a tap dance on the wall.

The caustic soda burnt a dark circle three-thirty-seconds of an inch in diameter into the dermis with no damage to the epidermis, and I repeated the procedure with every dot. Taking a pair of nail clippers, I carefully clipped the epidermis around the edge of each circle, exposing concave cavities filled with semiclear jelly — burnt skin. I then cleansed the cavities with ordinary soap and water and applied Elase, a salve with three-way healing properties: an enzyme to dissolve the burnt connective tissue lining the cavities; an antibiotic to prevent infection; and a local analgesic to alleviate pain.

Next I wapped my finger in gauze, then repeated the entire procedure on all finger and thumb pattern areas as well as my significant palm print characteristics. Within thirty days my fingers healed. I had obliterated any groups of characteristics. The total count on any one finger numbered fewer than ten points. Plus I had destroyed the cores and deltas, thereby making an accurate classification and ridge count impossible as well as changing the corresponding specifics and formulas. The healing process of severely damaged tissue, especially burnt tissue, permanently scars the epidermis, causing the misalignment of the ridge lines in the pattern area. Therefore, a before-and-after visual examination would show the fingerprints were similar but couldn't prove conclusively they were identical. And a before-and-after computer evaluation would indicate the fingerprints didn't match and conclusively weren't identical.

I started to get bored working with flowers at Pittsburgh, so I considered applying for employment in the prison abattoir. I thought the training I'd receive there would benefit me, but I wasn't sure I'd like the work. Recently I'd spoken to a number of slaughterhouse employees, and it seemed their temperaments had taken a turn for the worse, causing them to become increasingly meaner. This tendency even extended to the civil servant who supervised the slaughtering. He became embroiled in bar fights on a regular basis. So after weighting each pro and con, and still remaining doubtful, I thought the best way to reach a decision would be to watch the actual work being performed.

Upon entering the slaughterhouse, I noticed that the interior was pure white except for the bluish-gray concrete floor. The place was spotless, with no signs of the butchered animals anywhere. Even so, the stench of blood lay heavy on the air. Down a long, fenced runway an animal, a big-boned 900-pound steer, was herded into a steel-railed box stall. As it tried to continue on through an apparent opening, its efforts released a spring-loaded collar, which clamped shut, making it impossible for it to withdraw its head. Simultaneously a metal barrier slammed shut behind it.

The animal could sense something was wrong. Something was terribly wrong. It shivered with fright, even though it was a warm summer day. Teetering on the verge of panic, it sought an exit, but there was nowhere to run. The rails were too solid to break and the cage was too high to jump over. It looked around helplessly in nervous uncertainty, its big brown eyes frantic.

Though it didn't know what was about to happen, I did. But if I had known how the deed would be accomplished, I would have left immediately. A prisoner walked up to the steer, carrying a handgun that shoots a four-inch-long pointed steel bolt a quarter inch in diameter on a retractable spring by means of a blank .22-caliber cartridge. The steer poked out its nose for sympathy, then the man placed the barrel in the concave spot of its forehead, just three inches above and between its eyes, and pulled the trigger.

The steer dropped immediately to its knees and then to the floor. A lever was pulled, and the carcass rolled sideways down the ramp. A chain was flung around the animal's back leg joint and anchored by a hook. Then a hoist raised the steer off the ground. The supervisor stepped over with a five-gallon pail and placed it beneath the animal's head. Then he inserted the blade of a boning knife into the steer's neck just below the shoulder, gave a flick of the wrist, severing the main artery, and withdrew the blade quickly. A gusher of blood burst out equal in volume and velocity to that of the water from a bathtub faucet turned on fully.

It was then that I noticed the short, gasping breathing of the steer as it moaned — it was still alive! As I watched in horror, the steer uttered a number of desperate gasps, vainly trying to hold on to its life. Then the moaning subsided and there was silence.

I turned around and walked out of the abattoir, ashamed to be a member of the human race. I never went to work in the abattoir and I never went back to watch again, either. It took me a while to adjust to what I had seen. The steer had been alive while it was being butchered. I had seen its hopeless breathing and heard its moans of pain. And if that was our modern-day cattle "slaughtering" process at its finest, I couldn't imagine a more fitting word for it. All I knew was that I wanted nothing to do with the abattoir. It reminded me too much of my own suicide attempt.

In October 1982, after nine months at Pittsburgh Farm Annex, during which I got up to my old knaveries again, picking every locked door in the camp and having an exciting time doing it, too, I was granted a day parole to Kirkpatrick House in Ottawa, which is affiliated with the John Howard Society. The staff of both agencies were the most decent group of people I had ever met. They were completely dedicated to the assistance and rehabilitation of the ex-prisoner. They provided rides to employment interviews in their own vehicles free of charge and arranged employment with local businesses. Failing that, they created construction work around the House, for which you were paid a reasonable wage. Memberships were arranged for physical fitness clubs and organized sports outings. There wasn't anything the staff wouldn't do to help a person readjust to society and encourage him to embark upon gainful employment.

Many of the staff members were part-time university students trying to complete their degree in social work, which required them to do a short period of fieldwork at the house. These individuals were frequently pretty young women who were always exceptionally polite. I came to think quite fondly of a number of them because they acted just like my younger sisters. Many times I would go to sleep on the couch downstairs on the weekends because a girl was afraid to be alone at night.

Little did I know that on Saturday, July 6, 1985, a tragedy would befall the house. A dangerous twenty-eight-year-old sex offender named Allen James Sweeny sadistically raped and murdered an innocent twenty-one-year-old counselor named Celia Rygrok. Celia had just graduated from the Carleton University criminology program and was working alone in the house late that night. Sweeny, a resident of the house who had been paroled after a previous conviction for the second-degree murder of a twenty-seven-year-old Sault Sainte Marie woman in 1975, stabbed Celia six times in the chest in the furnace room in the basement. Her salary was only $4.50 an hour.

15

Armed and Dangerous

AFTER MY ESCAPE FROM THE MILL IN 1984, where I had once again been imprisoned following the Hepworth bank robbery with Steve after his fateful phone call in the early summer of 1983, and prior to embarking on a serious bank robbing career, I decided to polish my skills. I visited the local library and studied every available facet of policing, including recruitment qualifications, training, psychology, investigative procedures, forensics, equipment, robbery tactics, emergency task force strategies, surveillance techniques, canine training, special branches and individual forces, to name a few. The most comprehensive and latest texts were always by American authors. They were way ahead of us in the crime game. This additional information supplemented my previous studies in criminology, plus my personal experience.

Before I even entered a town to rob a bank, I had already memorized the entire street plan, the immediate area, plus the general area from topographical as well as road maps. They were available through the local main library. A blueprint of the bank itself was usually provided by the town hall. I knew what percentage of the population was employed in each town industry from the CN Railway Shipping Guide, and I studied the historical and cultural background using encyclopedias, magazine articles and the town newspaper. Any peculiarities that needed clarification were researched by telephone calls to leading citizens or major employers of the town on the pretext of being a news reporter or free-lance writer who was preparing an article. Any other idiosyncrasies could often be cleared up by chatting with the town bum or street sweeper, who always seemed to know everything about everyone. He knew when and where the police made their periodic appearances, who the bank manager and his staff were and even who was having an affair with whom. A quick listing of the license plates on the cars remaining in the bank parking lot fifteen minutes after closing time and a phone call or trip to the nearest license bureau revealed all sorts of information, including the owner's name, phone number and address, as well as the make, model and serial number of the car, not to mention the license expiry date and spouse's name. It was a simple matter of matching up the full names with the various name plates and corresponding positions or levels of authority within the bank's hierarchy. Surveillance of the bank opening and closing procedures revealed who was entrusted with what responsibilities, including the vault combination and schedule. And the rental of a safety deposit box gained me access to the actual interior of the bank vault itself.

Ultimately I became quite proficient in the art of robbing banks. I was exceedingly well trained and equipped. As an offensive weapon, I employed a twelve-gauge Winchester Defender pump shotgun with an eighteen-inch barrel. The Defender was one of the four combat shotguns respected by shotgunners as tried and true. Originally purchased, the weapon's cylindrical magazine contained a regulating plastic plug that limited its capacity to five three-inch shells. It was an easy task to unscrew the weapon's magazine cap and discard the plug to increase the capacity to six three-inch shells plus one in the chamber.

I unscrewed the silver bead front sight and replaced it with a bright orange fluorescent one that was clearly visible in low light. Police shotguns are usually equipped with front and rear rifle sights. However, in a fast and furious firefight one doesn't have time for precise aiming. Firing must be done instinctively and immediately without any hesitation whatsoever, and it must be accurate. In this respect standard rifle sights prove to be inadequate for bank robbing.

Next I unscrewed the rubber butt plate, which tends to throw a shooter's aim off by its rebounding action after each shot, and cut the stock to the correct arm length. A shotgun must fit a shooter properly for maximum results. Then I refitted the weapon with a solid steel plate and filed the edges to conform to the variance in butt size. Next I shaved and sculpted the stock grip and slide grip to conform to the proper palm and finger grips. This had to be done conforming to the correct shouldered firing position. I then fitted my "new" shotgun with a sling.

Once a week I went to the firing range and shot clay pigeons, running a series of fifty straight at various angles, speeds and heights. I fired from all directions with the weapon in a ready but not shouldered position. The shells I used in an anticipated combat situation were 000 buck interlaid with rifled slugs. Anyone proficient in shotguns and loads understands the massive destructive potential of such loads. The rifled slug at a maximum range of 100 yards will penetrate and completely shatter two two-inch wire-reinforced concrete patio slabs, and anything less formidable will explode upon slug impact. Three-inch Magnum 000 buck contains ten lead slugs each the diameter of a 9 mm bullet, and at a maximum range of seventy-five yards it will riddle anything in its path. In the hands of a trained shotgunner, the Defender loaded with this shell at close range has twice the firepower of the famed Israeli Uzi submachine gun. Using my Defender at urban combat distance, I would have gone up against any Canadian or American police officer, no matter what his chosen weapon was.

Supplementing the shooting range, for one hour every night I practiced every conceivable shooting position, whether standing, kneeling, sitting, lying, walking, running, turning, rolling or diving. To further hone my skills, I practiced night sighting in the dark on silhouette targets with a miniature flashlight inserted in the barrel. Situational shooting was important, too, so I found a vacant building in the country and practiced moving from one protected position to the next until running, dodging, ducking and firing became second nature. Speed chambering and rapid firing in the dark eventually enabled me to pump off five shots in 2.5 seconds with every shot hitting its mark at a distance of thirty yards. And I could shoulder and fire from any position to any direction in less than one-sixth of a second. Through constant cleaning I was able to disassemble and reassemble my weapon completely, including the trigger mechanism. The purpose of the shotgun was to stop any pursuing vehicle with a rifled slug in the engine block or 000 buck in the front tire. As well, it would enable me to lay down covering fire for escape purposes. A rear tire shot was an option, but only in extreme circumstances. If the gas tank wasn't full, a piercing bullet could spark an explosion from the gas fumes and barbecue the officer.

As a defensive weapon, I used the Colt mark IV/Series '70 Gold Cup National Match .45-caliber automatic pistol with a few modifications. It was ramped and throated to accept semiwadcutter and mushroom-tipped shells, and the butt edge was beveled to ease the insertion of clips.

The best grip is Pachmayr's black-checkered rubber wraparound model, which provides a secure, nonslip grasp. Pachmayr also makes a polished stainless-steel magazine with a rubber bumper that protects the clip from damage when it hits the ground during clip changes in completion matches. Plus the bumper helps to insert the clip, giving it that extra little extension that ensures it is locked in place.

I used a bright orange fluorescent front post sight cradled by a white-outlined rear sight, which lessened sighting time since the color combination allowed no mistake between front and rear sight focus. A flat finish on the top of the slide deadened sunlight reflection. My holster was a Biachi International 45 leather combat hip model with a tension-adjusting screw. It allowed me to perform all the various maneuvers such as diving, running and jumping that one would anticipate during a firefight without losing the gun. But when I drew, the Colt came out smooth and clean.

The pistol shells I used were 180-grain semiwadcutters, which made my practice hits more visible through the range scope. But in an expected combat situation I would switch to a 230-grain round-nose full metal jacket, which lessened the risk of a shell jamming and increased bullet penetration. The variation in grains had to be taken into consideration, since a 230-grain bullet trajectory differs slightly from that of a 180-grain bullet. Semiwadcutter and mushroom-tipped shells are fine if you want to cause massive bodily damage or death, but my goal was to stop a man neatly and cleanly with as little risk as possible to life and limb. In that respect the

230-grain round-nose full metal jacket shell was quite adequate.

Again, as with the shotgun, I could disassemble, clean and reassemble the .45 completely, including the hammer and trigger mechanisms. I knew how it shot, where it shot and why. I realized that if I didn't know my weapon as well as I knew my woman, it could cost me my life. My basic philosophy was that when you pick up a gun you had better know how to use it, because as soon as you point it at another person who has a gun, you have morally as well as legally given that person the right to take your life. If I had a choice, I would rather be robbed by a professional bank robber who is trained in weapons and an expert marksman. If he fires, he aims to warn or at the very most wound. An amateur bank robber who is untrained and inexperienced in firearms is more likely to panic out of fright and fire at the largest or most visible targets — your head or chest — with the intention of killing.

But being able to shoot wasn't good enough. I trained in the martial arts, specifically Shito-ryu karate, since a well-placed kick or chop is often far superior to a bullet in controlling any situation that arises. I trained in weapons and martial arts not to take lives, but to save them, mine as well as others. Ninety-nine percent of all bank robbers in Canada and the United States aren't qualified to rob banks.

During every bank robbery I was protected with a Kevlar sixteen-ply bulletproof vest covering both chest and sides. The vest could stop a .357 Magnum 158-grain mushroom-tipped slug at point-blank range. It was also equipped with a chest pouch for a lead plate that could stop a rifle slug. Additionally I was equipped with a Bearcat 100 crystalless programmable scanner tuned to the OPP, RCMP and municipal police force frequencies with a miniature earphone attached that I carried on my person at all times during a robbery. As insurance I also carried U.S. Army smoke grenades.

The vehicles I employed for bank robberies weren't high-powered muscle cars, but low-profile nondescript vehicles, which if seen by any person after the robbery would be difficult to remember. I wasn't concerned about a possible police chase because I was better equipped and trained than ninety-nine percent of all police officers. Even so, I never once experienced a confrontation with the police thanks to my pinpoint planning.

But even with such combat capabilities I shied away from sense-less violence. Violence is a stupid bank robber's method and a shortcut to the grave. If I couldn't rob a bank without using brute force, I was at fault, not the bank personnel or the police. Either my research was incomplete, my equipment inadequate or I had employed the wrong technique. Robbing banks was a business in the strictest sense, and I conducted it in a very businesslike manner, with no bias against the bank employees or the police, and with as much consideration as possible under the circumstances. They were just major pieces in a fast and furious match of speed chess, nothing more and nothing less. My opening move was Gunman's Gambit.

The initial reaction to a bank robbery by bank personnel and customer alike is mild shock and uncertainty, which last an average of three seconds, followed by two categories of responses that I classify as voluntary and involuntary. The voluntary responses orig-inate from presence of mind and experience and are as diverse as the individual imaginations that produce them. They include attempts to gain control of the progression of the robbery, thus ensuring the safety of everyone; attempts to obstruct the robbery by pressing the silent alarm button; attempts to overpower and disarm the robber; refusal to cooperate by professing ignorance of the vault treasury combinations; claims that key members of the staff are unavailable; refusal to cooperate, period; feigned ignorance of any robbery in progress; and finally, of course, full cooperation. Fainting is rarely done nowadays, since it isn't as fashionable as it once was. The involuntary responses are caused by intense fear and include urinat-ing, running, hyperventilating, crying, nervous breakdown, diving to the floor, laughing hysterically, jabbering senselessly and general all-round trauma.

When I first picked up a gun, I thought robbing a bank would be easy. All you had to do was walk into the bank, show the gun and everyone would throw bags of money at you just to get rid of you. That just isn't the way it happens. Trying to get money out of a bank is like trying to pull a bank manager's gold tooth out of his head. You have just slightly more credibility with your gun than a custo-mer falling behind in his mortgage payments. And the looks of utter contempt and hatred that shoot out of some tellers' eyes can shrivel all but the most intrepid of bank robbers.

It was in the first three-second period of suspended thought and motion that I had to seize complete control of a robbery. I issued direct, exact and clear orders to secure everyone's cooperation and avert any complications. It was usually the younger, inexperienced male bank manager or his assistant who was the most uncooperative and therefore the most unpredictable and potentially dangerous. He viewed the robbery as a personal affront, a challenge to his machismo or threat to job security, and was prone to react foolishly. The older, wiser, manager had usually experienced numerous robberies in the past and posed no potential threat. He realized that a bank robbery was just a bank robbery — no big deal. The money was insured, his job wasn't jeopardized and safety was of primary importance. His immediate objective was to get through the robbery as quickly and safely as possible, return home to his wife and grandchildren alive and leave apprehension of the bank robber to the police.

In order to prevent the potential injury or death that could result from an accidental discharge, I made sure that I never trained my weapons on the employees or customers. My guns were strictly for show, and self-defense in case the police got involved. If my reflexes and training weren't adequate enough to thwart anyone's approach and effort to disarm me, I wasn't qualified to rob a bank. I always maintained a minimum distance of at least two steps from any one person. Even with a gun, at the distance of one step, any black belt martial artist could ram your weapon into a very uncomfortable spot of your anatomy in a fraction of a second. I knew that through my own training in the martial arts. When the black belts fought for their dans, their martial arts masters, you couldn't even see their hands move. They were that fast.

I observed a three-point precautionary proviso: no prints, no face, no place. No prints meant I wore either a layer of liquid latex, leather epoxy or such coating on my finger and palm prints. Or I wore an expensive pair of leather driving gloves, which afforded both pro-tection against leaving latent prints but also gave the sensitive feel necessary to handle a weapon competently. No face meant I wore either a complete disguise or a balaclava to prevent a positive eyewitness or camera photo identification. No place meant I made certain I wasn't seen and possibly recognized in the immediate vicinity of the bank either immediately prior to or following the robbery. And I always left a bogus clue behind in the primary escape vehicle to mislead the robbery investigators. There was one other precaution I observed, which, although it wasn't objective, proved to be crucial time and again. It was my sixth sense. If the ambience of the robbery didn't feel right, aside from the normal level of tension I experienced anticipating the robbery, I would abandon it. There are old bank robbers and there are bold bank robbers, but there are no old, bold bank robbers.

I now considered robbing banks my profession. I didn't rob banks for kicks; I robbed them for money, plain and simple. It was a business. In the past I had engaged in a number of reckless activities just for the hell of it, especially when I was with Steve. But I had outgrown that. I had matured. I was forced to when I experienced the sentences imposed by the courts, when they put me in prison for nine years just for raising hell. Where the hell was the justice in that? We didn't hurt anyone. That was the time life ceased to be humorous. The music stopped and I became serious. If the judicial system could determine an aggregate sentence of nine years for a twenty-one-year-old man for minor break-and-enters and car thefts, and in the same breath sentence another man to seven years for his second manslaughter charge, with the penal and parole systems supporting these inconsistencies, then I could determine to concentrate my efforts on finances from that time onward. But no violence.

Every single time I walked into a bank, every single time I saw a female teller or employee, I saw Jacquelyn. And I would remember the day I lost my temper during a typical lovers' quarrel and put my fist through the bedroom wall. That little lady had crumpled like a child's sand castle in a storm. She had started to cry and shake. I couldn't even go near her without frightening her. It had taken me two days of hugging and kissing and reassuring just to settle her nerves down. And I had felt like the biggest jerk on the face of the earth. It was for that reason that I used a deep, commanding, no-nonsense voice when robbing a bank. I didn't want to hurt any women. I would never pistol-whip a female teller or shove her around the way some amateur bank robbers have been known to do. I wouldn't even so much as lay one little baby finger on her regardless of what she might have said or done, because there is no honor in hurting a woman. I've always been of the opinion that if you're going to break the law, then show a little class. But a man, a male bank manager or employee or the police. Well, now, that was quite another story. They were potentially dangerous opponents, and bank robbing was a form of combat.

Robbing banks is addictive. No bank robber will ever deny the rush, the natural high you get from robbing a bank. Your hands sweat, your chest gets tight and you feel light-headed. A glint of madness shines in your eyes and you become exuberant and extremely excited. Even counting the money afterward doesn't compare with that kind of immediate gratification. But I didn't really like to rob banks. My heart wasn't into acting barbarous. True, there was a high degree of excitement, but there was also an element of great risk involved. You could get your head blown off! A man would have to be a fool to crave excitement so desperately that he was willing to chance leaving his brains behind on a bank floor or wall.

The police have a nasty little habit of waiting for a bank robber to leave the bank, then ambushing him with a quick revolver shot to the head at point-blank range or a shotgun blast to the back as he runs toward his getaway car. Toronto and Montreal robbery squads are notorious for holding court right in the street, a modern-day trial by combat. The word from the Montreal Boys was that if you went to Montreal to rob a bank and the robbery squad came, you might as well just start blasting your way out, because there was no such thing as giving up. Surrender ensured a one-way ticket to the morgue.

Yet I robbed banks. And all money bought me was a little extra time, time to obtain more credible identification, time to put distance between me and the law . . . time until I had to rob another bank.

On a national average a man has seventy some years to live. The more time I spent on the street, the less time was available for prison. The authorities have a way of dealing with persistently ambitious and serious criminals. They age them like a piece of blue cheese. They lock them up until a person is too old, infirm and full of microbes to present a threat to society any longer. It's called warehousing. So I escape every chance I get. And it isn't a stroll through a rose garden. There's a price to pay.

There is nothing so dark and distant as the future. But there is nothing so clear and close as the hounds of hell behind you. That's what being on the run is all about. A considerable number of persons are under the impression that living a life of crime on the lam is wild and exciting. But it's not. It's a rough and rocky road and you walk down it alone and at night.

In 1984 I was in my early thirties, but I had yet to marry and father children. As men we like to think of ourselves as being pretty macho in one form or another, insisting that we really don't need anyone. But when it really comes down to what is important in life, few men will deny that their wives and children are the only things that really mean anything. There were times on the lam when I thought of becoming deeply involved with a woman. But to marry her, to have her bear my children, I would first have to love and care for her. And a few years later down the road, when inevitably the police would come crashing through the door of our home at three o'clock in the morning, her whole world would come crashing down around her. I just couldn't do that to the mother of my children.

I don't care for loose women. I have a penchant for ladies with a little class and I wouldn't have an affair with a woman I wouldn't marry. But no decent, sensible woman will have anything to do with a bank robber, and with a closetful of guns she'd know I was either working for the law or against it. So I was pretty much left to my imaginary lover. There was something missing in my life, an emptiness, a void. And that something was the love only a woman can give a man.

All you have on the run as a bank robber besides yourself is money and what it can buy you. And sometimes they aren't enough. You have no one to go to after someone has tried to kill you or you've almost killed someone — and there's very little difference between the two. You have to stand alone, tall and straight with your fears, worries, wants, needs and frustrations. You can never bend. You can never make that one fatal mistake that could bring disaster and ruin raining down upon you.

You have no permanent home and must be ready to flee at the first sign of the police. And you can't take a chance. Even if you're not sure they're onto you, you still have to run, because if you don't it could mean your life. You can never tell the truth, your whole life is a lie and your memory has to be flawless. You can never slip up. You don't know, when you go to sleep at night, if you're going to wake up in the morning alive. From 1972 until 1985 Canadian police officers claimed over 240 lives. They have an unwritten law reserved for murderous bank robbers, cop killers or "cop shooters" such as me. They surround your motel room, apartment or house in the early hours of the morning, fill it full of lead and then yell, "Police! Open up!" They are so skilled in surveillance these days that you don't even know they're there until it's too late.

You can't walk down the street or drive down the road without watching for that one person or vehicle, that same face in the crowd or that same make, model and color of car. Everyone is suspect. No one is a friend. Then, sooner or later, you have to rob a bank again and the whole crazy cycle starts once more, only intensified.

You can't have any family contact because family members are under surveillance. Their phones are tapped, the calls are traced and the police have paid informants living nearby. You can't jaywalk, speed, go out at night, frequent crowded places or do anything conspicuous or high-profile in case the police investigate you or someone recognizes your face. You're always living on the edge and you can never drop your guard.

Essentially you're free, but it's a highly restricted, guarded and controlled freedom. And after months or years of such stressful existence you truly are a hunted man. So why did I sentence myself to such a tense, precarious lifestyle? Because I'd rather die in the street with a gun in my hand than spend a lifetime of putrefaction in a prison cell. That's why. And so, at all times I was armed. And at all times I was dangerous.

16

The Eleventh Commandment: Thou Shalt Not Get Caught

BY THE END OF 1984 I WAS PRESENTING an elusive target for the law, living in Portland, Oregon, slipping across the border at intervals and robbing the occasional Canadian bank, then slipping back again to resume a normal lifestyle. One day I decided to contact Paul Marshall, whom I'd met in Millhaven.

Before my escape from the Mill Paul had provided me with a telephone number for just such an eventuality. Since he had been transferred to Joyceville Medium Security Penitentiary just weeks prior to my escape, I figured that by now he was on mandatory supervision, so I phoned Saskatoon, his hometown.

Paul was quite surprised and happy to hear from me. He was employed as a barber in a hairstyling salon, but he wasn't at all impressed with the poor attitude of the owner toward some female employees. Initially I was concerned that his phone might be tapped, but he assured me it was safe. Even so we spoke cautiously, only alluding to subjects, never mentioning key words. Our future intentions were a foregone conclusion. There was no question we would be taking down a bank. It was just a matter of the locale, timing, preparation and equipment. We discussed the basic objectives in general terms, and while Paul set about researching the bank and schedule, I busied myself assembling and testing the weapons and accessories. I had already amassed my own complete set of bank robbing gear, so it was just a simple matter of duplicating each item and checking for the customary defects. We agreed to contact each other after two weeks to discuss further developments, any problems encountered and a date for the bank robbery.

In the meantime I was a consistent and reliable student at the Oregon School of Martial Arts. I attended two one-hour classes every day, occasionally opened up the dojo for business in the morning, conducted warm-up exercises and taught junior belt classes. I was looking forward to becoming a black belt instructor after two and a half years. Most of the students liked me. I provided leadership and wasn't afraid to fight any of the black belts; after all, the worst they could do was knock me out. They followed my instruction willingly and showed respect for my discipline. I always awoke at 11:00 a.m., prepared brunch and left for the school in time to make the one o'clock class.

In keeping with the school's rules, it was necessary for me to advise my teachers of my forthcoming absence. I couldn't tell them I was off to rob another bank, so I used the subterfuge that I was going to visit my mother in Winnipeg. Two weeks later Paul and I were again in touch and at that time I learned he had cruised the mid-northern states, searching for a bank that met our requirements. After a lengthy period he finally hit upon the South Dakota State Bank in Mobridge, South Dakota. In the interim I had purchased a Colt .45, Winchester Defender, Second Chance vest and related accessories and performed the requisite alterations and tests. We agreed to a meeting in Portland, scheduled for the upcoming long weekend, to finalize plans and strategies and to familiarize Paul with his weapons.

One week later he arrived by plane under an alias unknown to customs officials and registered in a prebooked, low-profile hotel. I phoned to ensure he hadn't been tailed, then picked him up. After a series of taxi, foot and bus changes, designed to shake any surveillance he might have overlooked, we reached my apartment. Only then did I extend myself the luxury of an enthusiastic greeting. It had been a long time and hard men are hard to find. Paul was like an older brother to me.

The following day we took a trip to the local firing range with the shotguns and pistols and fired off a few boxes of shells. After leaving the pistol range, I could see a shine of exhilaration in Paul's eyes. I was amazed to discover that Paul's shooting skills were comparable to mine in view of the fact that his last opportunity to handle a weapon had been many years ago, and my abilities surpassed those of the state troopers I had come into contact with who regularly frequented the range.

After returning to the apartment, Paul smoked a joint of marijuana and we dismantled the guns, giving them a thorough cleaning and lubrication. As we were both deeply involved in cleaning the guns, Paul looked at me and laughed. "Two psychopaths all wound up with nowhere to go," he said. We both laughed, realizing there was obviously more than a little truth to the statement, at least where we came from. Up in Canada we would have been looked upon as psychopaths or gun nuts, but down in the States we were just a couple of good ol' boys.

On his last day in Portland I gave Paul a tour of the city, including the market on Seventh Street and Main, which always reminded me of a Turkish bazaar with its hodgepodge of contrasting shops, personalities and merchandise. Paul was like a little kid in a candy store. His eyes were wide with excitement and the wonder of it all, and he didn't know what to buy first! We made a pact to meet again in two weeks time to do the job, and Paul caught a plane back to Saskatoon that evening.

Two weeks passed and Paul again flew down to Portland. We packed our gear and boarded a bus to Butte, Montana, where we registered in a hotel. We intended to steal a car and continue on to Mobridge. In Butte that night we went to a shopping mall parking lot and Paul spotted a 1984 Olds Cutlass. As Paul watched for anyone's approach, I calmly walked over to the car, popped the door lock, climbed inside and picked the ignition. The engine came to life, he hopped inside and we drove out of the parking lot. We sped back to our hotel, quickly loaded our gear into the car and took the nearest exit to Interstate 90, leaving the city. Other than stopping once for gas, our trip to Mobridge went smoothly.

Once in Mobridge, Paul dressed up as an auditor, briefcase and all, and calmly walked into the South Dakota State Bank for a personal interview with the manager. He was passing himself off as a bank auditor sent down from the head office to examine the accounts.

After the interview Paul beamed with satisfaction. In reply to my query he said that not only was Mrs. Seeler, the bank manager, convinced of his authenticity, she actually was quite concerned. He had scheduled a further date for Wednesday to begin auditing the books, but this time he would be accompanied by his assistant — me. Since it was nearly closing time, Paul suggested I use the opportunity to watch the bank-closing procedure and the routine departure of the personnel.

We spent the following day masquerading as fishermen on vacation and lounged on a riverbank a half-hour's drive from town, basking in the luxurious sun and spectacular scenery. It was just wonderful. South Dakota is one of the most beautiful vacation places I have ever seen.

The entire time I was in the States I wore a partial Swede disguise. It involved stripping my hair and eyebrows completely of pigment and dyeing them blond. I had shaved off my mustache and beard, too. But in anticipation of the bank robbery I included a few additional changes to my appearance to make my disguise more complete. I reshaped my nose with hollow nose inserts and packed cotton batting in my cheeks to change their contours. Since the skin of a fair-haired person is usually lighter than that of a dark-haired person, I brightened my complexion with a light tone of woman's facial makeup. Most fair-haired persons also have light-colored eyes, so I wore a pair of contact lenses that adjusted my eyes accordingly. The most recent photograph the American authorities had of Paul had been taken twenty years earlier, so he had no reservations about walking into the bank without a disguise.

On Monday, April 29, 1985, at 2:30 p.m. we readied the equipment. We arrived at the bank, parked the car in the customer lot and climbed out. It was 2:45 p.m. Paul carried a briefcase containing his Colt .45. I carried a second briefcase with my .45 inside. The duffel bag containing two shotguns, two bulletproof vests, a stun gun, four smoke grenades, two tear gas bombs, four clips and a large supply of ammunition was in the trunk. I surveyed the town. The subdued activity around the bank was normal for this time of the day. Paul paused for a second, then asked, "Are you ready?"

I knew what he was saying. Once we walked through those bank doors there was no turning back, and maybe we wouldn't be walking back out again. Surrendering after the bank was surrounded by a SWAT team wasn't even a consideration. It just wasn't in our psychological makeups. It was more sad than inspirational to consider it, but feet first on a stretcher or guns bucking would be the only way we would surrender. And I remembered Paul once telling me he would save the last bullet for himself. He had no intention of getting caught robbing a bank. Nor would he ever go back to prison. So, to his question, I simply replied, "Yes."

"Let's do it," he said matter-of-factly, and we calmly walked into the bank.

Mrs. Seeler was busy talking to another customer, so we sat in the waiting area. We had deliberately arrived late for the audit. It was a tense period. I don't mind the action of robbing a bank. It's the waiting that kills me. The moments seemed to trickle by with excruciating slowness. Finally Mrs. Seeler ended her interview and Paul lured her into her office for a preliminary discussion. We intended to delay the conclusion of the discussion until at least 3:15, well past closing time. Finally, at exactly 3:30, after a lot of double talk between Paul and me, we decided it was time to talk business. He placed his briefcase sideways on top of her desk, snapped the locks open, lifted the top to shield his movements from the sight of any bank employees, showed Mrs. Seeler his .45 and said in a very low but unmistakably clear voice, "I have some good news and some bad news. The good news is we're not here to audit your books. The bad news is this is a robbery. Remain seated and remain calm and you won't be hurt."

She was slightly shocked but controlled herself remarkably. We asked for her full cooperation, advising her of our readiness to use the gun. Actually, what Paul said was "If you don't cooperate, I'll blow your head off and probably everyone else's in the bank, too." I sat there, trying my best to look menacing, and I almost burst out laughing. "For God's sake," Paul said, "don't do anything to get this guy going. He's a killer. There's no telling what he'll do if he gets upset. He's crazy."

"I won't," she said simply.

Paul then asked her to begin demonstrating her cooperativeness by putting a big smile on her face and keeping it there for the benefit of any inquisitive bank employee. After that he put his stratagem for luring the remainder of the bank personnel away from the alarm buttons into effect. He instructed Mrs. Seeler to call the nine women and two men over to the customer's lounge for cursory instructions. She agreed, and we walked out of the office. I moved over toward the tellers with my .45 in my briefcase in case any showed signs of hesitation and suspicion.

All the staff members were mildly surprised but came over willingly enough when beckoned; everyone except for one demurring lady, who asked what the reason for the meeting was. She just stood there behind the counter. I got into position to cover her in the event that she suspected something and pressed the silent alarm button. Nevertheless, she abandoned her post without further question after the second request by her superior. Paul arranged the chairs around in a cozy little circle. Then he sat down, called for everyone's attention, and with the most charming, disarming smile beaming from his face, he announced, "Folks, this is a robbery," and showed them his gun. I could tell he was aiming for an Oscar on this one. Everyone sat there looking glum and feeling slightly uncomfortable. But I was as happy as hell because we were going to get all their money! Then Paul gave everyone a summary of the robbery procedure, pausing to ask certain key questions concerning their safety.

I went out to the car and brought in the duffel bag with our weapons and ammunition. We would need it to get our asses out of the bank if we ran into trouble with the police. Upon my return I learned that the employees' lunchroom was occupied, so I went downstairs to escort the people up to the customers' lounge with everyone else. By this time we were about five minutes into the robbery, so I didn't know what little surprise might await me when I walked into the lounge. Up in Canada it was rare for a bank manager to have a gun. But down in the States everyone carries one around as if the country is about to be invaded by an army of mad Russians.

I padded softly over to the door and listened. Everything was quiet. With my pistol aimed at the ceiling, I slowly turned the handle, eased the door open a crack and peeked inside. I could see an older soldier sitting on the couch, but he wasn't alone. I stepped quickly into the room and commanded, "Freeze!" Then I saw the other person was his wife with their two small children. So much for dramatics. I put my pistol away and told them we were robbing the bank but assured them no one would be harmed. Then I asked them to follow me upstairs to join the rest of the group. The farthest thing from my mind was to harm the mother or her children. But I remained uncertain of how levelheaded the father was or how he might react, particularly if he sensed a threat to his wife or kids. He eased my apprehension by constantly asking, "How am I doing? Am I doing all right?" as if I were about to plug him on his first false move. He must have watched one too many *Miami Vice* episodes. When we got upstairs they took their places with the rest of the group.

Then Paul asked Mrs. Seeler to accompany him into the vault, which was still open to collect the bank's cash reserves. She replied that the treasury safe was locked and we would have to wait an additional fifteen minutes until the electric timer released the lock. But the head teller chirped up saying, "No, Mrs. Seeler, the treasury safe is still open."

As he squired her into the vault, Paul gave Mrs. Seeler a reproving frown and said, "Mrs. Seeler . . . don't fuck around."

As I was sitting in a lounge chair, minding the group, one gentleman who had remained silent and inconspicuous up until then started to get up out of his chair. What nerve, I thought! Here I was with a pistol and this man has the raw audacity just to get up and try to leave. I stepped smartly over to him and sat him back down in the chair. "What the hell's wrong with you?" I scolded. "Do you want to get yourself shot?" He didn't answer and seemed to be a bit confused. "What's wrong with him?" I asked the girl sitting next to him, still outraged. "Is he goddamn retarded?"

"Yes," she replied, "he is."

I looked down at him and I could see the childlike confusion registering on his face. That injected a little humility into my bearing.

After a few minutes, Paul reappeared with the briefcases packed with money. During my surveillance the first day I had noted a man standing outside the bank who waited for a bank employee, then departed. Paul asked Mrs. Seeler who he was waiting for and then instructed her to go to the front door and invite the man inside to wait for his wife. I accompanied Mrs. Seeler to the door to ensure she didn't go charging up the street, screaming, "Bank robbery! Bank robbery!"

Mrs. Seeler waved to the man, and soon enough he came striding cheerfully through the doors and, much to his surprise, right into a real-life bank robbery drama. We began making preparations for departure by handcuffing everyone together and putting them inside the vault. Everyone was standing in a circle as we were handcuffing them, and as we were busy doing so, one young woman began to tremble uncontrollably. I tried to calm her by reassuring her that she was in no actual physical danger. As I finished handcuffing her wrists, I whispered, "Don't worry. We aren't really going to hurt anyone. We're just bluffing." She really began to shake then, so I thought the best thing for me to do was to stay as far away from her as possible.

We expected to leave through a rear door, according to the information Mrs. Seeler had given us, but we should have known better. It was locked. So we wound up with no choice but to leave by the same doors as we had entered — the side customer entrance. We had been in the bank well over an hour by then. Any SWAT team would have had more than ample time to set up and be in position. Paul carried the briefcases filled with money, while I hefted the duffel bag. If there was going to be a firefight, we would know it by a shout or a bullet as soon as we stepped through the second door. I went first and Paul followed directly behind me. We walked purposefully out through the first door and scanned the parking lot. The coast looked clear. I stepped out into the bright South Dakota sunshine, my eyes darting back and forth, searching for any sudden movement or dark shapes in the thick hedges hemming the lot. All was still and quiet. We walked quickly to the car and placed the two briefcases in the back but kept the duffel bag with us in the front. Paul started the car and drove casually out of the parking lot, down the main street and out of town.

There were four main undivided highways leaving Mobridge. We took Highway 12, north to McLaughin. We had approximately thirty-five minutes of driving until we reached a secondary gravel road just before Route 6. I didn't feel too confident about the lengthy period of time we would be exposed to the highway patrols. Then, with five minutes left to travel until the next exit, we got stuck behind an eighteen-wheel transport truck. We had been roaring along between fifty and seventy miles an hour and the eighteen-wheeler was doing only forty. We would be on the highway and vulnerable for an additional five minutes at this rate of speed! And those few extra minutes could prove fatal.

Try as he might, Paul couldn't squeeze by. Every opportunity was snatched away by either a blind bend or an oncoming vehicle, causing him to swerve back in behind the truck again. We were in trouble. Eventually the trucker noticed our plight and gave the all-clear sign by flashing his passing indicator light. Paul hit the gas and we passed him in a flash. But just as Paul swerved back into the right lane again, a deputy sheriff cruised by, traveling in the opposite direction. Paul didn't react. We were pretty certain the bank employees would still be struggling to free themselves. And we also believed they definitely didn't know the make or model of our getaway vehicle. Little did we realize that not only had they freed themselves, noted the description of our vehicle and called the police, but the deputy had recognized our car as the getaway vehicle and immediately swerved into a frenzied U-turn in hot pursuit, only to be trapped behind the eighteen-wheeler just as we had previously been.

Nevertheless, unsuspectingly, we flew along until we finally reached the secondary road. Paul never even checked his speed as he made the transition airborne from one road to the other. He flew over the slight dip in road levels as he charged up the loose gravel, churning up a huge cloud of gray dust in his wake. Three miles later we stopped momentarily on the side of the road to retrieve our additional equipment and supplies, then we continued on. We were quite a few miles from the immediate area of the robbery by now. The most dangerous ground had been covered. There was no doubt we would make good our getaway. We began to relax.

Suddenly Paul noticed flashing red and blue lights in the distance through his rearview mirror. He slammed his foot down on the accelerator. I spun around in my seat but couldn't see any pursuing police car, yet Paul was adamantly positive he had seen the flashers. Then we realized our car must have been pegged, the deputy had spotted us and the predicament he must have been in with the transport truck. We swerved madly up the third road in our escape route.

We knew trying to leave the area by way of any main highways would be suicide, so we drove north through the boondocks until well into the night. We had purchased a number of road and topographical maps along the way. So detailed were they, in fact, that we went from a gravel road to a dirt road to a cart trail and we were still confident we knew exactly where we were; after all, we had the maps. And when the cart trail dwindled down into a river we were still confident we knew exactly where we were. And exactly where we were was lost! But we weren't concerned. We figured if we didn't know where we were, then neither did the police. The only thing we found particularly irritating and peculiar was that every piddling creek had a name posted on a sign, and sometimes the creek wasn't even big enough to float the post. If it wasn't Badger's Creek, it was Badger's Paw Creek or Badger's Paw Stuck in the Cow Pie Creek. It drove us nuts just trying to figure out where the hell we were on the maps, let alone what county we were in. Finally we had to retrace our route back twenty miles to the last paved road.

After having placed more than 150 miles between ourselves and Mobridge, at three o'clock in the morning we turned into a sportsman's access trail and bedded down for the night. We were still restless from the robbery and barely slept a wink. Early in the morning we awoke and drove into a small, secluded campground, where we built a fire and cooked breakfast. We left just as the other campers were stirring and drove north again until we came to a logging road, which extended down into a heavily forested valley. We parked the car behind a natural blind and climbed out into the warm North Dakota sunshine for a few hours of rest and relaxation.

Paul had estimated that our take would be a $100,000 in cash. We were slightly disappointed, though, when we counted only $76,000 in cash. But we weren't disappointed enough to give the money back. We converted the American value to Canadian and totaled more than $99,000. Not bad, put that way.

We remained in the valley until well into the afternoon, then sped to a nearby junction café to make a phone call. Paul contacted a close friend named Jake, who agreed to travel down to the small town of Fortuna, North Dakota, and pick us up. Paul would be let off one mile before the U.S./Canadian border. He would then hike through the heavy forest for another two miles and cross the border unseen by the patrols. Jake would then pick him up again on the other side. Meanwhile, I would take a bus back to Portland, Oregon.

Paul was on the phone for close to ten minutes. I figured we were pushing our luck parking the car at a dinky little redneck roadside café, especially since the robbery had even been broadcast over the radio with a complete description of the car, including the license plate number. I placed my shotgun on the front seat just in case a state trooper or local sheriff zeroed in on it. Ten minutes later Paul was still on the phone, and I had reached the limit of my patience. I started the car up and drove over to the phone booth to give Paul the hurry-up sign. He mistook it for the we've-got-trouble sign and cut short his call. Back on the road, he gave me hell for having to hang up on Jake without completing his directions, then stopped abruptly when a state trooper passed us heading in the opposite direction toward the café.

Just before sundown we drove the car deep into the valley and camouflaged it with an army net. As darkness fell, we walked up from the valley, backpacking our gear, and followed the country road to the nearest highway. All through the night we walked, resting frequently and occasionally diving into the ditch to avoid the headlights of passing cars. Finally, at daybreak, we reached Fortuna, where we were to meet Jake. Utterly exhausted, hungry and thirsty, we were heading at a determined, if somewhat mechanical, pace for the nearest restaurant, when Jake came cruising around the corner. Ensconced in his car, we divided up the money and paid Jake for his time and expenses. Then I took a bus back to Portland and Paul returned to Saskatoon with his money and the equipment.

Two months later Paul gave me a call. He had decided to relocate to Portland with his wife, Nancy. I took a bus up to Sweetgrass, Montana, to bring them across the border. At the appointed time they would be at the junction of Willow Street and Camrose Avenue in Coutts, Alberta. He would cross the border illegally, using the same route I did when I entered Canada to rob banks. I had told Paul I would keep an eye out for border patrols and flash a signal when the coast was clear. Then they could come across.

At 3:00 a.m. I spotted them with my binoculars. The coast was clear. I flashed the signal and they both ran across. I helped Paul with the duffel bag containing our cache of weapons and equipment. He carried a flight bag full of money. We walked to the bus depot, and Nancy went inside to go to the ladies' room. Paul and I paused for a second outside to scan the interior of the depot. Just as we were about to enter, he spotted two border patrol guards inside. Instead of going in, we casually walked past the door. But before we had walked more than twenty yards a border patrol cruiser pulled up beside us, and another one hemmed us in from behind. Two officers climbed out of the first vehicle and approached us separately, while the third officer got out and stood behind his vehicle. These men were professionals. We were trapped!

Paul's .45 was in the flight bag he carried, lying holstered on top of his money, with the fastener zipped shut. I had both our shotguns intertwined in the armholes of the bulletproof vests on either side of the duffel bag to keep them from clanging together and accidentally discharging as I carried them. While one officer questioned Paul another one interrogated me. The third maintained his vigil behind us. They never took their eyes off us for a split second. At all times they remained alert to the possibility of danger. Paul didn't have any false ID to give to the officer in response to his challenge, so he produced his Canadian birth certificate on the off chance they couldn't tap into CPIC, Canadian Police Information Checks, this late at night. I had an American birth certificate under the pseudonym of James Williams, which I willingly produced. The original James Williams was dead. He had been born in New York and raised in Portland, Oregon, where he had died as a child.

After the officer radioed in Paul's identification, he was immediately relieved of his flight bag and frisked. But since I was supposedly an American citizen, I was handled with kid gloves. As Paul was being placed in the rear of the first border patrol car, our eyes met for an instant. He looked so helpless. I knew what I had to do. He was counting on me. But I'd never be able to pull my shotgun out of the duffel bag fast enough, not with so many border cops around me.

Just then one of the border cops told me to stand in front of the cruiser's glaring headlights. He asked me what was in the duffel bag. It was the chance I'd been waiting for. I would no longer be boxed in by the vehicles or the officers, and it gave me the opportunity to reach inside the bag. I replied that it contained camping gear, a sleeping bag and a tent, and offered to show them to him. As I placed the bag on the ground, I unzipped it partway and groped around inside for my Colt .45. The safety was off, it was uncocked with a shell in the chamber and had a full clip of copper-jacketed 230-grain round-nose shells.

The second officer was standing eight feet away, facing me. He'd have to go first with a single snap shot to the chest. The telltale sign of a raised undershirt, indicating a bulletproof vest, was absent. The third officer was still standing behind his cruiser thirty feet away. My first double would have to go through both side door windows and into his chest, not a difficult shot.

The first officer by now was in his cruiser, receiving the results of his outstanding warrant and criminal record checks on our IDs. It would be touch and go if his reflexes were honed, but I was certain my second double through his windshield would either take him out or be enough to make him dive for cover. Then I would pull my shotgun from the duffel bag and it would be all over. The shotgun was fully loaded with 000 buck interlaid with rifled slugs.

I couldn't find my .45! It wasn't where I had packed it. The jostling around in the bag had probably displaced it. Desperately, uncertainly, I felt about in the dark for the angular, jutting butt of my gun, but it was nowhere within reach. The second officer by now was growing suspicious and began to shine his flashlight into the interior of the duffel bag, exposing the white sheaths of the bulletproof vests and the black gleam of the shotgun butts. He stiffened, and placed his hand on the butt of his .357 Magnum. "Move away from the bag," he ordered. I could still beat him to the draw. I continued to grope wildly, but still couldn't find my gun. "Move away from the bag!" he shouted, gripping his revolver.

As soon as he inspected the contents of the bag more closely and discovered the arsenal, he would realize exactly the caliber of illegal immigrants he was up against and throw down on me. And once I was placed in the back of the cruiser with Paul all would be lost. My only avenue lay in flight. As long as one of us remained free, the other had a chance. I stepped away from the duffel bag. As the second officer peered cautiously inside, I quickly turned and sprinted up the road. He immediately drew his revolver and started pursuing me, while the third officer jumped into his cruiser and roared up the exit ramp to cut me off. I thought I could easily outdistance the pursuing officer, but to my amazement he kept pace with me, screaming repeatedly, "Stop or I'll blow you away!"

I vaguely wondered what it would feel like when his bullet hit my back. When he stopped yelling, I knew I would have to lunge sideways, because that would be the split second he would be steadying his aim. The third officer in his cruiser swerved in front of me, so I dived for a decorative hedge of compact ferns carpeting the cloverleaf embankment of the ramp. To my surprise the ferns were so tightly knit that they threw me backward almost right into the outstretched arms of the pursuing officer, who was a mere ten feet behind me now.

We began grappling and I drove my fingers into his throat to grip his carotid artery and cut off the supply of blood to his brain, thus rendering him unconscious in seconds. But he flexed his neck muscles and tore away from my grasp. I couldn't hold him. He was too strong. So I caught him off balance and threw him over backward down the embankment. Then I dived back into the dense ferns before the third officer could rush to his assistance. He scrambled back up the embankment and began shouting for me to come out again, threatening to shoot.

While he cursed and ranted, I belly-crawled beneath the branches back in the direction of Paul and the first patrol car. The first officer had by now locked my duffel bag in the trunk. I could see him searching the rear seat of his cruiser, where Paul sat, for any additional weapons. I looked around frantically for a rock or club to knock him out with, but I couldn't find one. I couldn't believe it! Here I was right under the concrete overpass of a major highway with concrete slabs layering the embankment to guard against erosion and there wasn't a single rock in sight.

I hesitated, crouching in the shadow of the overpass, wondering what I could possibly do to win Paul's freedom. As soon as I bolted for the officer across the 100-foot gap, the other officers would be certain to spot me and race to his aid. Without some sort of weapon to overcome the officer instantly and take his revolver, the success of the attack couldn't be guaranteed. But I couldn't remain indecisive all night. Eventually the other officers would realize I'd given them the slip and extend their search area. I would be spotted and the chase would be on again, possibly with the opposite result this time. I didn't want to leave — it went against my grain — but I'd be no good to Paul sitting beside him in jail. I'd be back. They hadn't heard the last of me yet.

I dashed out from under the overpass and across a cloverleaf exit, heading back toward the bus depot. All that remained of my attire was a pair of soiled dress pants. My shoes had been lost in the race and my shirt had been torn off in the fight. I considered entering the bus depot and retrieving Nancy, but with the two other border patrol officers still inside, walking in half-dressed would only serve to draw attention to her. She would do better without me. My only option was to keep on the move and hope she made the best of it.

I ran toward the border, up the side roads and through backyards, expecting at any moment to be picked out by the piercing headlights of a border patrol car speeding toward me from the rear. I crossed the border, keeping to the shadows and wooded areas, avoiding roads and dodging vehicles with the utmost of caution until I reached the town of Coutts. By now it was early morning and the sun was rising. I picked the lock on a vacant cottage, scoured the closets for a shirt and pair of shoes, then caught the first bus to Lethbridge, Alberta.

I traveled to Saskatoon and learned from Paul's family that he was being detained in the Sweetgrass Jail. Naturally the Sweetgrass Sheriff's Department had seized the weapons and money pending further investigation. The arsenal wasn't a big issue. The Constitution of the United States of America stipulated that Americans had the right to bear arms, and three out of every four households did. But the substantial amount of untraceable cash perplexed them. A thorough search of Paul's personal possessions provided a lead — a name and address linking him to Baker, Montana. It was the address of a local businessman. An inquiry sent to the Baker Sheriff's Department concerning any recent major crimes quickly told the tale. Paul and a second accomplice were wanted for robbing a bank in Baker, Montana, two weeks previously. The FBI was called in, and Paul was to be extradited to Miles City to stand trial for the bank robbery.

My cover as James Williams was blown and so was my apartment. The police would easily trace my birth certificate back to Portland, Oregon, where I had applied for it, and lie in wait for me there. I needed to get back into the States and in some manner obtain Paul's release, but I needed identification to do it. I approached Jake, Paul's friend, with my problem, but now that the law was involved he began to suffer from severe fright. Some tough guy! Giving up on Jake in disgust, I contacted a loyal member of Paul's family, Luke, who agreed to furnish me with the necessary documents to get me back into the States.

I returned my hair to its natural color and grew a mustache. Then I picked up a tail in a shopping mall in Saskatoon, a gentleman in his mid-thirties dressed in a conservative, well-worn suit and loafers. I knew he was a cop the moment he walked in behind me. I had stepped into a hidden alcove for just such a reason, to see if anyone was shadowing me. And as he entered he glanced around expectantly for my location. I left through a side door, evading any further surveillance.

I went to Vancouver and attempted to fly to Portland, where I resolved to replenish my arsenal and break Paul out of the Sweetgrass Jail before they could extradite him to Miles City. But the customs officers refused me entry into the United States without photo identification.

I was disheartened. I knew I was Paul's only hope for freedom. If the customs officials wanted substantial proof of identity prior to authorizing my entry into the United States, then they were speaking to the right man. I purchased a one-way nonstop airline ticket on the first flight east to Edmonton.

Quite early in my criminal career I had realized that the most important precautionary measure involved in eluding the police and preserving my freedom after an escape or near capture was to possess genuine, credible and legitimate identification. By this I mean a person had to have actually been born under that name and birth date, the identification had to be composed of a minimum of three irrefutable pieces and it had to have been issued by the government. To qualify under these conditions, the source of the identification had to be a person who had died under the age of five, particularly an only child with both parents deceased.

There were two methods I employed in locating someone who met these standards. The first required a visit to the local main library, which, if the community was of any consequence, usually reduced and stored the leading newspaper on microfilm. I researched the approximate year, month and nationality I was interested in. With the newspapers it was a matter of cross-checking an obituary with an earlier birth announcement in the deaths, memorials and birth columns, which were, ironically, always adjacent to the comics page in every newspaper.

The second method involved a visit to the cemetery to survey the markers for a triple epitaph and cross-check the names and dates with the cemetery records. When I walked through the graveyards, they were always eerie and quiet, and although I wasn't superstitious, I did find something sacred about cemeteries.

After I found an appropriate subject, there were six pieces of information I needed: the father's full name; the mother's full maiden name; the deceased's full name; the actual place of birth; the exact date of birth; and the status of the parents. Through a variety of methods, which included researching public and private records, telephone calls and personal interviews conducted under diverse pretexts, I was eventually able to piece together all the above information from birth, death or memorial announcements; hospital records; community-based organizations; church or fraternity records; and distant relatives.

Once I had accumulated the required data I applied for a birth certificate in the most expedient manner possible — in person. At the Department of Vital Statistics, using the fictitious explanation that I had lost my identification and needed to travel to the United States to attend my grandfather's funeral, I was usually granted a birth certificate within twenty-four hours.

Now in possession of a primary document, I used a high-quality photocopier and my printing skills to flawlessly substitute the name on a stolen secondary document, usually a university degree. Then I sent both the certificate and the photocopy in an application to obtain a social insurance number. Upon the return of the SIN, I went to the Motor Vehicles Branch and received my beginner's driver's license. The next day I returned with a borrowed car and acquired my full driver's license.

With these three firm pieces of identification as my foundation, the potential for increasing and establishing a social history became boundless. I bought a Jeep, which supplied me with an ownership, then registered it and was issued a registration card. After insuring it, I was given an insurance certificate. Then I bought a motorcycle and repeated the entire process. I picked up a library card and became a member of the local Co-op store. The Liquor Control Board also provided me with photo identification, and checking and savings accounts further augmented my new identity. Any organization, club or fraternity, such as the YMCA, KOA or AAA were all accessible. The possibilities were as endless as my inventiveness. But the paper game stopped at the passport office of the Department of External Affairs. The passport people cross-referenced applications with death records. Here a different technique was used, which involved a confederate, usually paid, who agreed to substitute my picture for his in his revised passport application. Once acquired, the new identity provided me with time, versatility and protection. I could choose my business ventures more carefully, travel or change residences when and if the situation demanded and never be concerned about routine inquiries. But most important it gave me clear and unimpeded entry into the United States.

By the time I obtained my complete set of identification, Paul had been transferred to Helena, Montana, for an extradition hearing and subsequently to Miles City to stand trial for the bank robbery. I drove to Carway, Alberta, on the border, crossing into the States on Highway 2 in my Jeep. With my new identification I experienced no difficulty whatsoever. Then I drove down to Miles City with a trustworthy female friend and arranged to visit Paul in the Custer County Jail to make preliminary plans for his jailbreak.

The Custer County Jail was attached to the Sheriff's Department, so while I sat outside in the sheriff's waiting lounge, leafing through magazines, my friend walked in to visit Paul, pretending to be his sister. I had given her a false set of identification with the surname of Marshall. Paul was surprised at my nerve. I had the audacity to sit right in the sheriff's lounge while the FBI was searching everywhere for his partner in the Baker bank robbery. I had pondered a method by which I might discourage the witnesses against Paul, thereby winning his acquittal, but dismissed the tactic. There were just too many of them, a half-dozen at least. Through "Miss Marshall," I asked Paul what he wanted me to do. He replied that he wanted out. I would move heaven and earth to give him his wish. After the second visit, I figured I could safely visit Paul as his brother, Carl Marshall from Saskatoon.

The visiting room was secured by an electronically locked steel door controlled by the deputy, who also observed the proceedings on two video monitors from two closed-circuit television cameras from within the jail. Visitors were separated from the prisoners by a wall of bulletproof glass and steel. Conversations were held over telephones. Even so, visitors weren't searched for weapons or restricted from carrying briefcases into the room. Nor were they required to walk through a metal detector. The deputy had no actual physical involvement in the visits whatsoever. He logged the names from behind the bulletproof gun port separate from the visiting room and monitored the visits. I considered blasting the glass out with a rifled slug from my shotgun and shooting our way out through the Sheriff's Department, but only as a last resort if all else failed.

I was determined to win Paul's freedom regardless of the destruction unleashed. It was my job to see to it that he crossed the border safely and without being apprehended. I had failed him, and as a result he'd lost his freedom and $30,000. I owed him, and I pay my debts.

By alluding to various subjects and writing notes, we discussed the basic strategies, research and equipment needed to obtain his release, and before we knew it the visit was over. It crushed me to watch Paul being led back to the cell. But even as I waited expectantly he never even so much as turned around once to wave goodbye. And deep in my heart I knew why. If you let prison hurt you, you'll never live through the pain.

If I was to take Paul out of police custody by force, I would need

the firepower to support my bid. And I knew just where to find it —
in the classified ads of the *Little Nickel* newspaper in Portland,
Oregon. I could buy anything there from a Thompson submachine
gun to an H & K-91 assault rifle without identification, state resident
card or questions asked.

Within a few weeks I purchased my twelve-gauge Defender, Colts
.45, Second Chance vest, Bearcat scanner and all of the related
accessories. I returned to Miles City and rented an apartment from
a little old lady under a completely different alias from Marshall.
Then I assumed the profession of lecturer at the Miles City State
University and began orchestrating my plan to set Paul free.

From Paul I had learned that whenever he was scheduled to
appear in court for a remand, he was driven to the State Building in
Miles City by two armed deputies. They drove past the front of the
State Building, bypassing the public parking lot, to the back and
down a ramp to an underground garage with an electronically
controlled door. The interior of the garage was monitored by a
closed-circuit camera. Once in the garage they climbed a short flight
of stairs to a door leading into the basement corridor. They walked
around a corner and boarded an elevator to the fourth floor. Then
they walked through a metal detector, up a hallway and into the state
courtroom. After the court appearance, they retraced their steps,
exiting by the same route. Further investigation revealed that the
State Building also housed the FBI headquarters for the State of
Montana, and the building's security office was in the basement. Its
staff consisted of two armed uniformed officers and a number of
plainclothes men equipped with walkie-talkies.

Paul's next court appearance was scheduled for November 6 at
9:00 a.m., two months away. So for the next two-week period I rose
promptly at 7:00 a.m. and arrived at the State Building parking lot
an hour later with a pair of binoculars to survey the influx of vehicles
and persons at the underground garage. I recorded the make, model,
color and license numbers of each person's car, and their schedules.
Posing as the visiting nephew of one of the more prominent state
court judges, I asked a groundskeeper what the possibility was of
parking my vehicle in the underground garage to attend a number
of my uncle's court sessions. He informed me that it was a restricted
area and only vehicles authorized by the building security were

allowed access. Through a number of license checks at the motor vehicle branch, which was connected to the Sheriff's Department, I was able to identify, for a nominal fee, all the regular presiding judges as well as the key security personnel. I visited every agency in the entire building to familiarize myself with security measures. I even attended an illegal alien smuggling hearing to gain admission to Paul's slated state courtroom. But there was one area I was just itching to gain unobserved access to for a few uninterrupted minutes — the actual underground garage itself.

One morning I was parked at the rear of the multisectioned parking lot among a cluster of assorted vehicles. The two uniformed security officers who commonly haunted the basement corridors and the garage left, each driving a security vehicle. I couldn't believe my good fortune! This was the chance I'd been waiting for. I walked quickly down into the basement and knocked loudly on the security office door to make certain it was completely unoccupied. If anyone answered, I was prepared to embark upon a cock-and-bull story about a lost wallet. No one answered after the second knock, which meant the plainclothes guards were patrolling the upper levels of the building and the closed-circuit monitor connected to the surveillance camera in the garage remained unattended. I walked immediately down into the garage and scrutinized every single section, enclosure and exit. I noted the camera position, lens angle and blind spots. I carefully scrutinized the advantages and disadvantages of each security measure, analyzing, calculating and memorizing each related factor. Only when I was completely satisfied that I had explored every single aspect of the garage did I leave.

Procuring accessibility to the basement or the surrounding area for a relatively short period of time without arousing anyone's suspicion was a simple enough task in itself. But for what I had in mind I required a veneer of legitimacy. It was a problem that I spent a great deal of time musing over, since it would be the axis upon which my fortune would ultimately turn. One morning I noticed a white MES Courier Express car pull up in front of the State Building. The driver alighted, carrying a parcel, and walked inside. A few minutes later he came out, climbed back into his car and drove away. I had my axis!

I rented a single-car garage four city blocks from the State Building, then rented a second garage six blocks from my apartment. A few days later I bused the thirty miles northwest to Rock Springs, Montana, and stole a late-model car. I returned to Miles City and parked it in the first garage. The next day I painted the car white and changed its exterior to correspond with a genuine MES Courier Express vehicle. I ordered two MES Courier Express magnetic signs for the side of each door and fixed the red-lettered wording COMMERCIAL DOCUMENTS ONLY — NO CASH CARRIED, as was displayed on all MES courier vehicles. After obtaining a purple MES courier jacket and cap complete with company decal emblazoned on each, I supplemented my impersonation with a courier card pinned to my lapel. On MES shipment forms I typed in the address of the State Building basement maintenance service room number, authorizing shipment of three quantities of highly toxic cleaning chemicals shipped from an out-of-state chemical wholesale distributor. Then I typed in the authorizing name of a supervisor of building maintenance, who was away on vacation, and signed his name. Finally I attached the form to an MES clipboard.

After piling three empty, sealed cardboard boxes on top of one another, I glued them together to make it appear as if they were separate. In fact, they constituted one long-paneled compartment. With a utility knife I cut a fine line down the center of the entire length of the boxes, extending it four inches to the left at the top and bottom of each end. Then I sliced the interior layer of the corrugated cardboard along the bending seam, which gave me an elongated flap that would open easily from the inside but remain inflexible upon exterior pressure. I repeated the same procedure on the opposing right-hand side of the line on the bottom box only, reversing the slice along the bending seam to the outside, giving me a shorter flap that folded inside. I then cut out the inside panels, conforming to the shape of each section of the shotgun, much like the grooved panels in a gun cabinet. The bottom flap would collapse inward when I reached for the stock grip and the lengthier flap would break outward when the weapon was drawn. Upon each box, I taped the appropriate duplicates of each MES shipment form.

After my initial visit I couldn't continue to see Paul on a regular basis and still maintain my imposture as his gainfully employed straight john brother residing with a wife and children in Canada.

So we kept in touch through coded messages in the personal classified section of Miles City's leading newspaper, which Paul subscribed to. And every second Wednesday I entered the latest encoded developments. Just to make absolutely certain I wouldn't miss Paul in the event his next court appearance was unexpectedly updated, I stole two pocket pagers that I kept on me at all times. Each pager had its own individual access phone number, which Paul could reach me on within seconds with a secret message under the pretext of calling his lawyer from the pay phone in his jail cell block.

Eventually I ran into surveillance by three plainclothes officers in two unmarked cars from the Sheriff's Department, but I wasn't sure it was me they were watching or the three other occupants of my building. In any case I didn't spook. Even though I was always acutely aware that if I was arrested Paul's hopes would be dashed, I wasn't budging one inch until I had concrete indications that I was in imminent danger of being apprehended. Paul's freedom meant too much to me.

All my preparations were complete. Paul wanted me to take my time in setting the sting up properly and I spared not one second or one cent in the time-consuming research and coordination. It was the best planned, most expensive venture I had ever been involved in. Paul was scheduled to appear in court on Wednesday, one day away. I had driven the two most probable and direct routes at a normal rate of speed from the jail to the State Building, and each course took about fifteen to twenty minutes. Paul corroborated my calculations by advising me that he always left the jail around 8:00 a.m. and arrived at court at 8:20 or thereabouts.

On Tuesday afternoon Paul phoned to confirm that there had been no change in his court date — it was a go. Finally, after five months and $30,000, the day I had been eating, sleeping and breathing for was just one night away. That evening I thoroughly checked to make sure all the equipment was in order. Then I loaded it into the Jeep and drove down to the first garage and locked everything in the car. After that I placed a change of clothing and essential items for Paul in the second garage. Sleep didn't come easy. I replayed again and again in my mind all the possible combination of events and how I would react to each, and always, always, how I would in some stroke of determination achieve my ultimate goal — Paul's freedom.

Early the next morning I rose, ate a light breakfast and donned my old man disguise. I shaved two deep, U-shaped receding hairlines on each side of my crown, first with the trimmer on my electric razor, then with the rotary blades. I thinned my remaining hair with a pair of barber's thinning shears. My scalp was stark white due to lack of sunlight. I had to carefully pad diluted light brown makeup on with a small cloth to match the color of my face. It gave my scalp a naturally exposed and tanned appearance. I had obtained gray theatrical hairspray from a local theatrical shop. I brushed it in and combed my hair in a neat, conservative style. Then I thinned my eyebrows with an eyebrow plucker and brushed the gray hairspray on lightly with an eyelash thickener brush and also onto my eyelashes. I trimmed my mustache and again applied the gray hairspray. Next I dabbed liver spots indiscriminately on all my exposed flesh areas, using a cotton swab. Then I padded baby powder on my face, neck, crown and backs of my hands to give my skin a pallid appearance. Finally I put on a pair of horn-rimmed bifocals, a white shirt, a thin black tie, a pair of worn dark cotton pants, black oxfords, an old wristwatch and a wedding band. I had purchased all the items at a local Salvation Army store for a modest price. I looked in the mirror. An old man stared back at me.

Now everything was as ready as it could possibly be. One way or the other I would win Paul's freedom. I looked at my watch: 6:00 a.m. It was time. I drove to the first garage and put Paul's .45 and the scanner into the Jeep. After slipping on my bulletproof vest, I buckled on my holstered .45 and two extra clips in a clip holder. I drew my gun. It came out easy. One shell was in the chamber and seven were in the clip. The safety was off. I dropped it snugly back into the holster. I loaded the shotgun with straight three-inch Magnum 000 buck. Six shells were in the magazine and one was in the chamber. It was locked and cocked. I clicked the safety button off as I placed it carefully inside the boxes and reset the flaps. There would be no margin for error.

Dressed in the MES courier coat and cap with a pocketful of 000 buck and rifled slug shotgun shells, I was set. I drove to the State Building. The tire chains I had purchased to guarantee I would be able to drive back up the icy ramp rattled noticeably against the wheel wells of the car. I lessened my speed, and the noise subsided.

I turned into the parking lot and scanned the vehicles and glass front of the building. Nothing appeared to be out of the ordinary. I turned the corner and cruised down the ramped laneway leading into the mouth of the security garage and parked at the end of the loading dock.

It was exactly 8:00 a.m. Paul should arrive within fifteen to twenty minutes. I would wait on the outside loading dock by the car with the boxes loaded onto the dolly. Upon the arrival of the sheriff's car, I'd wheel the boxes into the basement through the loading dock doors and wait exactly thirty seconds. The timing was crucial. By then Paul would have entered the garage, alighted from the vehicle and be approaching the stairs, escorted by the two deputies. At that moment he would accidentally drop a sheaf of legal documents, spilling the contents all over the floor and stalling both officers. At that precise moment I would open the door and enter the garage, stepping onto the stair platform with the boxes, withdraw my shotgun and throw down on them. I had practiced that very same maneuver for hours every night for weeks on end until that shotgun had come out of the box as if it were spring-loaded.

Once I had drawn the shotgun, Paul would throw himself to the ground out of the direct line of fire. The officers would be caught off guard in a tactically disadvantaged position. There would be nowhere to run and nowhere to hide. Hopefully common sense would prevail, but there was no guarantee one or both deputies wouldn't try a John Wesley Harding routine and go for their guns. That would have disastrous consequences for them. As fast on the draw and accurate as I was with my pistol, I was faster and more accurate with my shotgun. They wouldn't have a chance. At a distance of fifteen feet they would both be blown into never-never land in an instant. If shooting erupted, it wouldn't be overheard by building security. But if it was seen on camera, it would all be over with before they had any opportunity to interfere significantly. Paul and I were both psychologically prepared to implement the most extreme measures if necessary.

Once I had disarmed the deputies, I would free Paul from his handcuffs. Then we would either handcuff and bind both deputies or leave them where they lay. That accomplished, we would run to the car, with me driving, and head to the first garage, lock the vehicle inside, set the garage on fire to destroy any evidence connecting me to the escape and switch to the Jeep. Once in the Jeep, Paul would turn the scanner on and we would drive to the second garage, where I would call an ambulance for the officers if the situation demanded. Then we would wait for nightfall, leave the city, drive west, cross the border and enter Canada.

I placed the three boxes on the two-wheeled dolly, sitting at the end of the loading dock. I could feel the solid weight of the shotgun inside ready for action. All I would have to do is pull and fire. A postal worker drove up in a large mail truck, parked and began loading parcels into the back. He paid me no mind. I checked my watch. It was 8:15. Paul should come cruising around the corner and down the ramp any time now. As soon as he came down the ramp, from that moment onward, he would be mine.

I picked up the clipboard and began to write on the shipping forms to appear preoccupied when they arrived. An FBI agent in a Jeep Cherokee sped in, suspecting nothing. I turned my back, not tempting fate, and busied myself with the boxes. I hoped he would leave the garage before Paul arrived. I didn't need a shootout with the FBI this early in the morning.

It was 8:20. I blew warm air over my clenched hands. My fingers were beginning to stiffen from the cold, but I didn't think it would seriously impair my weapon handling. I had practiced every possible combination of maneuvers that could happen during the encounter relentlessly. I could perform them with oven mitts on. Just then Paul's white-haired, middle-aged judge drove by in his late-model dark blue Pontiac sedan. If I had my way today, court would never be called to session.

Eight-thirty. Paul was late. Had something gone wrong? Could the police have suspected the escape plan? I had been standing idly on the loading dock for the past half hour. It was hardly the expected behavior of an express courier. One inquisitive building maintenance worker began to take more than a slight interest in my car. He asked me about its performance and compared it to his own car, which was the same make. I answered his questions politely enough, but not in such a manner as to prolong the conversation or encourage his continued interest. He went about his business, disregarding me.

Eight-forty. Something was definitely wrong. He should have

been there by now. If the Sheriff's Department or the FBI suspected a break, they would be lurking around somewhere, staking out my capture, but I couldn't detect any increase or decrease in normal activity. I would wait another twenty minutes and then go. I couldn't stay much longer without raising some suspicion. If I queered the setup, and Paul's hearing had been postponed, I wouldn't be able to come back in the afternoon or within the next few days under the same guise.

Eight-fifty. Still no show. I would have to scrap the schedule and phone Paul's lawyer to find out when his court appearance had been postponed to.

Nine. That was it. It was no go. I checked the security garage for the sheriff's car, which could conceivably have arrived prior to eight o'clock. It was empty. Then I hopped into the car and drove back to the garage. Once parked inside I took off the courier coat and cap, unstrapped my .45, removed the vest and locked everything inside.

Out of curiosity I drove back to the State Building in my Jeep, rode the elevator up to the fourth floor and got off outside the FBI head office. Then I checked my keys through the walk-through metal detector, saying a cordial hello to the old security guard, and walked to the courtroom where Paul was scheduled to appear. I peered through the glass windows of the double-panel doors and was astounded by what I saw. There was the back of Paul's balding head as he sat at the center table beside his lawyer, who was standing up addressing the judge!

Son of a bitch! I had missed him by a mere fifteen minutes. They must have slipped him by me in the time it had taken me to drive to the garage and back. A court security guard who was patrolling the hallways began to scrutinize me, so I walked casually down the corridor, around the corner and took the elevator to the basement. I checked the garage and, sure enough, the cruiser was there, parked in its prearranged parking space.

I hurried to my Jeep and raced back to the garage, redonning the vest, .45, coat and cap, and raced back to the State Building. Paul's remand wouldn't take long, perhaps thirty to forty-five minutes at most. I didn't have a moment to spare.

I loaded the boxes onto the dolly again and, with my clipboard in hand, wheeled them inside right down into the garage. I had made it in time. The cruiser was still there. This latest development would call for a slightly different strategy. The garage contained a filing room that housed multiple shelves behind a glass frontage secured by a locked door. The dark interior afforded me concealment from the normal comings and goings of the maintenance workers plus the camera. I had to act fast. At any moment I could be interrupted by security or a police officer. I tried to jimmy the lock, but it was a high-quality spring latch with a dead-bolt plunger and proved to be impervious. I punched a small round hole in the wire-glass window, reached inside, turned the handle and opened the door.

Quickly I checked the doorframe for any release button or magnetic open-circuit alarms, then closed and locked the door behind me. Moments later I taped a small cardboard sign over the hole: Authorized Personnel Only. Originally I had entertained the idea of using the room to lie in wait for Paul, but it had seemed too risky. I had no viable alternative now but to take Paul "after" they escorted him back to the car. The timing would have to be more precise. The chances of succeeding without gunplay were less. And the risks were greater. As soon as they passed by the filing room, it would be too late to step out, level my shotgun and command them to freeze. By then one officer would be within diving distance of the protection of the rear of the car. I would wait until both officers climbed inside the cruiser, then step quickly out and throw down on them three feet from the driver's side. The driver would be utterly helpless. He wouldn't be able to start the car fast enough and slam it into gear. Nor would I be close enough for him to throw the door open and knock my aim off. My angle would observe their every move. But the officer on the passenger side might attempt something foolish, like diving for cover out his door or drawing his weapon. He would never make it, of course, but his actions would decide whether he told the tale to his children from his armchair by the fireplace that night or from the hospital that afternoon. It was unfortunate, but I couldn't see any other option. Paul's court proceedings wouldn't extend past an hour at most. I would surely catch him on the rebound.

For two and a half hours I remained hidden in that room, clutching the shotgun, hoping no office workers would come down to retrieve any files. If they did, I would have no choice but to hold them until

Paul and his escorts arrived. Fortunately none did. Shrouded from view, I watched as the building security guards, deputy sheriffs and FBI agents passed right before my very eyes, not more than four feet away. They arrived and departed from the garage, and not one noticed the peculiar little sign advertising a foregone conclusion taped to the door. On one occasion six maintenance workers trooped into the garage, all dressed in dark green uniforms with attached decals, and began carrying steel doorframes back and forth across the garage for over forty-five minutes. I was certain they would most certainly notice and investigate the distinctive sign. They were more familiar with the normal goings-on of their immediate work area. But even they, too, seemed oblivious to the clue of my concealment. The thought of having to take the whole crew hostage wasn't a comforting one.

Finally at noon a plainclothes officer with a SWAT cap strode purposefully down into the garage, jumped into the cruiser, backed out through the door and sped up the ramp. I had feared that for security precautions or reasons of convenience the deputies might change their routine as I had seen officers do in the past with other prisoners. It appeared as if they had, taking Paul out of the building by way of the front entrance. I had missed him again. But just to verify my theory I placed the shotgun back inside the boxes, wheeled them out to the car and walked back inside up to the first floor to make a phone call to the court clerk. Using the pretense that I was an out-of-state visiting law student interested in viewing an actual state court case, I asked about the docket listings for the remainder of the day. After double-checking, she confirmed that Paul's hearing had concluded at noon. I was so depressed. If I could get just one shot, just one chance to free him, I knew I could do it or I would die trying. But I didn't even get that one chance, and I felt so helpless. I knew what he was going through in that jail, and it just ate at my guts. It felt like a part of me was imprisoned with him also. I wanted him out and I wanted him out now.

I waited until the weekend and then went in to visit him. The wretched disappointment clearly showed in his eyes. I was just speechless when he told me his court proceedings had lasted until 1:30 p.m. The court clerk had lied to me, and the deputies, suspecting nothing, had escorted him back down in the elevator to the basement garage and the waiting cruiser, not varying their routine in the slightest manner. We decided right then and there that rather than wait for his next scheduled court appearance in six weeks time, which would launch us well into winter, we would put a contingency plan into effect. For Paul that meant a trip to one of two local hospitals, where I would be lying in wait to liberate him. For the benefit of the bugged phones I ended my visit by informing Paul that I had some bad news for him: his wife had met another man and had filed for divorce. Immediately after leaving the jail I drove to both hospitals to check the security measures, staff routines and procedures. As well, I spent two hours in each facility to familiarize myself with the normal atmospheres.

On Monday night at the appointed time of 7:30 I was parked in the courier car in the public skating arena parking lot just one block from the Custer County Jail on Winnett Street in my old man disguise again and armed to the teeth. For the past two days Paul had been feigning extreme depression and suicidal tendencies over the abandonment of his wife. At 7:45 p.m. he slashed his wrists. As expected, an orange-and-red ambulance came speeding up the street with its emergency dome lights flashing and dodged out of view behind the Sheriff's Department to the rear entrance of the jail.

Twenty minutes or so later a single brown sheriff's van cruised casually out to the corner of Winnett Street. As I trained my binoculars on the three occupants in the darkened interior, I thought I recognized Paul's profile briefly outlined by the streetlight as it drove past. But I couldn't be certain. It would be just like them to sneak him to the hospital in a van, I second-guessed. As it turned the corner, I started the car and roared out after it. The van crossed a pair of railroad tracks midway down the street just seconds before a train came charging across, blocking my pursuit. Then I recalled that I had second-guessed the sheriff's routine twice previously, outsmarting myself and missing Paul. How could I justify chasing a brown sheriff's van all over the city all night long to Paul the next day? His emergency clearly specified the use of the ambulance as he advised me. I had just seen it go to the jail not more than twenty minutes earlier. I reversed direction and headed back to the arena parking lot to take up my watch once again.

Suddenly the ambulance appeared — it was time. I started the car and roared up the road after it. I expected to perform a great deal of artful driving in order to keep within visual contact to learn of its precise destination. But something was wrong. It didn't race from the security compound with dome lights flashing as I'd expected it to in a crisis situation. It just cruised slowly up the street. That was very peculiar. I peered through the double rear windows into the lit interior with my binoculars. There was a person dressed in the bright orange jail dungarees standing in plain view all right, but it wasn't Paul — it was a cop! It was a trap! They were waiting for me to hit the ambulance. I followed it to the end of Winnett Street, where it turned left into a dead end instead of right, confirming my suspicions. Son of a bitch, they had smuggled Paul out in the brown sheriff's van!

I sped into the nearby parking lot of a private clinic, viciously cranking the steering wheel and gunning the engine to perform a U-turn. I had to get to whatever hospital they had taken Paul to and catch him before he left. He would be stitched up and out of there in less than thirty minutes. The tires spun wildly on the loose, powdery snow, and the car snapped around. Then the engine choked and died. I cranked it over desperately, trying to coax it to life, but it wouldn't start. Of all the goddamn luck! After turning it over for five minutes, an employee drove into the parking lot and parked her car. I asked her almost desperately if she had any jumper cables I could borrow. She replied no, but possibly one of her colleagues in the clinic might. I told her that I would deeply appreciate it, since my wife was in labor and I was on my way home to take her to the hospital. She walked into the clinic, replying that she would see what she could do. I thanked her and waited, but no one came to my assistance. I gave the engine one last final try. Then it coughed to life and I shot out of the lot to the nearest hospital.

I still had a chance. I couldn't walk into the restricted emergency units without attracting some attention. But if I found the brown van, I would find Paul. I cruised the hospital's massive parking lots, earnestly hunting for the sheriff's van, but it was nowhere in sight. I walked past the ambulance emergency entrance, scanning the hallway. Neither Paul nor any vigilant deputies were there. They must have taken him to the other hospital.

Just to double-check, I headed into the public access emergency entrance, carrying my .45 holstered beneath my coat and walking past the open door of the security office, which was occupied by a lone deputy. I walked up to the receptionist's desk and asked her if a car accident victim with a lacerated wrist by the name of Marshall had recently been admitted. I informed her that I was his brother and had been told to come here by the Sheriff's Department, which had assured me he had been brought in not twenty minutes earlier. She punched the information into her computer, hesitated a second, then replied no, he hadn't been admitted. But she offered to call the other hospital and make inquiries for me. I thanked her but declined her assistance, stating that I didn't have the time.

I concluded that Paul must be at the other hospital and walked out of the emergency ward. I ran to the car and raced across the city, ignoring all traffic regulations and running the red lights. If I was pulled over for speeding, I would have no choice but to challenge the violation right in the street. At last I reached the second hospital and searched the parking lots. There was no brown van there, either! I walked into the emergency ward to see if any deputies were standing guard in any of the hallways. They were empty.

Then I realized I had been duped. Paul had been at the first hospital! The receptionist had lost her composure for just a brief moment before she'd informed me he wasn't registered. And she had been overly perturbed by my unwillingness to wait. Her phone call would have been to the deputy in the security office. They now knew I was prowling around.

I sped back to the first hospital. The police obviously had either dropped him off at the hospital in the van, intending to pick him up in a second vehicle, or switched vehicles in transit. An unoccupied ambulance exactly like the one Paul was originally supposed to arrive in was parked at the emergency bay doors. Was it possible they intended to transport Paul back to the jail in the ambulance? It was a million-to-one shot, but it was all I had. I chanced waiting between the double doors in the emergency entrance. I was dressed in my bulletproof vest, with my .45 under a doctor's smock. The shotgun was positioned just outside the door and around the corner within easy reach. I watched the activity behind me reflected in the glass. If the deputies accompanied Paul to the ambulance, I would casually walk through the outer door and stand by the corner within view. When they were caught between the first and second set of sliding doors, I would reach around the corner, retrieve the shotgun and throw down on them. Paul would know what to do. I would give them a chance to surrender, of course. But if they went for their guns, it wouldn't be pretty. The flying glass would have just as much of a traumatic effect as the 000 buck.

However, all my planning was for nothing. I waited for an hour, but they never showed. Finally I accepted the fact that I had missed Paul for the third time. If I hadn't been playing such a deadly little game, so earnestly, it would have been humorous. But it wasn't. I was awash in disappointment and failure. I had always believed that all any person needed to escape from any prison, jail or law-enforcement agency was one dedicated individual who was willing to go to any length to achieve his freedom, and I mean any length. But it wasn't so. Luck played a crucial role. I had never invested so much research, calculation, preparation, money and time in a project in my entire criminal career, yet I had met with nothing but disaster and misfortune. And I couldn't attribute it to being excessively complicated or bizarre with little chance of success. I had taken the greatest pains to keep it simple, direct, practical and not dependent on unknown factors. It should have been a routine operation. Escapes were what I specialized in. No one was more qualified than I to break Paul out — no one.

The next day I phoned Paul's lawyer to learn the date of his forthcoming scheduled court appearance. He informed me that the Sheriff's Department, as well as the FBI, had contacted him and told him they believed the suicide attempt was a ploy to escape, since Paul had mixed water with his blood to make it seem as if he'd lost more blood than was actually the case. And they also believed Paul's brother Carl was none other than his partner in the Baker bank robbery. A substantial security net had been thrown over Paul. Even his lawyer had to prearrange his soliciting sessions a day in advance of his arrival at the jail, no doubt to give the Sheriff's Department sufficient time to verify the authenticity of the visit and set up additional security measures.

I owned one of the four white Jeeps native to Miles City, but the only one with Canadian license plates. It wouldn't take a Sherlock Holmes to make the connection or an extraordinary period of time to put the final touch to the deduction by presenting me with a complimentary set of matching bracelets.

I thought it best to leave town for a while and let the heat die down. Since I was short on funds and it was the middle of November, I hastily packed a few personal items plus my .45 and left Montana, heading west in a semicircular route for Canada, the land of law and snow. I would rob a bank and return to Miles City in a month, then give it another crack. They couldn't cover every angle twenty-four hours a day, and eventually they would let down their guard. There were certain things I could depend on. They had to take Paul back and forth to court as scheduled. I had the advantage of the first move, and with it surprise. And there was no method on their part to predetermine which disguise I would assume next, be it man, woman or inanimate object. This time, if need be, I would take the sheriff's cruiser out as it went past the State Building parking lot, before they even reached the garage. And if I missed them coming, I'd get them going. One way or another I would free Paul this time, and it didn't much matter to me that Montana had the death penalty for capital offenses. I'd made Paul a promise and I intended to keep it. In this world of constantly changing morals, one compromises one's values in order to survive. I didn't. Loyalty — the last refuge of the criminal. We all choose the crosses we bear.

As soon as I entered British Columbia, I veered east on the Trans-Canada Highway through Banff National Park. I loved to drive, and even though I froze my butt off I thoroughly enjoyed every minute of it. The steady drone of the engine, the constant roar and flapping of the wind through the soft top and the jostling of the rigid suspension were all strangely comforting, as I cruised through Banff at midnight. And the solid walls of ice along the highway, which looked like frozen waterfalls, gave the park an eerie, otherworldly aspect.

Then, without warning, I came upon a large gory object lying right in the center of my lane. As I swerved to miss it, my headlights caught a young doe standing in the ditch with its head lowered. It was probably still too attached to its mother to leave, even though the scent of blood must have been overwhelming. I couldn't help but reflect upon my sentiment; it was a common trait among criminals. We were full of compassion for animals, yet willing to place ourselves in a life-threatening predicament that could result in the death of human beings. Curiously enough, too, most bank robbers had a tendency to give a lot of their money away to bag ladies, pencil sellers or skid row bums after putting their lives on the line to steal it. Many times I'd given away my last dollar to someone who needed it more than I did. It was the Robin Hood complex. It perplexed me. Perhaps we equated helplessness with innocence, or perhaps it was just an overcompensation for our own cruelty. But I preferred to think it was because we'd been there before, and we knew what it was like to suffer, to be in need. One thing was certain: there was a communication gap somewhere.

I thought back to when I'd robbed the Chilliwack bank in British Columbia more than a year earlier. I'd placed my pistol on top of the counter to show the teller I was armed and meant business. And as I'd peered intensely into her eyes, I could see a look of complete and absolute terror. And I'd thought, God, what a lousy way to make a living. Now, thinking back to that robbery, I wondered how many persons I had hurt in my life without ever knowing. And I remembered back to when I was just twenty-one with Steve. I'd been so young and fun-loving and innocent and had changed into something serious and cynical and dangerous.

At that point I made a new resolution: after I broke Paul out, I'd really go straight this time. Janet had connections to get me a job on an oil rig in northern Alberta. My increasingly conflicting emotions were beginning to appear less and less like the symptoms of a sociopath and more like those of a neurotic, which probably made me just about normal.

I arrived in Edmonton and phoned my sister with a coded message. She met me at a store on Calgary Trail, our usual contact place, and I watched her backtrail to make absolutely certain she hadn't been followed. She hadn't. We spent Christmas together with her five-year-old-son Nathanial. If we weren't racing each other around the track on his new electric race car set, we were tobogganing down Rabbit Hill or crashing into each other in the miniature cars at the West Edmonton Mall. He was a lot like his father, Steve, wild and impulsive. But he had the benefit of being daring like Janet. We got along great, just like an irresponsible uncle and an unschooled nephew should. That was the good thing about being an uncle. You could play the hero for a day but not have to assume any responsibility for anything afterward.

Still, I carried my .45 in a hip holster everywhere I went, even while walking around the mall with Nat and his mother. I was totally convinced the Canadian police would blow me away the first chance they got. And at night the gun was just an easy arm's reach away beside my bed on my night table. I wasn't going down without a fight. And I wasn't going down alone.

To replenish my escape reserves prior to returning to the States, I robbed the Toronto Dominion Bank on Saddleback Road in Edmonton just after Christmas. It was a basic "front end" robbery without the extensive planning, expense or risk required in either the Hepworth or Mobridge robberies. It was designed simply to provide me with traveling and expense money. I walked into the bank wearing a balaclava, declared my intentions and displayed my .45 for the benefit of any skeptics. Then I holstered the gun, cleaned out all of the tellers' drawers and walked out. I advised the manager that he was responsible for everyone in the bank, and anyone who attempted to follow me would be shot. An aspiring hero who was waiting outside in his small economy car did attempt to follow me down the back alleyway at the rear of the bank — one fool chasing another. In the early darkness of winter it was easy for me to vault through a few dozen residential backyards and circle back to my Jeep. Then I sped back to my hotel room on the southern outskirts of the city.

At the time Paul and I were planning to spring him, we also had the foresight to realize that even the best-made plans sometimes go awry. In the event that everything fell through, I would travel to Saskatoon and retrieve some negotiable bonds he had stolen in the Baker bank robbery. The reason for doing so was that the district attorney prosecuting Paul's case was threatening to sentence him to forty years unless $81,000 in negotiable bonds was returned. If the bonds were returned, he would be sentenced to twenty years. Paul had buried the bonds in the ground under an old desk in an open-ended shed on his brother Andrew's hobby farm.

Not desiring to dally too long in Edmonton after robbing the TD bank, a few days later I drove to Delisle, Saskatchewan. I intended to visit the farm and retrieve the bonds during the day when Andrew and his wife were at work. I thought it best not to tell Andrew I was coming. He had enough problems in his life as it was. He had just recently lost an eye while splitting firewood and was experiencing complications after the operation to replace it with an artificial eye. As well, he was employed in the frozen meat department of a supermarket and had premature arthritis, an affliction that would soon lose him his job and consequently his farm. He had a wife and two small children to feed. I decided to arrive at the farm in the morning, recover the bonds, conceal them in the spare tire of my Jeep, smuggle them back across the border and place them in the hands of Paul's counselor, who could negotiate with the D.A. from there.

At 11:00 a.m. I drove out to the farm. There was a big For Sale sign posted on the front lawn, which could only mean that Andrew had indeed lost his farm. I knocked on the side door to ensure no one was home, then peered inside. The house was unoccupied but completely furnished and still appeared to be lived in. I parked the Jeep in the carport. Then I located an ax and shovel and went to the equipment shed. The equipment in the shed had been moved and the ground appeared to have been disturbed. Following an hour-long battle with the ground, I dug down for about a foot and a half but found no bonds. Paul must have arranged for someone else to recover them. I filled the hole back in, replaced the desk, then cleaned and replaced the tools and decided to leave. But something nagged in the back of my mind. It didn't make sense. Paul wouldn't make other arrangements without telling me first. I knew him too well to underestimate his consistency. I climbed back out of the Jeep, returned with the ax and shovel and chopped down another six inches deeper. Sure enough, the bonds were there — inside a plastic picnic cooler. I hauled them out.

Then I heard a voice in the distance that sounded as if it were coming from a public address system at a factory. That was peculiar. There were no factories, construction sites or strip mines in the area that I knew of. Curious, I walked out of the shed and scanned the grounds. Everything seemed normal. I decided to investigate the matter later. I went back inside the shed and filled in the hole. Just then I heard a vehicle drive in behind the shed. I glanced out just in time to glimpse the tail end of a dark blue car going by. It had to be

Andrew returning home to find a strange vehicle parked in his garage. Now I would have to explain everything to him.

I picked up the bonds and was about to walk out and greet Andrew, when I glanced to my left. A man dressed in dark clothing was skulking toward me through the poplar grove 100 yards away. As soon as I spotted him, he commanded, "Hold it right there!" and pointed a black object at me, which I assumed was a gun, judging by his combat stance. I didn't know who the hell he was or what he wanted, but I sure knew who I was and what I wanted.

I dashed for the Jeep. As I flew past an RCMP cruiser behind the shed and a Mountie, I realized it was the police. I vaulted over the first rail fence. *Blam!* He snapped off a shot at me and yelled, "Halt!" He missed. I dived over the second fence. If I could reach the Jeep and my .45, there was still a way out. But it wasn't meant to be. I ran right into a third Mountie, standing between me and the Jeep with his gun leveled at my chest. I could run for the open fields, but with the heavy lumberjack boots I was wearing I didn't stand a snowball's chance in hell of getting away. It was early afternoon, with at least six hours left before dark. They would have a helicopter or search plane up in the air within the hour. Still, if there had been the slightest chance, I would have run the risk of taking a bullet in the back.

"Get down on the ground!" the Mountie shouted.

I stood there, waiting. If he made the mistake of coming too close, I'd karate-chop his radius bone, paralyzing his hand, and take his gun. The other Mounties circled me now, their guns leveled. There was no way out.

"Get down on the ground!" the first Mountie yelled, again advancing toward me.

I wasn't going to prostrate myself, not for him or anyone else, gun or no gun. He'd have to put me there, which he did, jamming his gun against my temple. I was handcuffed and placed in the back of a cruiser. I couldn't believe it. I was busted. It was January 2, 1986, two year and three months after my escape from Millhaven.

In the back of the police car I reminisced upon the latest events leading up to my capture. If I had to be arrested, I couldn't have picked a better way. I couldn't have stood idly by and watched Paul be sentenced to forty years — I'm just not built that way. He was forty-seven years old. He would die in prison. During his last sentence he had served sixteen years straight, no paroles, no passes, nothing. If I could have chosen to do it all over again, knowing I was almost certain to be arrested, I still would have tried to do what I could. I would have definitely changed my strategy and tactics, but I still would have done what I had to do.

Paul had helped me innumerable times in the past and I was still finding out things he had done without my knowing or asking, things that brought about unexpected and seemingly mysterious, fortuitous opportunities in my life. Through his manipulations, he'd orchestrated my first temporary absence pass from Collins Bay. He'd arranged my election, by proxy, to the Kingston Interval House planning committee. It had clinched my parole to Ottawa. And he'd mopped my blood up from my cell floor when it was thick enough to ladle after I'd slashed my arms over Linda. Yet he never once said a word when I asked him about it, just that silly goddamn grin of his spread all over his face as if he'd put one over on you, which he had, and that little twinkle in his eye. He didn't want to bask in the glory of approval or recognition. It was just good enough for him to know that he had done what he could. I didn't regret a goddamn thing.

I was transferred to Delisle RCMP detachment under the alias of Robert Scott Cross Stewart. I had nine pieces of legitimate government-issued identification to prove who I "wasn't." It only served to delay the inevitable. The head investigating officer, Corporal Emil Smetaniuk, guessed my identity. My fingerprints were sent off to Ottawa, and they sent back two sets of prints, both of which were mine! I was locked in a cell with an officer who sat outside on a chair guarding me all night long. In the morning I was transferred to the Saskatoon RCMP detachment cells. The sergeant of the detachment refused to accept the responsibility for holding me prisoner, so they transferred me to the Saskatoon Remand Centre, which got rid of me quickly. Two days later I was expedited to Edmonton Maximum Security Prison in Alberta.

The cell door slammed shut behind me and I was not a happy man. I was in prison once again. Prison — I hated it so much. I wondered how it was possible. I'd had nine pieces of identification and more tricks than a politician. I'd been two steps ahead of the FBI and three steps ahead of the RCMP. I'd been armed to the teeth and prepared to die for my freedom. Still I was sitting in a cell. How the hell was it possible?

17

Slip-Sliding Away

THE WARDEN OF EDMONTON MAX WAS Simon Trembley, a former nurse who woke up one morning to find himself in charge of a maximum-security penitentiary and, much to his bewilderment, right smack dab in the middle of the reality of life itself. He didn't know which way to turn, so he ran straight for the nearest paternal figure — Melville Weerts.

Melville was an old pig farmer who hadn't been endowed with the intellectual capacity to grasp the diverse complexities of the criminal mind and the motives concealed behind each prisoner's behavior or the solution appropriate to every individual problem, so he had one catchall solution for every problem: "Lock 'em up in the hole!" Melville was the assistant warden of security, which from my point of view was a very comforting thought. But Old Mel, although not breaking any IQ barriers, wasn't totally asinine himself. He practiced the art of ventriloquism and his dummy was Simon Crowder.

Slimon, as he was affectionately called by the prisoners, was the assistant warden of socialization, a pretty ambiguous term in itself. He presided as chairman over the Segregation Review Board and was penology's answer to Baron Münchausen. But no one could ever accuse Slimon of being prejudiced or discriminatory. He lied equally convincingly to everyone. If the prisoners weren't vociferously demanding his resignation, the guards or his colleagues were.

The rest of the prison administration ran around in a state of industrious disorder, doing as little as possible, as long as possible and as well as possible, and creating oceans of red tape with flair. The living unit officers desired the wage and job security of the guards but preferred not to suffer the uniform or the abuse that went with it, since they were within closest contact with the prisoners and too busy playing "confidant" to save their own skins. They collected their paychecks every second Friday with slightly less than steady hands. The guards pretty well ran the show by sheer weight of numbers, plus they were in control of security functions. They sabotaged the administration, the living unit officers, the prisoners and one another as often as possible, but they weren't really dangerous, because the head of their union, Mr. Spruyt, wasn't very bright.

The administration had me typed as some kind of commando and placed me in solitary confinement with a directive that I was to be considered an escape risk at all times. I submitted at least ninety complaints and grievances in protest but couldn't diminish the fear that gripped their little hearts. Their paranoia was so overwhelming that Slimon was cautioned not to interview me without bodyguards lest I take him hostage.

Naturally I wanted to get out into the population to "change my place of residence," so I finally arranged an interview with Slimon. After I told him what I thought was a pretty touching story, he looked at me incredulously and said, "You've broken out of every prison you've ever been in. You broke Cameron out of Prince Albert, shot a cop, robbed banks, changed your fingerprints, learned karate and trained in weapons, and God knows what else we don't know about. And you expect me to let you out into the population? In two days you'll have half the Indians charging for the fence with you."

"Yes," I replied. "I want out into the population. I've found God."

"You've found God all right," he said. "That's what the last warden said when you escaped — 'Oh, my God!' There's no way in the world I'm ever going to let you out into the population. You're not a maximum-security prisoner. You're super maximum."

In any prison it's the young guards who are the most provoking and aggressive. The older ones have experienced or seen enough beatings, stabbings and killings to mature them. Edmonton Max was no different. A six-foot-three-inch, 200-pound young bushwhacker named Butt repeatedly charged down the corridor with half a dozen of his crew at all hours of the day and night, striving to catch me in the act of manufacturing escape material, which of course I was.

There were three types of searches to contend with. A frisk search was a hand search from head to toe with clothes on, during the course of which certain guards with homosexual tendencies fondled my buttocks and groped around in my crotch. A strip search required me to undress while the same guards took perverse pleasure in ogling my genitals and anus. A body cavity search is self-explanatory and required my written consent for the physician to conduct an exploratory search of my body orifices — fat chance!

After Butt planted a knife in my cell, for which I was institutionally charged, I spit on him and challenged him to a fight. After all, he was a big boy and I wasn't anywhere near his size. I expected him to oblige me instantly. Instead, like the fearless correctional officer he was, he ran back to the office and charged me again. I began to lose my sense of humor then, so I phoned the Edmonton Police Department and had him investigated for smuggling drugs into the prison. The searches stopped.

During my time in solitary I immersed myself in a strenuous exercise program, practicing karate, speed and coordination, anticipating an eventual opportunity to escape from court or in transit. I hadn't obtained my black belt yet, but I knew enough about pressure points and blows to take a man's eyes out with a gouge, crush his larynx with a chop or smash his testicles with a kick, all in a flurry of blows designed to overwhelm an opponent in a fraction of a second. And my incarceration in the hole had put me in a murderous frame of mind.

Initially the federal custodial guards refused to escort me to court, and three armed RCMP officers were assigned the task. They made certain of my security by leaving the double-locked leg irons on overnight in the Edmonton RCMP detachment holding cell, but at times, due to a shortage of available staff, only one armed Mountie escorted me through the courthouse basement. The handcuffs and leg irons I could doctor to be removed within a split second by unlocking them with a handcuff key I had fashioned out of a Bic lighter and slipping one-sixteenth-of-an-inch slivers of razor blade between the meshing teeth of the clasps as they closed. I intended to disable the officer before he could draw his revolver, arm myself, then escape from the court cells. I had no qualms about using a weapon if necessary, regardless of the cost.

One morning I was transported in manacles and leg irons to Fort Saskatchewan Hospital for stomach X-rays. Three guards escorted me in the barred prison van. One RCMP cruiser led the procession. A second followed behind and a third blocked off traffic on the main highway leading into the community. A reception committee of three Mounties lined the sidewalk like toy soldiers, and a detective haunting the hallways greeted us at the hospital. No opportunity for a change of residence there! I always figured I could get myself out of anything I got myself into, but it was getting harder every time.

When it involved escape, specifically successful escapes, I was hard-pressed to find an equal. I studied every book and article ever written on escape, dating back to World War I POW camps, and I gleaned every scrap of information on Houdini ever published. I tried to be as knowledgeable about prison security as the deputy wardens in charge of prison security. I always developed my escapes well in advance, step by practical step, painstakingly perfecting, simplifying and allowing for error. I always retained information in an escape strictly on a need-to-know basis and kept assistance to a minimum of one or two trusted persons I had known for years to help with supplies only. Experience had taught me that when I depended on people, I was frequently disappointed. I upheld the pragmatic aphorism: If you want something done right, do it yourself.

I never confided in anyone about the actual method or even acknowledged the escape. Everyone in prison was always conspiring or scheming to do something, from killing someone to getting high, so my activities were always interpreted in a dozen different ways. It was easier to escape alone. Two persons meant twice as many complications. The disadvantages greatly outweighed the advantages. I had to guard against the additional exposure to danger a partner represented to my safety, and I was never certain of his reaction, aptitude or ability under stress. In most cases an accomplice was a millstone.

I had to know my construction materials and opposition's capabilities as well as I knew my own, and I never underestimated either potentialities. If anything, I overestimated. I had to be in exceptional physical condition, agile, strong, quick and able to think on my feet, and during an escape I never hesitated, not for one second. It could mean the difference between jubilant success and sudden death. I never relied upon outside help in an escape; that would be like counting your chickens before they hatched, plus it added one more security leak. If I could evade prison security without getting all shot up, the police would be the least of my worries. I always kept my escapes as simple, basic and direct as possible. The more complicated, technical and contingent the plan was, the more likely something would go wrong.

Immediately following an escape on foot, it was best to hide in the woods during the day and travel only at night. If it was necessary to move during the day, due to an intensive manhunt, I restricted my route to forests or low-lying areas and never got within sight of any buildings, no matter how derelict they seemed. I was even prepared to dig a small hole in the earth and bury myself with dirt, brush and foliage in case of a concentrated search. The soft, moist surface of a forest floor or any surface after a light rain was the most receptive to a man's scent, retaining it for a long time. A hard, dry surface such as rock or asphalt, with a good, warm breeze blowing, dispersed the scent the fastest. I had utilized various combinations of peppers, including red, white and black, but the most reliable method for suppressing my scent was to wash a clean pair of heavy cotton work socks in baking soda while wearing a pair of rubber gloves, then deposit the socks while still wet inside an airtight plastic sandwich bag, being careful not to contaminate them or the inside of the bag. Then, when I needed to lose my scent, I just slipped them on over my shoes. Another reliable trick was to spray the soles of my shoes with various animal musks, since tracking dogs were trained to disregard any animal scents that crossed a man's trail. The simplest way to terminate my scent trail, though, was to use a bicycle. Climbing trees or walking fences weren't reliable maneuvers, since anything touched holds a scent, and what goes up must come down. I've even employed domesticated animals such as horses and cows to carry me across particularly wide pastures.

After an escape it was imperative to leave the immediate area as quickly as possible and the general vicinity as soon as feasible. Depending on the intensity of the manhunt, one had to be prepared to leave the province, state, country or continent. One rule had to be adhered to: I couldn't go home or seek any manner of assistance from any family member, friend, associate or lover known to the police; it was foolish to underestimate the law's ability to gather intelligence. The French police have a saying pertaining to wanted criminals: "Cherchez la femme." I had to alter my facial appearance, habits, contacts and assume a totally new identity, and I couldn't contact anyone even remotely associated with my past after I had established my new identity. There was one further vital rule I realized I had to observe to maintain my freedom on a permanent basis. I had to eschew a life of crime. If I didn't, I'd inevitably be apprehended. It was as simple as that. Getting out wasn't a problem. Staying out was.

In prison it wasn't the sensational and idealized things I missed, like the excitement of fast women and new cars. I never really took a shine to such. I recognized them for just what they were — show. I missed the little things, like the mysterious scents of a woman I loved, her fleeting touch and piercing blue eyes, the contented bubbling laughter in her voice, the scent of perfumes mingled with the musky scent of lovemaking, the shared moments of intimacy afterward, falling unwittingly asleep in each other's arms, waking easily up to her and the smell of freshly brewed coffee on a mellow morning and the serenity of the evenings. I missed the wind in my hair as I cruised on my bike on a sunny October day down the long, deserted roads with their kaleidoscopic autumn colors. I missed the liberty to go where I wanted, when I wanted and for whatever reason. I missed the quiet things like the murmuring of a babbling brook on a crisp spring morning, the sound of a gentle wind rustling through dry leaves in the fall and the distant, carefree laughter of children. I missed the easy smiles of strangers, swimming, walking in the rain. I missed seeing an old couple strolling slowly hand in hand through a park or a mother excitedly coaxing her child to take that first uncertain step. I missed talking with sensible, rational persons and the consideration they show for no other reason than simply to be innocently considerate. I missed the few precious words of wisdom an old man gratefully gives you when you take the time to talk to him. I missed the little old ladies with their walking canes who always seem to make it only halfway across the street before the light changes, giving you the opportunity to play Sir Galahad by charging out to rescue them. I missed the mature and gentle women, each with their own special attractiveness, whether it be a friendly smile or cheerful laugh, and I missed my family. But most of all I missed my freedom, which forever aches inside my heart like a lost and special love. And sometimes when I look out through those prison bars to my freedom beyond, it hurts so much I can't help it, I just cry.

Everyone who has never been in prison is fascinated by it, somewhat like the fascination one holds for a snake. And everyone who has ever been in prison is fascinated that anyone could be fascinated by it — they are repulsed by it, somewhat like being bitten by a snake. A lot of people look upon professional criminals as modern-day folk heroes who have braved the wrath of the law by defying the oppressive powers that be, and all criminals wonder how anyone could be so naive. Nothing could be farther from their minds and farther from the truth. Their motives are the same ones that have been held by crooks since the beginning of time: personal profit and acquisitiveness. Most convicts don't have a very good opinion of themselves, but then again neither do most straight johns. Yet each one thinks the other does.

Being in prison is like having a steel box placed around your head with a very tiny peephole, a psychological pillory. In all the world there is no sound so heartbreaking as the hollow clang of a prison door. The door of the cell is like a wall, a dark, foreboding, invincible wall that is sealed for eternity.

A few prisoners, when they first come to the penitentiary, stroll conspicuously around the yard, looking up at the top of the wall, measuring, gauging, thinking, and they watch the tower guards calculatingly, but after two or three weeks they are crushed by the relentlessness of it all. They stop dreaming and their hopes flutter to the ground like a bird with a broken wing. They still walk around the yard, but with their heads bowed and eyes lost in the dirty puddles and mud, and never again do they look up, never again do they dare to dream. But most men walk around and around the yard in a circle like a gerbil on an exercise wheel going nowhere, and always counterclockwise, as if subconsciously attempting to turn back the hands of time.

You have to forget about everyone you've ever loved or cared about in prison. You have to close yourself in, cut yourself off, because if you don't, the pain will destroy you.

Since you have nothing to occupy yourself with, you sleep a lot, daydream a lot and spend as much time as possible doing mundane chores. It's escapism, waiting, always waiting for your release. And you pace: one, two, three, four, turn; one, two three, four, over and over again from the time you get up in the morning until the time you go to bed at night. The cell is only four steps long, and pretty soon you become so familiar with the pace that you can walk for hours at a time without ever missing a beat.

Young men come into prison at twenty-one years of age with long hair and longer sentences, and ten years later they are still inside and they still have the same long style of hair because time stands still for them. Almost everyone lifts weights, pumping up their arms to eighteen or twenty-one inches like physical fitness fanatics, but very few men develop their minds, so the classic picture of a huge muscle-bound weight lifter with a small head speaks a double truth for convicts.

A lot of men put tattoos on their arms, backs and chests. Some even go to the extreme and tattoo their faces and necks. And it's always hideous death's heads, daggers or snakes, always something that symbolizes either evil or death. It's almost as if they were drawing portraits of their lives on their own bodies.

Habitually men decorate their cells, adorning the walls with pictures, paintings and proverbs. They purchase stereos, televisions and street clothes. But I've never done that. I've never painted the walls, constructed shelves or grown plants. I've led a Spartan existence. I've never tried to make that cell homey and pleasant, because it is never home to me and prison is not pleasant. It's just a cruddy bus stop and I've never accepted my fate.

I am a prisoner, not an inmate or a resident or a convict in the derogatory sense, but a goddamn prisoner, an unwilling one at that, and I've never assumed the servile position of most convicts by calling the guard "Boss." No guard will ever be my boss. I am never happy where I am. I am never content and I'll never try to be, or even give the appearance. It tears me up inside to be where I am, and I'll never want it any other way, because I'd rather suffer with dignity than alleviate the pain with institutionalization. I've always had a theory: if you don't like prison, leave.

After fifteen or twenty years inside, you eventually wind up being somebody respected and admired by the younger, less experienced cons, who look up to you for your criminal exploits and reputation. But God, the price you have to pay for such trivial ego stroking — no family, no real friends, broken hopes and shattered dreams, no home, no money and all those wasted years. It's the old maxim: "Every nobody wants to be a somebody, and every somebody wants to be a nobody." And you've daydreamed all the way, the way it will be when you get out, the fine times, the money, the ladies — the way it never is. And all the people as a young criminal you looked up to, your heroes, all turn out to be informers, take their own lives, or worse, they turn out to be human, with the same weaknesses as everyone else.

And some die by another's hand inside the walls, never having again been given the chance to taste the sweet wine of freedom, and some turn homosexual, never again yearning for the gentleness of a woman's touch, and some lose their minds, falling helplessly into a world that we will never understand.

A cell is a slightly expanded coffin. One's emotional development through external experiences is in state of suspended animation. At first, back in prison, you remember the bitterness you felt toward the system, particularly the hatred of the guards, and wonder how you could have felt that way. But after a few months of confinement and the sadistic mind games the guards play, the spitting in your meals and urinating in your drinks, the old feelings come seeping back in and it is easy to understand how you had been filled with such a deep, silent rage. Having the guards constantly grope you during strip searches is so demeaning. You're being violated. You're constantly being violated, as if your dignity is being raped. The anger rises inside and you become so frustrated that it's all you can do not to explode and smash someone. All you have in prison is your personal dignity, your pride. Everything else has been taken away. Yet they still try to take your last possession away from you, too, and leave you empty and broken.

Being locked up in solitary confinement is like being locked in a room for a very long time with someone you really don't like but tolerate because you need him. But after a while you'd just like to get away from him for a while, maybe to be alone or talk to another person. But you can't, and after a little while longer you'll do anything to get away from him because he's driving you nuts with his constant yammering. And you tell him to shut up, and he does, but only momentarily. And you'd like to throttle the son of a bitch, but you can't because it will hurt you just as much as it will hurt him. So you just try to ignore him.

If you loved yourself, you'd be happy no matter where you were, even in prison. But then incarceration wouldn't work and they'd think there was something wrong with you. So one day you'd find yourself being moved to a clean, white room by a bunch of people you've never seen before, all wearing clean, white uniforms and all smiling sweetly, nodding in agreement, just like the little novelty puppy dog in your car's rear window. And they'd put you in a clean, white uniform just like theirs, promising to alter the sleeves that seem just a shade too long just as soon as they can. And in your new room with Big Brother watching, the ever-present electronic eye of a video monitor, you'd find yourself rethinking even your slightest move to appear as normal as possible. Every measured step would be graceful and relaxed with no wasted movement. You'd try to eat daintily and with regularity and precision, with manners that even your mother would be proud of. You wouldn't pick your nose or scratch your crotch, the things you regularly reserve for more private occasions. Somehow you'd even manage to sleep with your mouth closed and without driveling, and the whole pretentious affair would be just as insane as any one person can get. But the comforting thing would be that you'd never feel alone. Your silent friend would always be there. But you'd never look at him. He would always be watching, and he would know you knew it. But you'd pretend he wasn't and you'd never look.

But you don't love yourself. So you sit in the cell staring at nothing, assaulted by the deafening ring of silence emanating from cold, damp concrete walls and the stink, the stink from the urine and feces and blood and sperm. The walls are covered with human refuse where some men, after having been placed in the hole, paced back and forth and were filled with such hatred and turmoil that they spit at the end of each turn, layering the walls with thick, multicolored streaks of crusted saliva and mucus. Or, out of desperation for attention, they plugged their toilets, so that the human waste, mixed with shreds of used toilet paper, has adhered to the surface of the concrete floor in dozens upon dozens of miniature mounds like scabs on a diseased back. You try not to touch anything because everything is filthy. And you wonder how the hell you could have possibly gotten yourself into such an utterly wretched situation, again and again minutely reliving everything and anything that could have made a difference, even the slightest difference, to alter the course of events that brought you there. And you rebuke yourself for having been so stupid to ignore all of the warning signs that were so evident. Finally, flogging reasoning into the ground, you come to the conclusion that it was fate, predestined from the very beginning, and there was nothing you could have done to change it. It would have happened, anyway.

So then you delve into abstractions, philosophizing about life until you come to a revelation, some divine truth that makes sense of the predicament of man, all the while thirsting, hungering, dying for the voice of another human being. And you hope the echo of every footstep and every voice is for you, but it never is. You remember all the terrible things you've ever done in your life and wonder how you could have done them, what kind of a monster you must be. And eventually, after a period that depends on your strength of character, one of two things happens.

If you are relatively intelligent with a fairly active mind, you become slightly insane, exhibiting regressive signs of paranoia. You cling to the edge of reality by your fingertips from one day to the next, but then one day you slip unknowingly into the black abyss of the deranged. You begin to scream and howl and sing and whisper. You laugh like a madman and spit at the guards and anyone else who represents authority, or the persons who are directly or indirectly responsible for your being there and have caused you so much grief. You become extremely depressed and extremely bitter, and it's all you can do not to break down and cry. And you can't see the end of the tunnel because there is no end, and you are filled with so much pain. The walls close in on you, but you choke back your panic. Trapped in your own private hell, you feel so insignificant, and you wonder when it will all end. You feel as if no one loves you and no one cares and you might just as well be dead. And that's your second choice — to commit suicide. You finger the razor blade that shakes in your hand, testing the edge, hesitating in a momentary reflection. Then you make a decision. And those who choose one way live, and those who choose the other write their last thoughts in scarlet lines of dripping blood spurted onto the walls, finish with dark periods of ebbing dots on the floor and sign their testaments with one last unnoticed tear.

Eventually, after seven months of solitary, each day seeming to possess its own year-long lifespan, the assistant regional director of operations of the prairie region, A.J. Frank, "recommended" to the warden that I be transferred into the general prison population, much to the consternation of Old Melville. I was transferred to G unit, cell 007, and greeted upon my arrival by a number of the Boys.

I couldn't believe I had been let out, and it was like being free again, but I wasn't that far gone to believe I was. I took one look at the security measures and couldn't believe my eyes — the place was an escape artist's dream. There were so many ways out I didn't know which one to take first! I had no doubt the pig farmer would soon come to realize his greatest fears.

The notoriety of my escapes and alleged training had been relayed from the FBI and RCMP to the prison administration and subsequently to the general population, and I was, much to my amusement, heralded as the authority on escapes. The first week I was approached by six separate factions, all seeking advice on various methods of defeating Edmonton Max. But lifetime secrets are hard-earned and not to be squandered on half-baked conspirators who, in their lack of discipline, will only draw attention to security weaknesses, making it more difficult for the serious escape artist.

One group had the brilliant plan to employ the cherry picker the institution habitually used to change the light bulbs on the perimeter security lights. They intended to extend the cherry picker arm up over the double fences, then jump the sixteen feet down to the ground on the other side. The mastermind of this little scheme was a big six-foot, three-hundred-pound murderer who would probably have broken both his legs upon impact as soon as his three hundred pounds of blubber hit the ground. How they were ever going to manage to get the cherry picker from the outside of the prison to the inside of the two fences was an incidental problem that no one seemed to think warranted much consideration.

Another group wanted to shut off the main generator, which they were convinced was locked behind a mysterious door in the institutional services department. They were positive there was no backup generator, even though the PID system had clearly called for one for the past five years or more. It was a two-part plan. Part A was to break into the industry shop from inside the kitchen by bashing a hole through the cinder-block wall and camouflaging it with cardboard. For the next two nights, two pair of precision-made bolt cutters would be forged, even though the industry section had neither the tools nor the machinery to make any such implement. Part B was to sabotage the main generator, after which they would rush to the fence, climb almost to the top and cut a hole just beneath the roll of concertina. If they were going to climb the fence, I wondered why anyone would stop to cut a hole when they could just as easily continue to climb over the top. The last time I saw the leader of that group of saboteurs he was on his way to a hole of his own solitary. Rumor had it he was caught trying to unlock the kitchen door with a key stolen from another lock.

But the silliest idea was when one conspirator calculated he could escape by running along the top of the roof fast enough to build up speed to jump over the fifteen-foot space to the first fence. Both fences were separated by an eighteen-foot gap. I told him the idea was definitely original, the timing was good and it was well worth a trial run. I volunteered my services to mark off the distance with an Olympic long jump measuring tape and reassured him that if he broke both his legs after jumping off the fifteen-foot kitchen roof, we would know then that the plan definitely needed a little more calculation. For some inexplicable reason he seemed to lose interest in escaping after that.

The schemes were all very entertaining, but somewhat short-sighted and rash. Patience is a virtue I had long ago mastered. I knew my chance would come. I waited monklike, inscrutable, for my ingenuity, forever constant, forever faithful, to set me free.

After I was released from the hole, Rick Roache arranged my transfer to the kitchen.

Rick and I had first met in the hole in the spring of 1986. He was in Edmonton Max after being transferred from Prince Albert S.H.U. and was awaiting trial on a first-degree murder charge. I was there, of course, for breaking out of every prison they'd ever put me in. Rick was twenty-eight years old, five feet six inches tall, 160 pounds, with dark hair and a dark complexion, and a weight lifter and exercise enthusiast. I liked him because he was staunchly loyal to his friends, had a crude consideration for his associates and was inflexibly solid. But he had a cocksure attitude that antagonized a lot of the general population. The toughness was just a front, though. He was loud and aggressive because he'd taken another prisoner's life and he hated himself for it. The murder was the biggest mistake he ever made, he said.

I worked hard in the kitchen with Rick, and was making progress, too. All the kitchen stewards liked me, and things were different out in Edmonton Max — something I'd never anticipated. The prison administration didn't hate my guts the way they had back east in Millhaven, and they were more liberal. I began to think that maybe I'd do my time this time, and after a few years maybe they'd parole me again. I'd never really given myself a chance in life. I'd been too busy trying to beat the odds, trying to prove I could do the impossible. I'd put myself through more pain and torture than I would wish on my worst enemy and I had nothing to show for it. I figured it was about time I settled down, got married and raised a couple of kids while I was still young enough to enjoy them. Enough with guns and robbing banks. It was time I packed crime in before it packed me in, before I wound up dead.

Then, in the fall of 1986 on August 24, Rick was killed — murdered. The price? One quart of homemade brew. Rick had it and wouldn't share it, so they killed him.

It started out as a harmless fist fight one on one, uninitiated by Rick, though he did his best to defend himself. But Rick lost. Severely beaten, his face stomped on and smashed into the concrete pavement, he lay on the ground, exhausted and barely conscious. As he tried to drag himself up onto his hands and knees, struggling to take in deep, blood-gurgling breaths, someone stepped out of the surrounding crowd and plunged a homemade knife into his chest. He never had a chance. He gasped once and fell backward, his lifeblood spilling to the ground. Two friends tried to help him up, but he just did not have the strength to stand. The last time I saw him was through the common-room window as he was being unhurriedly wheeled out from the yard on a stretcher, his head lolling, all muscle control gone. The surgeons lost Rick on the operating table in the hospital one hour later. I knew he was dead before I even heard the news. I could sense it. Death hung in the air.

Alone in my cell that night I wept, my tears mercifully hidden by the darkness, because I'd known Rick, and one minute he was laughing and joking and the next he was cold and lifeless, and there was nothing I could do to bring him back.

Days later I walked by the spot where Rick had died. There were no telltale signs of blood or chalk marks on the ground. No one would even have known a man's life had been taken there. But I knew. And I knew that I'd never be able to walk by that spot again without thinking of Rick. The biggest mistake we make in prison is not when others treat us as animals, but when we cease to believe we are human.

How do you accept when a person is gone, when everything he represents is gone, too? When he is reduced to just a memory? When you know you'll never see his face again or hear his voice? When you can never talk to him again, share his ideas, his laughter, his feelings? The worldly space that person occupied is empty, and you'll live with the knowledge of his death for the rest of your life. You've tried to make sense of life, and at times you almost have. Then something like Rick's murder happens, and you realize you never will. Rick didn't have to die. There was not one flash of sense in his death. It embodied most prison murders — embroiled in treachery and deceit. God, it just made me sick.

Rick used to say he'd had enough of deception. But he'd been scared of losing his life and had felt he had to project an image of being tough, of being a wolf, to keep the wolves away from his door, from going for his throat. It didn't work. They killed him, anyway.

Prison treachery and perversion are sicknesses that eat away at the center of your soul like terminal cancer, diseases you'll never recover from if you lie on a deathbed in the ward for the criminally insane.

It seems as if prison has been just one long series of con jobs where I'm being had over and over again. Every time I start to care about people, to find some compassion in my heart for others, something comes along and throws my feelings into the mud. Disillusionment falls with the weight of consciencelessness, a convict's status isn't based on benevolence or philanthropy and the Convict Code is a farce. If we aren't killing ourselves, we're killing one another or the guards are killing us, and I look but cannot find an end. I know there are places in this world where a man doesn't have to murder to survive or live a tortured life. It's a long road back through the penal forest to Crystal Mountain, but for me there is no way back, and a broken man I'll never be.

The strongest bonds are not those of prison chains or bars, but the subconscious chains of defeatism in every prisoner's mind. I picked up my stopwatch and walked resolutely from the cell toward the yard. As I lounged on the bleachers, the patrol truck roared past and I hit the stop button — fifteen seconds. Not bad, but not good enough. Where there's a will there's a way, and soon I'll be free. I'd rather be wanted than had.